PRAISE FOR HARVEY'S SEVEN *NEW YORK TIMES* BEST-SELLING BOOKS

"If anyone can 'write the book' on sales success, it's Harvey Mackay. He is a proven leader in sales. My advice: Follow the leader to a stellar sales career!"

—John C. Maxwell

"Harvey Mackay is a champ at sales—and he doesn't pull any punches with his heavyweight advice."

—Muhammad Ali

"In today's world the only thing that you have going for you is YOU. But are you the best YOU you can be? Now a book that can guide you to be more and have more."

—Suze Orman

"Don't share this book with your competition; share it with your people. I'm going to do just that. Will it make a difference? Your competitors won't like the answer."

—Ken Blanchard

"There are three kinds of business experts. There's an expert, there's a world-class expert, and there's Harvey Mackay—THE world-class expert."

—Jeffrey Gitomer

"A mother lode of timely, hard-earned, bite-size, street-smart golden nuggets . . . invaluable for job seekers, employed or unemployed."

—Stephen Covey

"He is fast, smart, funny . . . and frighteningly right."

—Gloria Steinem

"Harvey's business acumen shows through on every page. . . . There's so much warmth, wisdom, and wittiness in this book that it would be well for everyone to read every page."

—Billy Graham

"Harvey Mackay is the only person I'll listen to while standing in shark-infested waters . . . real stories from the real world with real solutions."

—Larry King

"Harvey Mackay is one of the greatest writers of our time."

—Norman Vincent Peale

"Enjoy Harvey's cookbook for success. . . . It gives the reader the best of his wisdom . . . truly the best kind of chicken soup for anyone and everyone in business and in life."

—Mark Victor Hansen and Jack Canfield

You Haven't Hit Your Peak Yet!

You Haven't Hit Your Peak Yet!

Uncommon Wisdom for Unleashing Your Full Potential

Harvey Mackay

WILEY

Published by John Wiley & Sons, Inc., Hoboken, New Jersey.
Published simultaneously in Canada.

For general information on our other products and services or for technical support, please contact our Customer Care Department within the United States at (800) 762-2974, outside the United States at (317) 572-3993 or fax (317) 572-4002.

Wiley publishes in a variety of print and electronic formats and by print-on-demand. Some material included with standard print versions of this book may not be included in e-books or in print-on-demand. If this book refers to media such as a CD or DVD that is not included in the version you purchased, you may download this material at http://booksupport.wiley.com. For more information about Wiley products, visit www.wiley.com.

Library of Congress Cataloging-in-Publication Data:

Names: Mackay, Harvey, author.
Title: You haven't hit your peak yet : uncommon wisdom for unleashing your
    full potential / Harvey Mackay.
Description: Hoboken : John Wiley & Sons, Inc., [2020] | Includes index.
Identifiers: LCCN 2019050431 (print) | LCCN 2019050432 (ebook) | ISBN
    9781119658603 (hardback) | ISBN 9781119658771 (adobe pdf) | ISBN
    9781119658658 (epub)
Subjects: LCSH: Career development. | Success in business.
Classification: LCC HF5381 .M1973 2020 (print) | LCC HF5381 (ebook) | DDC
    650.1–dc23
LC record available at https://lccn.loc.gov/2019050431
LC ebook record available at https://lccn.loc.gov/2019050432

Cover image: Stephanie Rau
Cover design: Valerie Boyd

Printed in the United States of America

V10016248_121119

To my loving parents, Jack and Myrtle Mackay, who were my first teachers. Without their love and guidance, I would probably have never made even the first step that would lead me eventually to the exciting career I have been lucky enough to enjoy. Thanks Mom and Dad—you always were the best!

To my amazing family, my beloved wife, Carol Ann, and our children, David, Mimi, and JoJo—who have taught me so much over the years. Many people have great families, but I know each and every one of mine is truly extraordinary in so many ways, and they will always be the very heart of my life.

To my 11 grandchildren, each of whom I love dearly, and who have kept me up-to-date on this always-changing world we inhabit. These kids teach me something new every day and are the perfect recipe for staying young at heart!

To our employees who have continued over many years to make us all proud of how much we will do to keep our customers happy. They take unbelievable pride in manufacturing something as simple, but necessary, as an envelope and have made us all proud to say we are MackayMitchell Envelope Company.

To my readers and audiences, whose feedback inspires me.

To my friends, who always make me practice what I preach.

CONTENTS

FOREWORD

I've had the pleasure of calling Harvey Mackay my friend for more than 35 years, since he recruited me—hard—to consider a job coaching the University of Minnesota Golden Gophers football team.

Once you meet Harvey you never forget him. He has a tremendously commanding presence. He's the kind of guy who could convince the Saudis to buy sand.

In December 1983, I was fired from my job coaching the University of Arkansas football team. Harvey called me on the phone within hours, singing the praises of his alma mater. In his signature style, he managed to get me to visit the Twin Cities in the dead of winter and convince me that it was the warmest place on earth.

The only thing I knew about Minnesota was that every time I looked at the back page of *USA TODAY*, the temperature there was in the single digits or teens, sometimes above zero. Minnesota had lost 17 of 18 games by an average score of 47–13. Harvey is such a salesman that he told me the Gophers only lost to Nebraska by 10. He forgot to mention it was 10 touchdowns. The school was without a head coach not because it was taking its time and being choosy, but because the five people to whom it had offered the job had all turned it down.

Harvey picked me and my family up at the airport and the wind chill was 45 degrees below zero. He knew I hated cold weather, so he threw a raccoon coat around me, a raccoon coat around my wife, Beth, stuffed the two kids in the backseat of the car, drove us to the downtown Marriott, and kept us in the hotel for two solid days of negotiations. He never let me go outside once. And he wouldn't take no for an answer.

We ended up having a wonderful two years in Minnesota and took the Gophers to a bowl game in our second season and beat Clemson. The people were friendly, the fans exuberant, and the climate not quite arctic. Plus Harvey and I became best friends. We joke that we're like brothers from another mother.

I suspect some of that affinity stems from the fact that we are both extremely competitive. For example, we have played more than 100 rounds of golf together, and we have a traveling trophy to mark the occasions. To protect the identity of the innocent, I won't tell you what the stats are.

This competitive streak started for Harvey at a young age. He was a champion golfer in high school and won two St. Paul City golf championships and was runner-up in the State High School Championship when he three-putted the last hole. And he has never forgotten that. He went on to play varsity golf for his Minnesota Gophers. He also won the state table-tennis championship for 16 and under. He has run 10 marathons and was the number 1 ranked senior tennis player in Minnesota.

Harvey has carried that spirit through to his business life. And now he's once again sharing his best strategies with his readers.

Harvey has done it all. He took a failing envelope company and built it into the $100 million MackayMitchell Envelope Company in Minneapolis. In addition to his *seven New York Times* best-selling books—three that hit #1—he's been writing his nationally syndicated column since 1993. He's also one of the best speakers I've ever heard and is in several speakers' halls of fame. Toastmasters International named him one of the top five speakers in the world.

Harvey has made giving back to his community a priority in his life. For seven long years, he was the chairman of the Hubert H. Humphrey Metrodome task force in Minneapolis, and was rewarded by throwing out the first baseball when that stadium was built. He played a key role in landing the 1992 Super Bowl for Minneapolis, and he was a catalyst in obtaining an NBA franchise for the city—the Minnesota Timberwolves.

Harvey has been a board member of more than 20 nonprofit organizations committed to helping people and communities, and has served as president of many of these organizations. He was president of the Minneapolis Chamber of Commerce, Envelope Manufacturers Association, and the national University of Minnesota Alumni Association. Harvey was a member of the Board of Trustees of Robert Redford's Sundance Institute for 12 years, and served on the boards of the Minnesota Orchestra, Guthrie Theater, American Cancer Society, and American Heart Association, to name only a few.

Perhaps his biggest honor was receiving the coveted Horatio Alger Award in the Supreme Court Chambers. This prestigious award is given to distinguished Americans "who demonstrate individual initiative and a commitment to excellence, as exemplified by remarkable achievements accomplished through honesty, hard work, self-reliance, and perseverance."

What I like best about Harvey is his fanatical attention to detail and his follow-through. If he promises you something, he always delivers more. When I left Minnesota, he told me he's my 9–1–1 for anything I need. And boy, has he delivered.

Few people know it, but Harvey has told me plenty of times that if he had his life to do over again, he would be a high school or college coach because he loves to share his knowledge or, as he calls them, street smarts.

I beg to differ: Harvey has already been a coach all his life. He's been coaching millions of people through his books, speeches, and nationally syndicated column. Now he's written what I think is his best book yet. As the title says, *You Haven't Hit Your Peak Yet!* Harvey was born to write this book, and maybe he's finally reaching his peak. This book is a culmination of his illustrious business career.

As I've already mentioned, Harvey is a super salesman. Well, I believe a coach is fundamentally a salesperson. Before I became a coach, I was a salesman in the business world, and one of the most important lessons I ever learned was: "You don't sell anyone. You help people get what they want."

Harvey has spent his entire life helping people get what they want. He has once again shared the kind of wisdom that they don't teach in school, covering an incredible range of topics that will help everyone from aspiring entrepreneurs to seasoned pros hit their peak. It's a long climb, and Harvey is there every step of the way.

I could go on for pages about what this man can do, but I think I should let his words speak for him. Soak up his lessons and go tackle that mountain!

—Lou Holtz
Sports commentator, analyst, and Hall of Fame football coach

ACKNOWLEDGMENTS

At the top of the peak for helping with this book was Mary Anne Bailey, who has been part of my "kitchen cabinet" since the 1990s. Her help in researching, organizing, fact checking, and proofreading was insurmountable. She has a mastery in polishing prose and is a consummate professional with unlimited knowledge and patience.

The term "chief of staff" understates the pivotal contributions Greg Bailey has made to this book in every way. Greg continues to be my right hand—and so much more—in the entire spectrum of my professional life. He has an effortless ease in sourcing topics and keeping the book and me on schedule, all with a fanatical attention to detail.

My sister and editor Margie Resnick Blickman has an eagle's eye for detail and remains as astute and valuable as ever. She has been a tremendous sounding board over my entire career.

No matter what I write, I run it by Neil Naftalin, a member of my "kitchen cabinet" and best man at my wedding. His meticulous eye is great for checking the elusive fact.

The Wiley team, starting with publisher Matt Holt, made me feel like a teammate, even though I was a rookie to their imprint. Senior Editor Zachary Schisgal was my key contact during this entire book and couldn't have been more responsive. He was always there with an answer or an update. His judgment and advice are unparalleled. Kelly Talbot proved to be a terrific book editor whose stellar advice kept my lessons lively and timely.

My cover photographer, Stephanie Rau, brought the best out of me and managed to find my "good side."

Valerie Boyd of Valerie Boyd Design has designed several of my book covers as well as other publications and lent her creativity to this project as well.

Christi Cardenas was the right hand of my very first agent, Jonathon Lazear, and continues to be a terrific sounding board.

My Mackay Roundtable members—all 35 of them—have had a tremendous impact on my life, as we continuously seek each other's advice.

Our executive assistant, Karen Thompson, keeps the home/office fires burning and is always there with a witty and often humorous quip that has earned her a Nurse Nag tagline.

My business partner, Scott Mitchell, CEO of MackayMitchell Envelope Company, and all of our hard-working employees who practice the principles in this book, keep me on my toes in this always-changing business world.

And my family, my wife of nearly 60 years, Carol Ann, and our three wonderful kids: David, Mimi, and Jojo, and their families keep me forever grateful. They may be last here, but they are first in my heart always.

INTRODUCTION

I'll be the first to admit that I have lived a somewhat charmed life. No, I didn't start out with any specific advantages, with one exception: tremendous parents who encouraged me to reach for the stars. They imparted simple, lasting wisdom that launched me on a remarkable journey.

Building my envelope manufacturing company, becoming a New York Times #1 bestselling author and motivational speaker, and volunteering to spearhead some amazing events and projects have provided me with experiences that money can't buy. More than five decades of business have taught me that I still have plenty to learn, and I am grateful for the wisdom that my family, friends, and mentors have shared with me over the years.

Through my seven *New York Times* best-selling books (three that hit #1) and nationally syndicated columns, I've shared advice and offered information in brief snippets. I usually address one subject at a time in the hope that busy readers can benefit from the message and apply it to their own situations.

But this book truly is my master class, a compendium of the best lessons I have learned over a lifetime of work with people who have picked up where my parents left off. My love of storytelling is a gift from my father—an Associated Press newspaperman through and through—and my mother, a teacher who instilled in me a love of lifelong learning. Family, friends, business associates and competitors, community leaders, and a long list of acquaintances have presented me with opportunities that have stretched my imagination. They encouraged me to share what I've learned, what worked, what didn't, what I would change, and what I am so thankful for.

And that is what led to this book. I hope you can find inspiration on the following pages and live your best life.

My message to you is, first, don't be afraid to fail. But more importantly, don't be afraid to succeed.

1

ADVERSITY

ADVERSITY CAN BE YOUR BEST FRIEND

Nearly three thousand years ago, the classical author Homer opined, "Adversity has the effect of eliciting talents which in prosperous circumstances would have lain dormant." Homer is something of an expert on adversity, having penned the great story of the Trojan War in *The Iliad* and *The Odyssey*.

On the other side of the world, the Chinese symbol for crisis has a dual meaning: danger and opportunity. That's an intriguing thought, really. Life is fraught with both danger and opportunity, and when cool heads prevail, opportunity wins most of the time. An Asian adage says, "When fate throws a dagger at you, there are only two ways to catch it: either by the blade or by the handle."

Remember Mother Teresa's response to dealing with adversity? "I know God will not give me anything I can't handle. I just wish that He didn't trust me so much."

As you can see, coping with adversity is not unique to any particular culture or any specific era. Modern commentator Paul Harvey put it this way: "In times like these, it helps to recall that there have always been times like these."

Adversity is a constant in this world, and none of us are immune to it. It can also be the precursor to wonderful change. A business associate told me he has just learned to "cooperate with the inevitable." More often than not, he has conquered the inevitable with that attitude.

Retailing giant J.C. Penney was asked the secret of his success. He replied, "Adversity. I would never have amounted to anything had I not been forced to come up the hard way." I've dealt with my own share of ups and downs. I'd have to agree with Mr. Penney: The tough times have not only made me smarter, they've made me stronger.

I'm not very adept in the kitchen, so I was curious when a friend sent me a cooking story. She heard it in a sermon at church and thought I'd get some inspiration from it. It inspired me, to be sure. But more than that, it reminded me that no matter what adversity comes my way, the way I respond will mean the difference between defeat and triumph.

A young woman went to her mother and told her about her life and how things were so hard for her. She was tired of fighting and struggling. It seemed as soon as one problem was solved, a new one arose.

Her mother took her to the kitchen. She filled three pots with water and placed each one on a high fire. Soon the pots came to a boil. In the first she put some carrots, in the second she placed some eggs, and in the last she added ground coffee beans. She let them sit and boil, without saying a word.

In about 20 minutes she turned off the burners. She took out the carrots and placed them in a bowl. She removed the eggs and put them in a bowl. Then she poured the coffee into a bowl.

She asked her daughter, "What do you see?"

"Carrots, eggs, and coffee," she replied.

Her mother brought her closer and asked her to feel the carrots. She did and noted that they were soft. The mother then asked the daughter to take an egg and break it. After pulling off the shell, she found the hard-boiled egg. Finally, the mother asked the daughter to sip the coffee. The daughter smiled as she tasted its rich aroma. The daughter then asked, "So what does it mean, mother?"

Her mother explained that each of these objects had faced the same challenge: boiling water. Each reacted differently. The carrot went in strong, hard, and unrelenting. However, after being subjected to the boiling water, it softened and became weak. The egg had been fragile. Its thin outer shell had protected its liquid interior, but after sitting through the boiling water, its inside became hardened. The ground coffee beans were unique, however. After they were in the boiling water, they had changed the water.

"Which are you?" she asked her daughter. "When adversity knocks on your door, how do you respond? Are you a carrot, an egg, or a coffee bean?"

I'll still let others take care of the cooking, but I will never look at a cup of coffee the same way again.

MACKAY'S MORAL

When adversity is on the menu, make sure you order it well done.

Bouncing back
from deflating times

Failure is all too common in business. Anyone who has ever run a business wakes up regularly with nightmares about the what-ifs.

Successful businesspeople, however, know that even if adversity strikes, they can work around it. They are resilient.

In the mid-1990s, Microsoft was dominating its market and Apple Computer's sales were sagging. Steven Jobs, who had co-founded Apple in 1976, left in 1985 after a power struggle with the board of directors. Apple struggled too, until Jobs returned as CEO in 1997. He recognized the big problem and fixed it by establishing a spirit of innovation at the company. If brands like iMac, iPod, iTunes, and iPhone ring a bell, you'll know what Jobs had been up to at Apple. And you will see one of the best examples of resiliency in an ever-changing industry.

Tylenol currently controls about 35 percent of the North American pain reliever market. But in 1982, you couldn't give Tylenol away. A psychopath put cyanide into some Tylenol capsules, causing eight deaths. Although it was clear that Johnson & Johnson had done nothing wrong in the manufacturing of the pills, the company accepted responsibility and pulled more than 31 million bottles from the shelves at a cost of $100 million. The company also offered to exchange the capsules for tablets, taking another financial hit.

But their response, putting customer safety before corporate profit, helped restore confidence in both the company and the brand. Then-CEO Jim Burke said, "It will take time, it will take money, and it will be very difficult; but we consider it a moral imperative, as well as good business, to restore Tylenol to its pre-eminent position." Sales recovered quickly. Resilient? You better believe it.

Sure, those are two extreme examples. But if those companies can bounce back on such a large scale, they should inspire others facing smaller challenges.

Sales slumps, production slowdowns, labor issues, and changing customer preferences affect many businesses. The strong survive not because they are determined to conduct business as usual, but because they find ways to rise above the issue at hand.

Remember, you can't live life with an eraser. You can't anticipate every possible problem, no matter how hard you try. But you can resolve to face challenges as they arise. Keep your mind wide open for solutions, listen to those around and under you, reprogram your brain for success, and dig in.

Remember, you can't live life with an eraser. You can't anticipate every possible problem, no matter how hard you try.

Many events and technologies could have spelled disaster for envelope companies like MackayMitchell Envelope Company. Fax machines, email, instant messaging, online catalogs, online bill paying, the 2001 anthrax scare, 9/11, recession—you name it. There was one threat after another. We could have been in the tank 20 times.

But we changed our business focus as necessary, cultivated new business, and managed to survive and thrive. Sometimes during great challenges, the same work hours did not always apply, vacations for our employees were put on hold, and wages held in check. It wasn't forever, but it was survival. We would have had a hard time telling our employees that we weren't resilient enough to provide them with jobs. It wasn't just about us. We had a lot of families depending on our flexibility. And we still do. We are always looking for ways to protect our business against the next threat, even if we haven't identified it yet.

When it comes to dealing with adversity, keep in mind this story of the oak tree:

A great oak grew on the bank of a stream. For 100 years it had withstood the winds, but one day a violent storm felled the oak with a mighty crash into the raging river and carried it out toward the sea.

The oak came to rest on a shore where some reeds were growing. The tree wondered how the reeds still stood after the strong winds.

"I have stood up against many storms, but this one was too strong for me," the oak said.

"That's your problem," the reeds replied. "All these years you have stubbornly pitted your strength against the wind. You were too proud to yield a little. We, on the other hand, knowing our weakness, just bend and let the wind blow over us without trying to resist it. The harder the wind blows, the more we humble ourselves, and here we are!"

It is better to bend than to break. Companies and workers who can bend and not break have the gift of resiliency that lets them bounce back from adversity.

MACKAY'S MORAL

Don't let hard times turn into end times. Let them lead to your best times.

THE WORST FAILURE
IS THE FAILURE TO TRY

Failure can become a weight or it can give you wings.

That is the message I hear every spring when I attend the Horatio Alger Awards Ceremony in Washington, D.C., where 10 new members are inducted annually. I was honored to be one of them in 2004. During the short speeches given by new members to the audience, which includes more than 100 scholarship students, the message I hear over and over again is: Don't be afraid to fail.

The Horatio Alger Association of Distinguished Americans is a nonprofit organization based in Alexandria, Virginia, that was founded in 1947 to emphasize the importance of higher education and to honor the achievements of outstanding Americans who have succeeded in spite of adversity. The association is named for Horatio Alger Jr., a 19th-century author of hundreds of stories in the "rags-to-riches" genre, extolling the importance of perseverance and hard work.

The association gives the annual Horatio Alger Award to people who exemplify its ideals. It also grants scholarships and is one of the largest providers of need-based scholarships in the United States. All scholarships are funded by the generosity of Horatio Alger members and friends. Since the inception of its scholarship programs in 1984, the association has awarded more than $180 million in need-based college scholarships to 25,000 young people.

Perhaps the most important lesson these young scholars learn is that failure is not fatal. They hear about pathways to success that include episodes of difficult times, the temptation to give up, and the persistence to carry on. The members reinforce that failure is merely an opportunity to start over again, wiser than before. Inspired by these real-life success stories, combined with scholarship help and an amazing ready-made network of resources, these young people have opportunities to earn college degrees and jump-start their professional aspirations. And they have a clear understanding that failure is not the end of the road. It is potentially a new entrance ramp to the highway of life.

No one sets out to fail intentionally. Still, failure happens, sometimes because of bad luck or uncontrollable circumstances, but other times from entirely preventable causes. Whatever your career goals or personal objectives are, your chances of avoiding failure will improve if you address these all-too-common errors:

- **Wasting time.** Planning is essential, but too much planning can consume the energy you need in order to execute your plan effectively. Set clear deadlines. Be realistic, but ambitious. Don't obsess over getting every last piece of data before taking action.

- **Excluding people.** You don't have to like all your coworkers in order to work with them. Don't limit your partnerships and alliances to people who agree with you 100 percent. Be willing to bring in experts with different points of view, and listen to their opinions. You need honest feedback, not blind encouragement.

- **Fighting the wrong battles.** You've got to know when sticking to your position is going to be worth the time and energy, and when to back down in order to conserve your resources for the next confrontation. You don't have to succeed all the time to win in the end.

- **Ignoring the short term.** Yes, you have to think about an endpoint that's far in the future, but don't focus on it so intently that you forget to generate results in the meantime. You won't have the chance to succeed in the long run if you fail in the short term, so look for some significant initial wins you can point to as evidence that you're on the right track.

- **Playing it too safe.** In order to succeed, you've got to be willing to fail. The people around you will catch on to your dislike of risk if you never take on a difficult project or an ambitious challenge. Don't be reckless, but don't shy away from hard work if you want your boss, or your teammates, to believe in you. No risk, no reward.

The heroes in Horatio Alger's stories demonstrate that you can't avoid setbacks and disappointments. As Robert F. Kennedy said, "Only those who dare to fail greatly can ever achieve greatly."

MACKAY'S MORAL

Make your stumbling blocks your stepping stones.

2

ATTITUDE

TAKE CHARGE OF YOUR ATTITUDE

A mother was ready for a few minutes of relaxation after a long and demanding day. However, her young daughter had other plans for her mother's time.

"Read me a story, Mommy," the little girl pleaded.

"Give Mommy a few minutes to relax. Then I'll be happy to read you a story," the mother replied.

But the little girl was insistent that Mommy read to her now. Hoping to buy a few precious minutes, the mother tore off the back page of the magazine she was reading. It contained a full-page picture of the world. She tore it into several pieces and told her daughter to put the picture back together, and then she would read her a story.

A short time later, the little girl announced the completion of her puzzle project. To her astonishment, the mother found the world picture completely assembled. When she asked her daughter how she managed to do it so quickly, the little girl explained that on the reverse side of the page was the picture of a little girl. "You see, Mommy, when I got the little girl together, the whole world came together."

Each of us has the responsibility to put our world together. It starts by getting ourselves put together. We can become better parents, friends, spouses, and employers. The first step is adjusting our attitude.

Webster's Dictionary defines attitude as a "mental position." Successful companies and employees take the position that change is positive and challenge is good. They accept their environment and look for opportunities.

And opportunities are everywhere. It just depends on your attitude. Change can be difficult, or it can be exciting. You get to decide, so make sure your attitude puts you in the winner's circle. Winners are positive and believe in themselves. They are committed and don't easily give up. They take charge of their own attitude. Don't let it take charge of you.

Change can be difficult, or it can be exciting. You get to decide, so make sure your attitude puts you in the winner's circle.

There's a terrific description of attitude in one of my all-time favorite books, *Think and Grow Rich* by Napoleon Hill and Dennis Kimbro: "Our attitudes set the stage for what will occur in our lives—good attitude, good results; fair attitude, fair results; poor attitude, poor results. Each of us shapes his own life; and the shapes of our lives will be and are determined by our attitude.

"Your mental attitude is a two-way gate on the pathway of life. It can be swung one way toward success, or the other way toward failure."

Success and happiness depend as much on your attitude as on your resources and advantages. To develop the right mindset, keep these precepts front and center:

- **Control.** Ultimately the only control you have in life is over yourself: your thoughts, actions, responses, and behaviors. Don't obsess over what you can't control. Concentrate on what you can.

- **Positivity.** Stop yourself when you feel negative thoughts taking over. Instead, ask what's the best or worst that can happen. Then plan your response accordingly. Surround yourself with positive people, and see how quickly your own attitude changes.

- **Results.** It's easy to fall into routines and patterns that emphasize the process instead of the outcome. Learn the rules, but apply them with an eye on what you want to achieve.

- **Gratitude.** You'll stay positive if you remind yourself of what you already possess. Spend some time every day thinking about your health, your family and friends, and the advantages you have, instead of focusing single-mindedly on what you lack.

- **Example.** Realize that you are setting an example for those around you. Attitudes are contagious, and you will be a welcome carrier of this condition!

The good news is that anyone—absolutely anyone—can improve his or her attitude. As so often happens, we can draw the greatest inspiration for attitude adjustments from those who seem to have the greatest obstacles to overcome.

El Capitan is a granite wall in California's Yosemite National Park that shoots 3,700 feet (two-thirds of a mile) straight into the air. Mark Wellman was the first paraplegic in the world to climb El Capitan. When Mark reached the top, journalists asked him how he did it.

Mark's reply was, "I never thought of it as two-thirds of a mile. I thought of it as 7,000 six-inch climbs."

MACKAY'S MORAL

No platitudes about attitude, just think positive!

A SMILE ADDS FACE VALUE

I am a big fan of Dale Carnegie, the master of making friends. I carry a poem from one of his books with me and often share it when I am speaking to groups. It's called "The Value of a Smile," and I hope you learn as much from it as I have.

"It costs nothing, but creates much. It enriches those who receive, without impoverishing those who give. It happens in a flash and the memory of it sometimes lasts forever. None are so rich they can get along without it, and none so poor but are richer for its benefits.

"It creates happiness in the home, fosters goodwill in a business, and is the countersign of friends. It is rest to the weary, daylight to the discouraged, sunshine to the sad, and nature's best antidote for trouble.

"Yet it cannot be bought, begged, borrowed or stolen, for it is something that is no earthly good to anyone until it is given away. And if in the hurly-burly bustle of today's business world, some of the people you meet should be too tired to give you a smile, may we ask you to leave one of yours?

"For nobody needs a smile so much, as those who have none left to give."

I learned years ago that one of the most powerful things you can do to have influence with others is to smile at them. Smiling makes you more attractive and helps you make a good impression. We are naturally attracted to people who smile, because they appear warm and kind. They are more approachable. People who are constantly smiling appear to be more trustworthy than those who are not. And don't forget that the more you smile, the happier other people around you feel. Never underestimate the value of a smile. The person who is smart enough to keep smiling usually winds up with something good enough to smile about.

I learned years ago that one of the most powerful things you can do to have influence with others is to smile at them.

People all over the world smile in the same language. A smile should be standard equipment for all people, both at work and at home. It takes only 17 muscles to smile and 43 to frown—so really, you have no excuse. Put on a happy face!

People who smile are more productive and more creative. A 2010 study by Andrew Oswald, a professor of economics at Warwick Business School in England, proved that employees who smile more often are significantly more productive and creative in the workplace. And a 2013 study from the University of California, San Francisco, found that men who were happier had a more comprehensive approach to problems, improving their ability to think of more solutions than their negative-minded counterparts. The researchers connected this finding to the release of dopamine triggered by happiness, since the neurotransmitter is involved in learning, processing, and decision making.

Smiling also improves health. Studies have proven that when people smile, endorphins are released, making people feel happy and less stressed. The more you smile, the happier and more relaxed you become. Surprisingly, this also works when faking a smile or laugh, as the brain can't differentiate between real or fake smiles. Endorphins also act as natural painkillers. The added oxygen from smiling and laughing benefits your body while improving your immune system. Smiling releases more white blood cells, which protect the body against infectious diseases.

In a 2012 study published in the journal *Psychological Science*, University of Kansas psychological scientists Tara Kraft and Sarah Pressman studied 170 participants who were told to hold chopsticks in their mouths in three formations, making them smile to various degrees without realizing it, after performing a stressful task. The experiment revealed that subjects who smiled the biggest with the chopsticks experienced a substantial reduction in heart rate and quicker stress recovery compared to those whose expressions remained neutral.

Finally, smiles are contagious, just like yawns. So smile and start an epidemic.

Of all the things you wear, your expression is the most important. That's why you should not only smile from "ear to ear" but from "year to year."

MACKAY'S MORAL

Smiles never go up in price nor down in value.

ARROGANCE AND BUSINESS DON'T MIX

In a village long ago lived a young boy who loved nothing as much as competing in athletic contests. Because he was fit and strong, he usually triumphed and grew to love the adulation he received from the villagers around him.

One day he challenged two other youths to a race from one end of town to the other. The villagers all lined up to watch. The boy won, and the townspeople cheered wildly.

"Another race!" the boy demanded, greedy for more praise. "Who else will race me?"

Two more young men stepped up, and again the boy won handily. He laughed with pride as the villagers cheered—though they were a little less enthusiastic than before.

"Who else wants to race me?" the boy said. "Come on, are you all afraid?"

An elderly woman was watching the races, and she grew annoyed at the boy's arrogance. So she prodded two elderly men to challenge him. They could barely make their way to the starting line, but they seemed willing to compete.

"What's this?" The boy was puzzled. How could he win the applause he craved by beating two old men who could hardly stagger two steps?

The old woman walked up and whispered in his ear: "Do you want applause for this race?"

"Of course," said the boy.

"Finish together," the woman said. "Just finish together."

The boy did as he was told and received the loudest applause of his life when the three of them reached the finish line, side by side.

That boy learned a valuable lesson that day. No one likes arrogance. Have you ever worked with someone who is arrogant? It's not a pleasant experience.

Of all the human failings that can destroy a person or a business, arrogance is the deadliest. It is the most readily acquired, the easiest to justify, and the hardest to recognize in ourselves. Arrogance can infect all employees in a company with the silent destructiveness of a computer virus.

Herb Kelleher, the now retired head of Southwest Airlines, understood this danger very well. He said, "A company is never more vulnerable to complacency than when it's at the height of its success." Kelleher began his 1993 annual letter to all employees by describing the major threat to Southwest Airlines in the 1990s in these words: "The number one threat is us!" He went on to say, "We must not let success breed complacency; cockiness; greediness; laziness; indifference; preoccupation with nonessentials; bureaucracy; hierarchy; quarrelsomeness; or obliviousness to threats posed by the outside world."

There is nothing at all wrong with being proud of your company and the work you do. In fact, if you don't take pride in your work, you are probably not doing the best job you can do. But pride is not arrogance.

Arrogance is defined as engaging in behaviors intended to exaggerate a person's sense of superiority by disparaging others. It's not the same as narcissism, which is self-admiration. Nor is arrogance the same as confidence, which I consider a positive trait.

Unfortunately, many leaders today confuse confidence with arrogance. Confidence in one's ability is a critical element in the willingness to take risks while still steering the ship. Arrogance takes risks by assuming everyone will get on board even when the boat has a hole in it.

According to a 2012 article in *The Industrial-Organizational Psychologist* by Silverman, Johnson, McConnell, and Carr, arrogant people inflate their self-importance and see themselves as better than others, purport to be more knowledgeable than others, consider their own behavior acceptable, make others feel inferior, avoid blame and pin blame on others, discount feedback, don't perform their jobs well, and are less likely to help others.

I would add to that list that arrogant people are name droppers, avoid eye contact, frequently interrupt conversations, seem to have an opinion or an answer for everything, and aren't afraid to blast their competitors.

If you recognize yourself doing any of these offensive acts, check your behavior. It's nearly impossible to be a team player if you think you are better than everyone around you. Before long, you will be looking for a new team. You'd better hope your reputation doesn't precede you.

As Elvis Presley said, "If you let your head get too big, it'll break your neck."

MACKAY'S MORAL

Don't let arrogance get in the way of "finishing together."

HAPPINESS BREEDS SUCCESS

What makes me happy? It's a question we all should ask ourselves periodically, since all of our actions should, in some way, be directed toward achieving happiness. Initially, thoughts of riches beyond imagination may fill your mind. Or your thoughts may center on the car/house/job of your dreams. But if you are honest, you will probably find it to be a more difficult question than you would expect.

Abraham Lincoln is purported to have once said, "Most folks are about as happy as they make up their minds to be." Abe knew what he was talking about, and in the final analysis, I think you will find that the only "thing" that can make you happy is you.

Happiness is just a state of mind. So are anger, sorrow, disappointment, and loneliness. The mind is the most powerful tool in the universe, but you are the one who controls it. Like your car, if you see your mind heading in the wrong direction, you can steer it the other way. You need to recognize when you have negative feelings and try to steer your mind in a different direction. You don't want to be dwelling on the situation that brought you to that emotional state.

The mind is the most powerful tool in the universe, but you are the one who controls it.

Of course, it is easier to steer your mental car toward happiness if you have directions. That brings us back to our question, "What makes me happy?" By answering this question, you will be drawing the map. Try an easier question if you are stuck: "What has made me happy in the past?" My guess is that it was not material things.

My definition of happiness is not the fleeting, live-in-the-moment feeling that accompanies a birthday present. Rather, I think of happiness as a way of life. Truly happy people may have difficult times, but they know how to bounce back because they know better times are possible—and probable. They are content to have more positive thoughts than negative ones. They also understand that their happiness depends largely on how much happiness they share with the people around them.

Happiness is a powerful, addictive narcotic. Step into the bliss often enough and you'll carry it with you and seek situations that perpetuate it. Build a powerful reserve of positive feelings that will carry you through the tough situations that life throws at you.

Studies have shown that too much stress can inhibit your immune system, causing many of the health problems that plague our society. Heart disease, rheumatoid arthritis, ulcers, migraine headaches, mental illness, and even cancer are just a few of the health issues that have been linked to excessive stress. So in addition to improving the quality of your life, reducing your level of stress and increasing your happiness may also help to save your life.

Researchers at the Institute for Aging Research at Albert Einstein College of Medicine questioned 243 people age 100 or older. They found that centenarians tend to share certain personality traits (in addition to other factors, like genetics). In general, these long-lived people are:

- Outgoing,
- Positive-minded about other people,
- Full of laughter,
- Open with their emotions,
- Conscientious and disciplined,
- Unlikely to obsess about anxieties or guilt.

The scientists point out that these characteristics don't necessarily represent a cause-and-effect relationship. They did notice, however, that in many cases the personality traits they observed weren't necessarily lifelong tendencies, but behaviors their subjects learned as they grew older. Focusing on the good and not worrying about the negatives may have a positive impact on overall life expectancy.

So now that you know what finding your bliss could do for your quality of life, why wait? Organize your life so you have time to do the things you love.

I am not advocating that you abandon all responsibility. Life's pressures are going to prevent you from playing golf seven days a week, and even sunsets start to look alike after a while. You may not be able to just quit your job to become a professional singer. But the more attuned you are to what truly makes you happy, the more your life will align itself with the things you value and treasure.

As Albert Schweitzer said, "Success is not the key to happiness. Happiness is the key to success. If you love what you are doing, you will be successful."

MACKAY'S MORAL

Only you can draw the map of the road to your happiness.

3

BELIEVE IN YOURSELF

PEOPLE ACHIEVE TO THE DEGREE THEY BELIEVE IN THEMSELVES

"This is the worst day of my life. I must have been nuts to think I could do this."

Those were the words of my chief of staff, Greg Bailey, one summer as he climbed Mount of the Holy Cross in the Vail area, one of Colorado's famous 14,000-foot peaks commonly referred to as the "Fourteeners." He took his two boys on a mountain climbing expedition as part of an extended family father/son bonding in what he thought sounded like a fun hike or adventure.

Once he got down from more than eight hours on the mountain and recovered, he had a completely different perspective. He wanted to climb another "Fourteener" … of course, at a later date. He told me climbing that mountain was the hardest thing he had ever done in his life. He had never pushed himself to this level before.

Why do people push themselves to another level? What makes them accomplish or even attempt things that others think are not attainable or are even crazy to try? Is it the excitement, adventure, stimulation, or just plain challenge?

Remember the four-minute mile? People had been trying to achieve it since the days of the ancient Greeks. In fact, folklore has it that the Greeks had lions chase the runners, thinking that would make them run faster. They also tried tiger's milk—not the stuff you get down at the health-food store, but the real thing.

Nothing worked. So they decided it was impossible. And for over a thousand years everyone believed it was physiologically impossible for a human being to run a mile in four minutes. Our bone structure was all wrong. Wind resistance was too great. Human lung power was inadequate. There were a million reasons.

Then one man, one single human being, proved that the doctors, the trainers, the athletes, and the millions before him who tried and failed, were all wrong. And miracle of miracles, the year after Roger Bannister broke the four-minute mile, 37 other runners broke the four-minute mile, and the year after that 300 runners broke the four-minute mile.

So what makes people successful? Is it sheer determination? The thrill of accomplishment? The desire to achieve? The will to persevere?

I learned long ago that there are three kinds of people in the world: the wills, the won'ts, and the can'ts. The first accomplish everything. The second oppose everything. The third fail in everything.

I learned long ago that there are three kinds of people in the world: the wills, the won'ts, and the can'ts. The first accomplish everything. The second oppose everything. The third fail in everything.

Greg's mountain climbing story reminded me of another involving two tribes who were at war with one another. One of the tribes lived in the lowlands and the other lived high in the mountains.

One day the mountain people conducted a raid on the lowlanders and plundered a village. During the raid, they kidnapped a baby of one of the lowlander families and took the infant with them back up into the mountains.

Enraged at the loss, the lowlanders resolved to recover the kidnapped baby no matter what the cost. But they didn't know how to climb the mountain. They didn't know any of the trails that the mountain people used, and they didn't know where to find the mountain people or how to track them in the steep terrain. Even so, the lowlanders sent out a rescue party of their best fighting men to climb the mountain and bring the baby home.

The men tried one method of climbing first and then another, all to no avail. After several days of effort, they had succeeded in climbing only several hundred feet up the mountain. Thoroughly discouraged, the lowlander men decided that the cause was lost, and they reluctantly prepared to return to their village below.

But, as they were packing their gear for the descent, they suddenly saw the baby's mother walking toward them. They stood silent gazing at her in the realization that she was coming down the mountain they had totally failed to climb.

Then they saw that she had the kidnapped baby strapped to her back. They all stared in amazement. How was that possible?

The first man to greet her said, "We couldn't climb this mountain. How did you do so when we, the strongest and most able men in the village, couldn't do it?"

She shrugged her shoulders and replied, "It wasn't your baby."

MACKAY'S MORAL

The only thing that matters is if *you* say you can't do it.

GIVE YOUR SELF-CONFIDENCE THE BOOST YOU NEED

Walt Disney used to talk about the four Cs to success in life: curiosity, confidence, courage, and consistency. He believed that if you applied these four Cs to your life, you could accomplish practically anything. But there was one C that Walt said was the greatest of all: confidence. He said, "When you believe a thing, believe it all the way, implicitly and unquestionably."

When people think of Walt Disney—the man—they think of success and the empire he created. But that wasn't the case for Walt early on. He was anything but successful. He had several business failures and was told by an editor at the *Kansas City Star* newspaper that he "lacked imagination and had no good ideas."

Maybe that's why confidence was so important to him. He certainly was no quitter.

Self-confidence is extremely important in almost every aspect of our lives, yet many people don't believe in themselves as they should, and they find it difficult to become successful.

Would you buy a product from someone who is nervous, fumbling, or overly apologetic? No. You would be suspicious of their product, their trustworthiness, and their ability to provide follow-up service. You would prefer someone who is confident and speaks clearly and knows their stuff.

Confidence enables you to perform to the best of your abilities, without the fear of failure holding you back. It starts with believing in yourself.

Confidence enables you to perform to the best of your abilities, without the fear of failure holding you back. It starts with believing in yourself.

As one of my favorite motivational authors, Norman Vincent Peale, said, "Believe in yourself! Have faith in your abilities! Without a humble but reasonable confidence in your own powers you cannot be successful or happy." One word in particular in that quote stands out: *humble*. Confidence does not mean arrogance, in fact, quite the opposite. Humility is a quality that must accompany confidence in order to instill trust.

You don't acquire confidence overnight. You can't wake up one day and think you are good. You have to work at it. You have to practice the right concepts, get the best coaching you can, and develop mental toughness. You have to think like a winner.

Coaches and managers can tell their players and employees to be more confident, but if they don't prepare and work hard enough, confidence will always be lacking. It's easy to fire people up, but they also have to be willing to prepare and pay the price to achieve a high level of confidence.

My friend, the late Jack Kemp, told me the story of how his coach motivated him when he played quarterback at Occidental College.

Before the football season started, the coach called Kemp into his office for a private meeting. He said, "Jack, you are my guy. You are the leader on this team. You are the one I can count on. Every year I pick just one player, and you are that player. If you live up to your potential, you have what it takes to achieve greatness. But it's important that you don't tell anyone else."

Jack told me that when he left that room he was ready to run through a brick wall for that guy. What he didn't know until after the season was that his coach said the same thing to 11 other players.

Kemp went on to play pro football for 13 years, served nine terms in Congress representing western New York, and was Republican nominee Bob Dole's vice presidential running mate in the 1996 presidential election.

A wonderful accompaniment to confidence is a sense of humor, as the following story illustrates. Being able to laugh at yourself is the ultimate demonstration of confidence.

A New Yorker fresh from a business trip to Texas was telling his associates about his experiences. One of them asked, "What impressed you most about the people there?"

"Their confidence." The man thought for a moment. "Here's an example. We went duck hunting on Saturday. We sat in a blind all day long and never saw a thing. Then, right about sundown, this one duck flew over our heads. One of the guys stood up with his shotgun and fired. And the duck kept right on flying.

"Nobody said a word for a moment. Then the shooter shook his head and said to me, 'You're seeing a miracle! There flies a dead duck.'"

MACKAY'S MORAL

Confidence is keeping your chin up. Overconfidence is sticking your neck out.

Humility, success make good business partners

As Will Rogers used to say, get someone else to blow your horn and the sound will carry twice as far.

Humility is becoming a lost art—in an era of self-promotion and making sure you get all the credit you deserve, it's refreshing indeed to come across coworkers, bosses, or even customers who have enough self-confidence to let their work speak for their abilities and achievements.

And even after all the boasting and bluster, most folks have already figured out who will get the job done ... and who won't drive them crazy in the process.

A very thin line separates confidence and conceit. People who are confident in their abilities are described as "capable," "intelligent," "efficient," and "dependable." Anyone would be pleased to have those adjectives associated with their reputation. Conceited people, on the other hand, earn titles like "phony," "arrogant," "obnoxious," and "unpleasant."

I learned my lesson from none other than my wife when I invited her to join me at a speaking engagement. I did all my usual homework and preparation, gave the speech, and was thrilled to receive a standing ovation from the audience.

Feeling rather smug in the car on the way home, I turned to her and asked: "Sweetheart, how many great speakers do you think there are in the world today?"

She smiled and said, "One fewer than you think, dear."

Touché.

It was at that point that I realized the human body is designed so that we can neither pat our own backs nor kick ourselves in the backsides too easily.

Humility is not difficult to practice. It doesn't involve downplaying your achievements. It doesn't mean that you won't be recognized for your contributions. It does mean that you realize that others have been involved in your success, and you are prepared to be involved in theirs.

You start by giving credit where it is due. The coworkers who participated in the early stages of a project surely deserve some recognition, and the folks who mopped the floors and kept the lights on so you could work late are team players too.

Have you ever noticed how long the credits take at the end of a movie? They identify everyone from the stars to the caterers to the pyrotechnical wizards. The project couldn't be completed without all of those people.

If you want a real lesson in humility, volunteer. Jobs go begging every day, so you surely won't have any problem finding something to do. Putting yourself in a position where your performance will not result in a raise, promotion, or fancier job title has a way of refreshing your perspective.

Here's a story that perfectly illustrates the point:

A couple hundred years ago, a rider on horseback came across a squad of soldiers who were trying to move a heavy piece of timber. A well-dressed corporal stood by, giving urgent commands to "heave." But try as they might, the squad couldn't budge the timber.

The rider was curious, and asked the corporal why he didn't help his men.

"Me? Why, can't you see I'm a corporal?" he replied.

The rider dismounted and offered to help. He took his place among the soldiers, smiled, and said, "Now all together, men, heave!" The big timber slid into place. He silently mounted his horse and turned to the corporal.

"The next time you have a piece of timber for your men to handle, corporal, send for the commander-in-chief." With that, George Washington rode off, much to the amazement of the soldiers, and I suppose, the dismay of a very embarrassed corporal.

MACKAY'S MORAL

Just remember, when you put yourself on a pedestal and elevate yourself above the rest of the world, the size of your funeral will still depend a lot on the weather.

4

BUSINESS BASICS

THE BEST JOB LESSONS
I EVER LEARNED

The *San Francisco Chronicle Examiner* recently called me to participate in a story on "What job taught you the most lessons?" I had 100 words or less, which is pretty tough, especially for someone like me.

I had to think about that for a while since I've only had a couple jobs in my adult life. My first job out of college was for another envelope company, where I toiled for nearly five years. I learned plenty in that job, of course, but most significantly, that I wanted to own my own company. In 1959 I bought a failing envelope company, and the rest is history. I learn something new in this job every day.

After giving it some thought, I realized that the job that taught me the most was possibly when my father, who headed the Associated Press Bureau in St. Paul, Minnesota, encouraged me to sign up for a paper route at age 10. I learned many valuable lessons at an early age.

Here are some of the lessons I remember learning:

- **Hard work.** Seven days a week, I had to get up at 4 a.m. when it was pitch dark and possibly snowing or raining, and deliver my papers by 6 a.m. There were no days off. And nine months of the year I had school to look forward to after my route. Child labor laws would probably prohibit this now, but I'm pretty sure it didn't hurt me.

- **Focus.** I knew I had to get up early every morning, so I knew I had to get my homework done and get to bed early. I've always felt that if you put your mind to it, you can do anything.

- **Persistence.** I dealt with all kinds of people, including many who didn't like to pay their bills. But I had to keep after them. I learned that there are good days and bad days at work, but you work on all of them regardless. Pretty soon the bad days get better.

- **Customer service.** I learned how to deal with people face-to-face on a paper route. Also, sometimes I had to apologize for things that were out of my control, which is a tough thing to teach to anyone, especially a 10-year-old. But when newspapers were late in getting to me, I was in turn late in getting them delivered. It wasn't my fault, but I still had to personally apologize to my customers. And then there were other elements like the weather that can cause havoc. Who likes a wet newspaper? We didn't have little plastic bags to put papers in back in those days. It was also important to remember who wanted their paper between the doors, in the milk box, or under the mat.

- **Accountability.** I was accountable for my route to make sure my customers received their newspapers in a timely fashion and paid their bills. That's pretty cut and dried, especially when you are a one-man show.

- **Handling money.** Collections and keeping financial records were also important, as well as learning how to handle money. A 10-cent boo-boo then was as important to me as a 1,000-dollar mistake is to me now. The adding and subtracting end of the business also helped with math class.

- **Salesmanship.** Most importantly, I learned my number one skill . . . the art of selling. If people paid in advance, I earned more. If I could get my customers to pay for the newspaper one or two months in advance, I was in candy heaven. Likewise, if I could get people on my route or within my sales territory to start subscribing to the newspaper, I made more money. That should be a good incentive for anyone. I learned that I loved to sell and knew it would be my life's work.

Now after working with another kind of paper, I can honestly say that the job that launched my career was pivotal. Everyone has to start somewhere. You never forget your first job.

No matter where you go to work, you are not an employee—you are a business with one employee . . . you. Nobody owes you a career. You own it, as a sole proprietor. You must compete with millions of individuals every day of your career. You must enhance your value every day, hone your competitive advantage, learn, adapt, move jobs and industries—retrench so you can advance and learn new skills.

It's as simple as having a paper route.

MACKAY'S MORAL

Your first job on any job is to learn.

How not to ride a dead horse

Dakota tribal wisdom says that when you discover you are riding a dead horse, the best strategy is to dismount. That's a no-brainer if I've ever heard one. However, in business we often try other strategies with dead horses, although I'm not sure why. Among the possibilities:

- Buying a stronger whip.
- Changing riders.
- Saying things like, "This is the way we have always ridden this horse."
- Appointing a committee to study the horse.
- Arranging to visit other sites to see how they ride dead horses.
- Appointing a tiger team to revive the dead horse.
- Creating a training session to increase our riding ability.
- Comparing the state of dead horses in today's environment.
- Changing the requirements, declaring that "This horse is not dead."
- Outsourcing contractors to ride the dead horse.
- Harnessing several dead horses together for increased speed.
- Declaring that "No horse is too dead to ride."
- Providing additional funding to increase the horse's performance.
- Doing a cost analysis study to see if contractors can ride it cheaper.
- Declaring the horse is "better, faster, and cheaper" dead.
- Promoting the dead horse to a supervisory position.

If any of these ideas sound remotely familiar, it's time to make a few large-scale changes. No amount of CPR is going to save that horse, and every minute that your staff invests in trying to change the situation is costing your company money.

First, run your staff through a session on identifying the central issue. What we have here is a non-productive, non-salvageable, soon-to-be-stinking mess that deserves a swift and merciful end. Imagine what other serious work you could be doing, rather than just postponing the inevitable. The dead-end projects in any department should be acknowledged for what they are, and should be put in the big "learning experiences" file.

Second, hold your managers accountable for projects. Suggestions like the pathetic efforts above indicate a serious lack of leadership. The biggest mistake a manager can make is failing to provide guidance to subordinates. As Warren Bennis and Burt Nanus put it: "Managers do things right. Leaders do the right things."

Third, demand results, not excuses. Excuses don't do much for the value of your company's stock. Following the big break-up of AT&T, Bell Atlantic made it clear that excuses were not an option: the company established a structure where each department was required to bill other departments for their services. Before this practice, the information systems department could easily respond to requests with excuses such as "we can't do that," "we don't have time," or "we don't have the money/staff." With the new plan in place, and the information systems department needing to show a profit, the response changed dramatically, because excuses were not an option.

Finally, acknowledge mistakes, and then move on. Everybody, every company, makes mistakes. Do not be too hasty to equate mistakes with failure. One dead horse shouldn't mean you lose the farm. At the same time Babe Ruth held the career record for home runs (714), he also held the record for career strikeouts (1,330 times). Henry Ford forgot to put a reverse gear in his first car. Thomas Edison once invested more than $2 million (the value in his era, not ours) on an invention that turned out to be useless.

Don't let a mistake keep you from doing great things. But don't let a mistake take on a life of its own either. If you are dealing with the same mistake you dealt with last week or last month or last year, identify the central issue and deal with it. You'll be glad you did.

MACKAY'S MORAL

Don't horse around when you're dealing with mistakes. Get back in the saddle and grab the reins.

DISCIPLINE IS THE ORDER OF THE DAY

Most people aim to do right; they just fail to pull the trigger. For whatever reason, they just don't have the wherewithal to finish the job. They are lacking discipline.

"Discipline is the foundation upon which all success is built. Lack of discipline inevitably leads to failure," said the late motivational speaker Jim Rohn.

It doesn't matter whether you are pursuing success in business, sports, the arts, or life in general. Hope is not an option. The difference between wishing and accomplishing is discipline.

It doesn't matter whether you are pursuing success in business, sports, the arts, or life in general. Hope is not an option. The difference between wishing and accomplishing is discipline.

Bob Knight, one of college basketball's winningest coaches, said: "It has always been my thought that the most important single ingredient to success in athletics or life is discipline. I have many times felt that this word is the most ill-defined in all of our language. My definition of the word is as follows: (1) Do what has to be done; (2) When it has to be done; (3) As well as it can be done; and (4) Do it that way all the time."

Julie Andrews put it a little differently. She said, "Some people regard discipline as a chore. For me, it is a kind of order that sets me free to fly."

Arthur Rubenstein, one of the greatest pianists of all time, said: "If I miss one day of practice, I notice it. If I miss two days of practice, the critics notice it. If I miss three days of practice, the audience notices."

Discipline is all about sitting down and setting goals, figuring out a schedule to achieve those goals, and then following your plan.

It's the old adage: the more you put in, the more you get out.

"You can't get much done in life if you only work on the days when you feel good," said Jerry West, the former Los Angeles Lakers great who was nicknamed "Mr. Clutch."

Health and fitness clubs get very busy at the beginning of each year. New Year's resolutions result in large numbers of people joining, wanting to get fit or lose weight. What happens in February, March, and April? The number of people at the club starts to thin out, but the well-intentioned folks who lacked discipline didn't thin down.

Good intentions aren't enough. People have good intentions when they set a goal to do something, but then they miss a deadline or a workout. Suddenly it gets a lot easier to miss again and again and again.

Golfing great Byron Nelson said: "The only way one can become proficient at anything is self-discipline and dedication. The people who succeed are the ones that really do not let personal feelings get in their way from giving their all in whatever they choose to do. The superstar golfers are people who are willing to do and give a little bit more than the others who do not succeed."

The legendary football coach Vince Lombardi maintained: "A player's got to know the basics of the game and how to play his position. Next, you've got to keep him in line."

That's discipline, which is a trait that every good manager must have. It's not enough as a manager to teach your employees how to do the work. You also have to provide the motivation that keeps them moving forward. Perhaps most importantly, a good manager must model self-discipline.

To me it is better to prepare and prevent instead of repair and repent.

I like the way Jim Rohn described discipline: "It is the bridge between thought and accomplishment . . . the glue that binds inspiration to achievement . . . the magic that turns financial necessity into the creation of an inspired work of art.

"Discipline is the master key that unlocks the door to wealth and happiness, culture and sophistication, high self-esteem and high accomplishment and the accompanying feelings of pride, satisfaction, and success. Discipline will do much for you. More importantly, though, is what it will do to you. It will make you feel terrific about yourself."

MACKAY'S MORAL

If your willpower doesn't work, try your "won't" power.

WINNERS SET GOALS, LOSERS MAKE EXCUSES

Ask any successful CEO, superstar athlete, or winning person what their keys to success are and you will hear four consistent messages: vision, determination, persistence, and setting goals.

A new year is a perfect time to set your goals for the year, for the decade, or for the rest of your life. After all, if you don't set goals to determine where you're going, how will you know when you get there?

Remember the Italian proverb: You never climb higher than the ladder you select.

My friend Lou Holtz is a firm believer in setting goals. In 1966 while unemployed, Holtz listed 107 lifetime goals, most of which he has already achieved. He dreamed of having dinner at the White House, appearing on *The Tonight Show*, coaching the Notre Dame football team, and winning the national championship. And what do you think Holtz will do when he achieves all 107 goals? He'll make a new list.

All of us know that it is easy to get sidelined or distracted in trying to reach our goals. One of the most common goals is to lose weight. But did you ever notice how your goal always seems to run into a snack?

Let me tell you a story about the fellow who used to wear the grapes in the Fruit of the Loom commercials. He became obsessed with losing weight and went on a crash diet, losing more than 100 pounds within three months. However, the dramatic weight loss left him hospitalized. After recovering, he decided to learn how to lose weight safely through good nutrition and proper exercise. He was so thrilled after learning this, he set a goal to share his knowledge with people who struggle with obesity, and he determined to make it fun and entertaining. Richard Simmons became a household name for his weight-loss crusade. He couldn't have done it without setting goals and sticking to them.

You must stay focused on your goals above all else. Truly dedicated individuals won't let anything interfere with attaining their goals. That's why so few people become champions. It's not easy.

Famed Boston Celtic coach Red Auerbach was one of the most successful basketball coaches in history. He believed that the basic principles for success are the same in business as athletics. At the top of his list was setting goals. Good teams always share common goals. When the goals of some members differ from the rest of the team, then the team will usually not do well. That's why teams with outstanding individual talents sometimes do poorly, while others are able to blend average abilities into championships.

I witnessed this first hand at the 2000 Olympics in Australia when the huge underdog Lithuanian basketball team took the U.S. Dream Team to the final seconds before losing.

Goals give you more than a reason to get up in the morning; they are an incentive to keep you going all day. Goals tend to tap into deeper resources and draw the best out of life. Achieving goals produces significant accomplishments.

Goals give you more than a reason to get up in the morning; they are an incentive to keep you going all day. Goals tend to tap into deeper resources and draw the best out of life. Achieving goals produces significant accomplishments.

Most important, goals need to be realistic: beyond your grasp today, but within your reach in the foreseeable future.

I remember a particular Peanuts cartoon in which Charlie Brown is having a bad day. He strikes out for the third straight time. In disgust, he says, "Rats!"

Back in the dugout, he buries his face in his hands and laments to Lucy, "I'll never be a big-league ballplayer. All my life, I've dreamed of playing in the big leagues, but I just know I'll never make it."

Lucy responds, "You're thinking way too far ahead, Charlie Brown. What you need are more immediate goals."

"Immediate goals?" asks Charlie.

"Yes," says Lucy. "Start right now with this next inning. When you go out to pitch, see if you can walk out to the mound without falling down."

MACKAY'S MORAL

A goal is a dream with a deadline.

ETHICS IS ABOUT WHAT IS RIGHT, NOT WHO IS RIGHT

If you have integrity, nothing else matters. If you don't have integrity, nothing else matters.

That pretty much sums up ethics.

Peter Drucker, management consultant and author, said: "As to 'ethical problems' in business, I have made myself tremendously unpopular by saying, again and again, that there is no such thing as 'business ethics.' There is only ethics."

Ethics are more scrutinized today than in any previous era. That might be hard to believe for some, in light of all the corporate malfeasance and other ethical issues that seem so pervasive. We are demanding more and higher ethical standards than in the past, and ethical breaches become front-page news. Cheating, under-the-table deals, and hoping no one will notice are dangerous practices in the 21st century. The make-money-at-all-costs mentality of the 1980s and 1990s is now viewed as greedy, excessive, and just plain wrong.

Many companies are going beyond the usual degree of ethics. For example, Raytheon has a director of ethics compliance. All wrongdoings, difficult personnel issues, and ethical quandaries are reported to the same person. Honeywell also has a corporate director of ethics to try to make it easier for employees to detect what's right and wrong. Companies can't mandate morals, but they can surely ask employees to bring their ethics to work with them.

Many of us encounter an ethical dilemma in the workplace, whether it's someone swiping office supplies or witnessing a coworker's questionable actions. To guide you to make better ethical decisions, ask yourself these questions:

- **Is it legal?** This is a given, but you'd be surprised how many people don't know local, state, and federal laws. Knowing what's right doesn't mean much unless you do what's right.

- **How will it make you feel about yourself?** Ask yourself how you will feel about yourself if you do or don't act in a given situation. Abraham Lincoln was once asked about ethics and he quoted an old man he had once heard speak at a church meeting in Indiana. The old man said, "When I do good I feel good; and when I do bad, I feel bad."

I'm reminded of Hall of Fame golfer Bobby Jones at the 1925 U.S. Open, where he insisted on penalizing himself a stroke when his ball moved slightly in the rough as the blade of his iron touched the turf. Nobody else could possibly have seen the ball move. The penalty dropped Jones into a tie with golfer Willie McFarlane, who went on to win the playoff.

Golfer Tom Kite did the same thing 53 years later in 1978. The self-imposed penalty caused him to lose the Hall of Fame Classic at Pinehurst by one stroke. Reporters asked both men why they took the penalties. And both said essentially the same thing, "There's only one way to play the game."

- **How do others feel about it?** I have a "kitchen cabinet" of people I can talk to and bounce ideas off of. Two heads are better than one, and three heads are better than two. These are trusted friends and coworkers. Get their opinions on a situation. Don't always trust your gut. You want to see all sides.

- **How would you feel if your actions were made public?** No one ever wants to see his or her name linked to anything bad. Conscience is like a baby. It has to go to sleep before you can. If you don't want coworkers, family, and friends to know about something, then it's a sure bet the action is questionable.

- **Does the behavior make sense?** Will it hurt others? Is there a hidden motive in your actions?

- **Is it fair?** Ethical decisions ensure that everyone's best interests are protected. When in doubt, don't.

- **Will people in authority approve?** What would your supervisor say? Get a manager's opinion. We have an open door policy at MackayMitchell Envelope Company for employees to discuss anything with managers.

- **How would you feel if someone did the same thing to you?** The Golden Rule is always an appropriate standard.

- **Will something negative happen if you don't make a decision?** Sometimes not taking action can result in harm to others.

MACKAY'S MORAL

Honesty is the best policy, even if it comes at a high premium.

5

COACHING

Lessons from John Wooden: Build a pyramid of success

If I could come back in a second life, I'd be a high school or college basketball coach. First off, I love basketball, and second, few can have a greater influence on young people than a coach or teacher.

I've long admired John Wooden, the legendary UCLA basketball coach who won 10 NCAA championships in a 12-year period. He has won countless awards and even received our nation's highest civilian honor, the Medal of Freedom. Not surprisingly, Wooden was named the Greatest Coach Ever by *Sporting News*.

Coach Wooden was a masterful molder of young men. Bill Walton, a member of the National Basketball Association's Hall of Fame, wrote, "After my father, Coach Wooden has had the most profound influence on me of anyone in my entire life."

Coach Wooden, in turn, credited his father for grounding him in the principles on which he based his life and career.

"When I graduated from our little three-room grade school in Centerton, Indiana," said Wooden, "my father gave me a little card on which he had written out his creed." At the top of the card was written, "Seven Things to Do." They are:

1. Be true to yourself.
2. Help others.
3. Make each day your masterpiece.
4. Drink deeply from good books, especially the *Bible*.
5. Make friendship a fine art.
6. Build a shelter against a rainy day.
7. Pray for guidance and count and give thanks for your blessings every day.

Wooden remembered that all his father said to him when he handed him the card was, "Son, try and live up to these things." Wooden certainly did.

Coach Wooden might be best known for his Pyramid of Success. He drilled it into his players over and over. Basketball great Kareem Abdul-Jabbar, who played his college years under Wooden, once told a reporter he thought the Pyramid was kind of corny when he first saw it, but he later came to the conclusion that it had a great effect on his career and later life.

You can construct a visual picture of Coach Wooden's Pyramid. On the bottom layer, draw five rectangular blocks and label them: industriousness, friendship, loyalty, cooperation, and enthusiasm. On the next layer above, fill in four blocks with these labels: self-control, alertness, initiative, and intentness. On the third layer toward the top of the pyramid, place three blocks and label them: condition, skill, and team spirit. On the fourth layer, place two building blocks and label them: poise and confidence. The fifth and next to last layer has only one block. It bears the label: competitive greatness. Finally, the triangular crown of the pyramid is divided into two halves with the labels: faith and patience.

Wooden always maintained that the order and placement of each block was essential to the pyramid's success. Considering his success with this teaching tool, who can contradict him?

What a lot of people might not know is that John Wooden was a three-time All-American at Purdue University. "My coach at Purdue, Piggy Lambert, constantly reminded us: 'The team that makes the most mistakes will probably win.' That may sound a bit odd, but there is a great deal of truth in it. The doer makes mistakes. Coach Lambert taught me that mistakes come from doing, but so does success. The individual who is mistake-free is also probably sitting around doing nothing. And that's a very big mistake."

Like all great coaches and teachers, Wooden did not teach basketball. He taught life.

If you learned a little basketball on the side, well, so much the better. Among my favorite Wooden quotes:

- "Too often we get distracted by what is outside our control. You can't do anything about yesterday. The door to the past has been shut and the key thrown away. You can do nothing about tomorrow. It is yet to come. However, tomorrow is in large part determined by what you do today. You have control over that."

- "Develop a love for details. They usually accompany success."

- "Failure is not fatal, but failure to change may be."

MACKAY'S MORAL (COURTESY OF JOHN WOODEN)

"Talent is God-given, be humble. Fame is man-given, be thankful. Conceit is self-given, be careful."

Good bosses
improve good employees

With so much focus on finding or keeping jobs in this economy, one significant employment factor seems to get moved down the pros and cons chart: What kind of boss will my next supervisor be?

Interviewing with a human relations specialist…. Meeting folks up and down the line…. Putting your best foot forward while they are all doing the same…. The process may not present a completely accurate picture of the day-to-day environment.

Bosses know the importance of a good hire. Assuming the best candidate has accepted the offer, and has shown up on time for a few weeks, does the boss realize how critical retaining that new employee is? Does the boss know how to be a good boss?

In short, will the boss be a buddy or a bully?

Bosses have tremendous power over those they supervise. Whether dealing with the owner of the company or a middle manager, employees understand that the person they report to can be their biggest cheerleader or their worst nightmare.

I prefer to think that the people I have hired put me in the first category. Having made a significant investment of time in hiring them in the first place, I must have recognized the sort of talent, personality, and energy that would improve our company.

I want the folks I hire to love their jobs enough to come back raring to go after a lousy day, because everybody has a lousy day once in a while. I want them to look to me for inspiration. I want them to respect my work ethic. I want them to want to get better at what they do. I want them to know that I will help them get better. I want them to learn from my example, even when I am not directly mentoring them.

Of course, none of that happens unless I know how to come back revved up after a miserable day, demonstrate a stellar work ethic, and keep improving myself. What goes around comes around.

Study after study has concluded that the most important factor in job satisfaction is a positive work environment. Praise is vital, and salary is important, but nothing ranks as high as loving what you do. Location matters, but people are willing to go great distances for a job that makes them happy. Titles aren't even near the top of the list.

Study after study has concluded that the most important factor in job satisfaction is a positive work environment. Praise is vital, and salary is important, but nothing ranks as high as loving what you do.

The determining factor is often closely related to the boss. A truly great boss will engender loyalty before any of those other factors will. A committed boss works hardest at positive leadership and a professional environment. A perceptive boss remembers her own early challenges and draws on those experiences. A responsible boss understands that mentoring his staff and helping them develop skills reflect positively on him.

I admire the bosses on those popular television shows who concealed their identities and went to work on the front lines for some "real-world" lessons about their companies. They were quite courageous to expose their own weaknesses to the world. But the exercise resulted in enhanced awareness of the importance of every single employee.

If you dare, try that experiment in your organization. You likely cannot be anonymous, but working side-by-side with staff and reinforcing that you won't ask them to do anything that you wouldn't ask of yourself demonstrates your understanding of their challenges.

If all this sounds too overwhelming, step back and examine your motives. Are you ready to let someone else have a share in the glory? Are you willing to listen to options? Are you threatened by others' successes? Can you take responsibility for failure?

Many bosses are promoted without any formal leadership training. A good boss learns quickly that listening to employees will serve them better than a superior attitude.

Now here's the most important piece of boss advice I will ever give you: Your employees don't really work for you. They work for your customers. Customers are their real bosses. And yours too.

MACKAY'S MORAL

Be a mentor, not a tormentor.

A GREAT WORK ENVIRONMENT
IS AN EXCELLENT MOTIVATOR

People do things for two reasons: they have to or they want to. Which reason works better? My money is on the work that is performed because someone wants to do it.

But that other work still needs to get done. Is it possible to change a "have-to" job into a "want-to" job?

Motivation results from actions that satisfy inner needs. If you show people how to get what they want, they will usually move mountains to get it. And that often involves both the have-to and the want-to chores. The secret is in the motivation.

As a manager, you frequently need to be a motivator and a cheerleader. Here are a few tips:

- **Create a favorable environment and attitude for learning.** Try to capture the attention and curiosity of the person you're trying to motivate. Provide training that helps that person diversify his or her skills and expand job opportunities.

- **Provide incentives to promote learning. Incentives can be praise, privilege, or actual material rewards.** It can include paying tuition for pertinent classes, recognition at a sales meeting, a plaque for the office, a bonus, or any one of 100 other ways to let your employees know you appreciate their willingness to go the extra mile.

- **Try to boost internal motivation that does not have to be rewarded all the time.** Otherwise, the person may not find her own true motivation in the long run. I have found that some of the most motivated individuals are simply content to be a part of a really great organization. Claiming ownership in a company's success is powerful motivation.

- **Sometimes, you just have to wait until people are ready to learn.** Give your employees a little time to get used to a new way of doing business. Change can be scary when the old way has worked for a long time. It's important to have workers buy into the concept.

- **Pay attention to how the information you are trying to get across to the learner is organized.** If management doesn't look motivated to take the time to present information well, the message is that maybe this new system isn't that great after all. It can make a difference in whether the learner is motivated or not.

- **Recognize that learning new concepts can make people anxious and uncomfortable—and prepare to deal with their concerns.** The person who is trying to motivate and teach should understand that patience is more than a virtue—it's an absolute necessity. Create an atmosphere in which employees can take risks, fail, and try again without fear or humiliation.

- **Remember, business should be fun.** Fun is a powerful motivator. Going to work should never be drudgery, no matter what the job involves. I have a dentist friend who loves to do root canals—not because she's a sadist, but because she knows her patients benefit so greatly from the result. I've always said that if you find something you love to do, you'll never have to work a day in your life.

- **Finally, give your employees credit.** Letting people move ahead without interference is also an effective way to motivate. When you trust employees enough to let them make decisions that affect their work, you have recognized their intelligence (and your own, for hiring them in the first place).

The late Bartlett Giamatti, on his first day as president of Yale University in 1978, issued the following memo to everyone in the university: "I wish to announce that henceforth, as a matter of university policy, evil is abolished and paradise is restored. I trust all of us to do whatever possible to achieve this policy."

What an ideal work environment—just do whatever you know you should to make things perfect. It's up to you to figure that out, and the results should be easily quantified and obvious. I've spoken at a number of colleges and universities, and I can tell you that there are places like this. It works in businesses, too.

MACKAY'S MORAL

Ability is what you're capable of doing. Motivation determines what you do. Attitude determines how well you do it.

RECOGNITION DOES WONDERS FOR YOUR SENSE OF HEARING

U.S. President Harry Truman once said, "It is amazing what you can accomplish if you don't care who gets the credit." That is especially true when a manager doesn't take the credit for himself and instead gives it to his team. A little recognition here and there can go a long way to help employers attract and retain the best workers. It's human nature for everyone to want to be appreciated for doing a good job.

According to a survey by WorldatWork and the National Association for Employee Recognition, 84 percent of the responding companies have an employee recognition program. More than half of the companies that don't have such a program said they are considering implementing one in the next 12 months. And nearly half of those companies that have a recognition program plan to expand it in the next year.

Survey participants said recognition programs create a positive work environment by "reinforcing desired behaviors, motivating high performance, increasing morale, and supporting organizational mission and values."

It's no wonder then that Napoleon was always inventing new military medals. One day, someone asked him why he wasted time on these "toys." According to folklore, Napoleon replied, "Men are ruled by toys." Like all great military leaders, Napoleon understood that recognition, honor, and glory are the kinds of rewards that warriors work for.

The WorldatWork survey examined medals and other types of awards used by employers. Topping the list was gift certificates, followed by cash, office accessories, jewelry (lapel pins), household items (vases, china), watches, electronics (cameras, TVs), travel, and debit cards.

I've always found that cash works wonders. There's nothing quite like crisp, crunchy, crackly, cold hard cash. At MackayMitchell Envelope Company we also recognize our employees with tickets for sporting events, theatre, orchestra, and dinners. We like to celebrate our employees' accomplishments.

The survey also looked at the ways companies recognize employees. One-on-one with managers was first at 71 percent; followed by special events like banquets/luncheons, 65 percent; during staff meetings, 60 percent; and during company-wide meetings, 42 percent.

I've always tried to give recognition in front of a group. Single people out among their peers. Why not give others something to strive for and show them how you value good performance?

I've always tried to give recognition in front of a group. Single people out among their peers. Why not give others something to strive for and show them how you value good performance?

Ever meet a person who didn't like recognition? No way. The child who says, "Mother, let's play darts," expresses it brilliantly. "I'll throw the darts and you say 'wonderful.'"

Listen to what Dale Carnegie had to say on the subject: "Tell a child, a husband, or an employee that he is stupid or dumb at a certain thing, that he is doing it all wrong, and you have destroyed almost every incentive to try to improve. But use the opposite technique; be liberal with encouragement; make the thing seem easy to do; let the other person know that you have faith in his ability to do it, that he has an undeveloped flair for it—and he will practice until the dawn comes in at the window in order to excel."

One of the great examples of that is Jackie Robinson, the first African-American to play major league baseball. When Robinson was signed with the Brooklyn Dodgers, he became a target for racial hate mail and even death threats. Before one game, Robinson received a threatening phone call that left him so shaken that he was unable to concentrate on the game.

Robinson struck out in one inning with bases loaded. In another inning, he committed a fielding error. The crowd screamed obscenities at him. A time-out was called and the Dodger shortstop, Pee Wee Reese, walked up to the shaken Robinson, put his arm around him, and said: "Jackie, you are the greatest ballplayer I have ever seen. You can do it. And I know something else. One of these days you are going into the Hall of Fame. So, hold your head up high, and play ball like only you can do it."

Robinson was so encouraged by these words that he went on to deliver a game-winning hit for his team.

Many years later, Robinson recalled the incident when he was inducted into the Baseball Hall of Fame. He said of Pee Wee Reese: "He saved my life and my career that day. I had lost my confidence, and Pee Wee picked me up with his words of encouragement. He gave me hope when all hope was gone."

MACKAY'S MORAL

A person may not be as good as you tell her she is, but she'll try harder thereafter.

LOU HOLTZ COACHES YOU ALL THE WAY TO #1

Do you have what it takes to be successful?

Few people know more about success than my close friend Lou Holtz, the only Hall-of-Fame college football coach to lead six different programs to bowl games, and the only coach to take four different programs to the final top 20 rankings. Along the way he guided Notre Dame to the 1988 national championship.

Lou believes there are four things any person or organization needs to be number one. "First," he says, "you have to make a commitment to excellence." Second is complete attention to detail. "It is the teams that pay strict attention to little things that win," says Holtz. The third thing is to have sound fundamentals. "You can't be bored with such basic things as blocking and tackling." The fourth requirement is discipline. "Virtually nothing is impossible in this world if you just put your mind to it and maintain a positive attitude."

Let me give you my take on all four:

Commitment to excellence. When you are interested in doing something, you do it when circumstances permit. However, when you're committed to something, you accept no excuses, only results.

Commitment is a prerequisite to success. Commitment is the state of being bound—emotionally, intellectually, or both—to a course of action. Commitment starts with a choice and is sustained by dedication and perseverance. Actions speak louder than words.

Commitment is a prerequisite to success. Commitment is the state of being bound—emotionally, intellectually, or both—to a course of action.

Have you ever seen a team run on the field yelling, "We want to be number two?" Everyone wants to be number one. Those who actually achieve it are those who are willing to put the blood, sweat, and tears into their effort.

Attention to detail. I like to add one word—*fanatical* attention to detail. The difference between failure and success is the difference between doing a thing nearly right and doing it exactly right.

Having a fanatical attention to detail is a mindset. It must be an obsession. It has to be part of a company's culture or an individual's mentality. You can't just talk about it. You have to practice it every day for years.

It is not enough just to do the best you can. You also have to do everything you can. There are no shortcuts in the world of sports—or life. If it were easy to become the best, everyone would do it.

Sound fundamentals. Look at the great athletes and musicians. There are no walk-ons at the Super Bowl or Carnegie Hall—or in corporate boardrooms for that matter. The level of performance in those exalted places is only partially a reflection of talent. Those people also had to practice sound fundamentals to earn their place there.

It's kind of like a stonecutter hammering away at his rock, perhaps 100 times without making a dent in it. And yet on the 101st blow the rock splits in two. And it was not that blow that did it, but all that had happened before. If you're not willing to practice—and practice until you get it right—you will never make the 100 blows that make the breakthrough on the 101st.

Whatever it is you do, you can be better at it if you just keep on learning and practicing. The minute I persuade myself that I have learned all there is to learn about a subject and can relax, that's the moment my competition will hand me my head and slam me into the pavement.

Discipline. Most people want to succeed, but they lack the discipline to get there. Discipline requires that you set goals, map out a plan to achieve them, and then follow that map.

The formula is the same for athletes, business people, and students: have a no-nonsense attitude, work hard, and improve every day. Arrive early and stay late if that's what it takes to get the job done. Go the extra mile. It is one stretch of the highway where there are seldom any traffic jams, and few people are trying to pass you.

MACKAY'S MORAL

There aren't any rules for success that work unless you do.

6

COMPETITION

KNOW THY COMPETITORS

Competition can be compared to the two hikers who spotted a mountain lion stalking them. One of the hikers calmly sat down, took off his hiking boots, and began putting on his running shoes.

"What good are those shoes going to do you?" asked his buddy "You can't outrun a mountain lion!"

Lacing up his running shoes, the friend responded, "I don't have to outrun the lion. I just have to outrun you."

Competition is generally good. No one ever set a world's record competing against himself or herself. If competition can make General Motors, GE, and the U.S. government improve their performance, just think what it can do for you.

When I'm out speaking to Corporate America, one of the lessons I always share is, "Know thy competitor." You'll profit a lot more by trying to learn from your competition than by trying to destroy them.

You need to recognize that your competition is not just the outfit that's selling the same kind of stuff you are. If you sell envelopes, for example, your competition is not just other envelope manufacturers; it's also email and fax. The competition is whoever affects how your product is used, even if it seems like a stretch.

I remember reading a plaque on a businessman's office wall that was printed in the great little publication *Leadership*. It read:

- My competitors do more for me than my friends do. My friends are too polite to point out my weaknesses, but my competitors go to great expense to advertise them.

- My competitors are efficient, diligent, and attentive. They make me search for ways to improve my products and service.

- My competitors would take my business away from me if they could. This keeps me alert to hold on to what I have.

- If I had no competitors, I would be lazy, incompetent, and inattentive. I need the discipline they force on me.

- I salute my competitors. They have been good to me. God bless them all.

Most business heavyweights know the importance of keeping tabs on their competitors. Former GE CEO Jack Welch regularly asked his top managers in the company's 14 major businesses to answer a series of questions, one of which was "What actions have your competitors taken in the last three years?"

Sam Walton, creator of Walmart, the world's largest retail chain, had his own rules for success. One of them was "Know your competitors and what they are doing so you can communicate everything you can to your employees." The more they know, the more they will understand. Information is power. In his autobiography, Walton tells a great story about how a clerk at a competitor caught Walton roving around their store with a tape recorder.

In *No Thanks, I'm Just Looking*, author Harry Friedman points out that you can't sell against your competitors if you don't know anything about them. Visit your competitors' stores and websites. Sign up for their email lists. Being aware of what's going on around you can put you in a superior position. Here are a few more reasons you should familiarize yourself with your competitors:

- You'll know their pricing structures and whether or not they're offering sale prices for the same or similar merchandise.
- You'll be able to compare products they sell to products you sell.
- You'll know what competitors are saying about your business.
- You can get merchandising and display ideas.
- You can spot trends in your industry.
- You'll know their credit options.
- You can be the expert your customers expect you to be.

Become the industry standard if you really want to beat the competition. Coca-Cola got a law passed that said that if you order a Coke, and the restaurant doesn't have it, they must tell you that they don't have it and would a Pepsi (or whatever substitute) be okay instead? Could that approach backfire? Sure, if the consumer tastes the competition and decides the flavor is better. But Coke knows which soda most people ask for by name—and that keeps its competitors up at night trying to get the same name recognition.

MACKAY'S MORAL

Competition is a lot like cod liver oil. First it makes you sick. Then it makes you better.

How to beat your competition

Woody Allen said, "Eighty percent of success in life is just showing up." I like to take that several steps further.

Just show up. *You're a winner 80 percent of the time.* Some accounts are won because nobody else is calling on them.

Show up on time. What could be more annoying than a salesperson who can't deliver the first thing he's promised, his or her own body? Mars, Inc., known around the world for its M&M's, 3 Musketeers, Snickers, and Mars candy bars, is a $35 billion privately held company. The multinational corporation really places a premium on showing up on time. Everyone punches a clock, including the president of the company, and every associate (employee) who punches in before 8:30 a.m. receives 10 percent added compensation called "The Punctuality Bonus." Talk about positive reinforcement—that's certainly nothing to "Snicker" at! Do it when you say you'll do it, and *you're a winner 85 percent of the time.*

Show up on time with a plan. Okay, you're there. So what? You have to know your prospect's strengths and weaknesses and be able to anticipate his or her concerns. Give your prospect a clear understanding of what the product benefits are and the specifics of price/delivery/service. Don't expect to get by with vague, offhand answers to any objections to your proposition. If there are going to be any problems you know about, don't try to evade them. Let your prospect know up front. By being truthful and accurate in your answers, you'll receive orders that others, who may actually meet the customer's needs better than you, won't get. Do it right, and *you're a winner 90 percent of the time.*

Show up on time with a plan and a commitment to carry it out. If you don't believe in what you're selling, how can you expect anyone else to? Lack of commitment shows through like rust on a used car. It will kill a deal even faster. You have to look, act, and feel like you mean it. That's why motivation is the single common denominator you'll find in all topflight salespeople and the hardest attitude to maintain. If you have it, *you'll win 95 percent of the time.*

Show up on time with a plan and a commitment to carry it out, and then execute it. Nothing is more deadly to a sales relationship, or any relationship, than a broken promise. Whatever you say you're going to do, you'd better do it. And if you find you can't do it, then the price/service/

delivery concessions better be so generous that the buyer is glad you didn't. Once you've put the other elements together, if you perform—or better yet—if you deliver more than you promised, *you'll beat the competition 100 percent of the time.*

Show up on time with a plan, a commitment to carry it out, execute it, and give 110 percent. Go beyond giving more than you promised. Keep in frequent contact with your customers, and those whom you hope will become your customers. Ask for feedback on everything from your product to your service. Fix absolutely everything that you can. If your product specs aren't exactly what the customer needs, find a way to meet that need, even if on occasion you must tell them that you honestly can't be their vendor. Then keep working with your R & D department to make things work better next time. Not only will you beat the competition, but *you'll know you have a customer for life because of your intense interest.*

Knute Rockne, the legendary Notre Dame football coach, said: "I don't like to lose, and that isn't so much because it is just a football game, but because defeat means the failure to reach your objective. I don't want a football player who doesn't take defeat to heart, who laughs it off with the thought, 'Oh, well, there's another Saturday.' The trouble in American life today, in business as well as in sports, is that too many people are afraid of competition. The result is that in some circles people have come to sneer at success if it costs hard work and training and sacrifice."

MACKAY'S MORAL

There're plenty of people out there willing to beat you, so don't beat yourself.

COMPETITION TEACHES YOU TO OUTSWIM THE SHARKS

Codfish are a delectable treat in America's Northeast. But when attempts were made to ship them fresh to distant markets, the cod did not taste the same as they did closer to home.

To deal with this, shippers decided to freeze the cod and then ship them. But the fish still didn't taste right. Then the fish merchants tried shipping the codfish in tanks of seawater, but that proved even worse. Not only was it more expensive, but the codfish still lost their flavor and, in addition, their flesh became soft and mushy.

Finally, some creative soul solved the problem in a most innovative way, according to Charles R. Swindoll in his book *Come Before Winter and Share My Hope*. The codfish were placed in a tank along with their natural enemy—the catfish. From the time the codfish left the East Coast until it arrived at their westernmost destination, those catfish had chased the cod all over the tank. And, as you may have guessed, the cod arrived at the market tasting as if they had just been pulled from the ocean. If anything, the flavor was better than ever.

What a competitive environment and daily challenge can do for codfish works for humans as well. Competition and challenges make us better.

But a problem I see all too frequently is that people are afraid of competition. Perhaps it's because they fear losing, but I suspect a better reason is that they know they are not as prepared as the competition. They are not willing to put in the necessary hard work, training, and sacrifice. They think things will be easier for them than for others, possibly because others have made things look easy.

Former New Jersey Senator Bill Bradley was a basketball star at Princeton University and later with the New York Knicks. When he was at Princeton, Bradley's father used to tell him, "Son, when you're not out practicing, someone else is. And when you meet that person, he's going to beat you."

The Incas of ancient Peru played a sport similar to basketball, the object of which was to shoot a solid rubber ball through a stone ring placed high on a wall. The winner was traditionally awarded the clothes of all spectators present. The loser was put to death. (You can check out more of these fascinating facts in *The Best, Worst & Most Unusual* by Bruce Felton and Mark Fowler.)

It's the same in business, except the part about the clothes and being put to death. When it's crunch time, you want the people who are willing to roll up their sleeves and jump in. You want gamers. You want people who are confident in their abilities.

When it's crunch time, you want the people who are willing to roll up their sleeves and jump in. You want gamers. You want people who are confident in their abilities.

As much as I love to come out on top, I'm too realistic to believe the "winning is everything" philosophy. After so many years in business, I know that you can't win 'em all. But there is no excuse for not giving it your best shot. And you can be the winner more often than not.

Athletes and actors have long hired coaches to help prepare for a specific competition or role. But today there are coaches available to help people in any field improve their "game." If you think that leaders don't need coaches—that if you're already at the top, a coach couldn't offer you anything new—think again. Why does someone like tennis champ Serena Williams have a coach, whom she could handily defeat on the coach's best day? For the same reasons all high-performing individuals have one, says professional coach Daniel Pendley: "(1) We cannot see our own mistakes; and (2) If we are not getting better, we are getting worse."

Your competitive urge is sometimes the only real advantage you have. Someone else will always have more money, more resources, more connections, or more experience. You will compete with larger companies, smarter people, and less ethical organizations. Use these experiences as opportunities to improve your game.

MACKAY'S MORAL

As I like to say, you CAN swim with the sharks without being eaten alive!

WINNERS THRIVE ON COMPETITION

I hate to lose.

That said, I am proud to admit that competition has made me a better businessman, a better golfer, and a better person. And when there isn't another company or business to compete with, I try to outdo myself. If that sounds simple, well, it is. I always want to be at my best and show my best side.

People can exceed expectations when motivated properly. This story, told by Andrew S. Grove, former CEO of the Intel Corporation, the California manufacturer of semiconductors, is a perfect illustration:

For years the performance of the Intel facilities maintenance group, which is responsible for keeping their buildings clean and in good shape, was sub-standard. No amount of pressure or inducement seemed to do any good.

Then Intel initiated a program in which each building's upkeep was periodically given a score by a resident senior manager. The score was then compared with those given the other buildings. Result: The condition of all of the buildings improved dramatically—almost immediately. Nothing else had been done. People did not get more money or other rewards. What they did get was the stimulus of competition.

Competition drives performance. It drives people to work harder and dig down deeper to deliver more than they ever thought they could.

According to the tutor2u website, the many benefits of increased market competition include:

- Lower prices for consumers.
- A greater discipline on producers/suppliers to keep their costs down.
- Improvements in technology with positive effects on production methods and costs.
- A greater variety of products from which to choose.
- A faster pace of invention and innovation.
- Improvements to the quality of service for consumers.
- Better information for consumers, allowing people to make more informed choices.

There's nothing like a little competition to boost productivity. Look at industry studies and you will consistently see that competition helped improve results.

I am and have always been very competitive. I understand that some people don't like competition, but you have to accept that competition is unavoidable in life. That's the way our society works. And it's my firm belief that our society improves with competition.

Some parents don't want to engage their young children in competition. I understand their reluctance in situations where unrealistic expectations are set. But friendly competition is good. It is critical to prepare children and teenagers to compete in the real world. As they grow older, they will face competition in schools, getting a job, even buying a house.

A University of Florida study found that participating in sports is a healthy way to teach kids about the positive aspects of competition. Playing sports helps kids understand how competition works in a friendly environment and that if you try your hardest, you have a better chance at succeeding, not to mention improving your health and self-esteem.

In competition, when you don't expect enough out of yourself, your competitors will beat you every time. When I was in London at the Olympics, I heard an interviewer ask an athlete to predict the outcome of his race.

He said, "I'll come in fifth."

Sure enough, that's exactly where he finished, even though he could easily have placed third, or even second, since two other major competitors fared poorly.

Contrast this with Manteo Mitchell, who broke his leg midway through the 4×400 meter relay but kept running to allow the U.S. team to reach the final.

I cannot emphasize enough that all my business life I have faced competition, and I believe it has made both me and my company better. When competitors improve their products, we improve ours more. When a sales prospect mentions service, I ask what the other company promised them and then exceed it. We know our customers better here at MackayMitchell Envelope Company. It's our real leg up on the competition. We hate to lose a customer. We take tremendous pride in beating the competition, because that means we are serving our customers better.

There is an old saying in Africa that goes like this: Every morning a gazelle gets up and knows that it must out-run the fastest lion or it will be eaten. And every morning, a lion gets up and knows that it must out-run the slowest gazelle or it will starve to death.

So, whether you are a gazelle or a lion, every morning when you get up, you'd better be running.

MACKAY'S MORAL

If you go the extra mile, you will almost always beat the competition.

7

CREATIVITY

CREATIVITY DOES NOT REQUIRE GENIUS

Based upon an independent survey of advertising and marketing executives, which was reported in *USA Today*, there are three common misperceptions about creativity:

- That the time of day when people tend to be the most creative is at night,
- That the common causes of creative block are lack of inspiration and concentration, and
- That the best way to prevent creative block and keep ideas flowing is to focus harder on the task at hand and talk to others to gain their perspectives.

The truth of the matter is that most people are more creative in the morning. Most of us do not work better under a tight deadline. And taking a break is the best way to avoid creative blocks.

Notice I said *most* people. Everyone is different. Beethoven poured cold water over his head when he sat down to compose music, believing that it stimulated his brain's creative process. And no one ever doubted his creative genius.

In my case, I'm sharpest in the morning after a good night's sleep, or when I'm exercising. But ideas hit me at all times during the day and night. That's why I always carry a pen and paper with me, or make a voice recording if I can't take time to write. If I get an idea during the night, I have a pad of paper and pen on my nightstand, and I get up and write it down. Sometimes I even check my phone messages to jar my memory in the morning. I don't trust it to memory alone. I hate to waste an idea, even if it doesn't turn out to be great when exposed to the light of day.

One of my favorite cartoons in the *New Yorker* magazine showed two assistants preparing for a sales meeting in a conference room. One says to the other, "And don't forget the little pads in case one of them has an idea."

Like many people, I don't think well when I'm hurried or under pressure. I tend to go a mile a minute, but I think better when I'm relaxed. Did you know that some truly creative people spend their most productive time looking out the window? They are thinking. It's one of the most important things we do.

Every one of us can become more creative, and we can help each other learn how. When I speak to groups, I give them this lesson: If I give you a dollar and you give me a dollar, we each have one dollar. But if I give you an idea and you give me an idea, we each have two ideas.

Thomas Edison, who was awarded more than 1,000 patents, was a prime example. He said, "The ideas I use are mostly the ideas of other people who don't develop them themselves."

Edison visited Luther Burbank, the famed horticulturist, who invited everyone who visited his home to sign the guest book. Each line in the book had a space for the guest's name, address, and special interests. When Edison signed the book, in the space marked "Interested in," he wrote "Everything!"

That was an understatement. In his lifetime, Edison invented the incandescent light, the phonograph, the hideaway bed, wax paper, underground electrical wires, an electric railway car, the light socket and light switch, a method for making synthetic rubber from goldenrod plants, and the motion picture camera. He also founded the first electric company.

Edison refused to let his creativity be stifled. He was curious about everything. See a connection?

"Ideas are somewhat like babies," said the late management guru Peter Drucker. "They are born small, immature, and shapeless. They are promise rather than fulfillment. The creative manager asks, 'What would be needed to make this embryonic, half-baked, foolish idea into something that makes sense, that is feasible, that is an opportunity for us?'"

I like that thinking. It validates all my little scraps of paper and two-word dictations, among which are my best ideas in infant form. Developing them and watching them grow, seeing where they go from a little seed— and seeing what other bright ideas grow right along with them—that's what gets my creative juices flowing.

MACKAY'S MORAL

Creativity has no script; it is inspired ad libbing.

CULTIVATE CREATIVITY
TO GROW SUCCESS

Paul was majoring in zoology at college. One semester he took a course in the study of birds—ornithology. For the final exam, Paul studied until he had the textbook nearly memorized. He knew his class notes backward and forward. He was eager to take the exam, certain of getting a good grade.

The morning of the exam, Paul took a seat in the front row of the big auditorium where the class was held. Over 100 students were in the class with him. On a table at the front was a row of 10 stuffed birds, each one with a sack covering its body so that only the legs were visible.

The professor announced, "For this test, which counts for 80 percent of your final grade, I want you to identify each bird up here by its legs, and then discuss its species, natural habitat, and mating patterns. You may begin."

Paul stared at the birds. All the legs looked the same to him. After spending half the exam period in growing frustration as he tried to determine which bird was which, he picked up his exam and threw it on the professor's desk.

"This is ridiculous!" he shouted. "I studied the textbook and my notes all night, and now you're asking me to name these birds by looking at their legs? Forget it!"

The professor picked up the exam booklet and saw that it was blank. "What's your name, young man?"

With that, Paul yanked one leg of his pants up. "Why don't you tell me?"

Paul's response probably didn't earn him a passing grade, although I must admit, I admire his creativity!

"Creativity is a great motivator because it makes people interested in what they are doing. Creativity gives hope that there can be a worthwhile idea," said English psychologist Edward de Bono. "Creativity gives the possibility of some sort of achievement to everyone. Creativity makes life more interesting."

Everyone is born with the ability to be creative, but some people seem to lose it as they grow older, whereas others are better at accessing their creativity throughout their lives. Studies show that there is no correlation between IQ and creativity.

Everyone is born with the ability to be creative, but some people seem to lose it as they grow older, whereas others are better at accessing their creativity throughout their lives.

Here's how to regain or retain your creative spark:

- **Be aware of what's going on around you.** Just as a scientist needs to analyze all available facts and every bit of research, you need to stay on top of current business trends. Learn from other people's ideas and mistakes.

- **Explore.** Examine all of your options and alternatives, no matter how far-fetched they may seem at first. Don't rule anything out as you look for solutions and new approaches.

- **Be courageous.** You've got to be fearless and not worry about what others may think. Don't try to be like everyone else. Take your own approach, whatever you're doing. Prepare to accept some criticism, but don't take it personally.

- **Rely on your instincts.** As you assimilate the information around you and assess the possibilities, factor in your instincts to come up with creative solutions. As legendary film director Frank Capra said, "A hunch is creativity trying to tell you something."

- **Assess your options.** Sort your ideas into categories, and rank them. Try combining ideas, and eliminate any that don't fit what you're looking for.

- **Be realistic.** Step back and evaluate how your idea or solution is likely to play out in the real world. Look at the upside, but consider the downside as well. Not all great ideas will work, but they may lead to other solutions.

- **Stick with it.** You need to be persistent if you want to achieve anything significant. A novel takes a long time to write; a successful business may take years to build. Keep a detailed picture of the intended result in your mind to help you stay focused and move forward.

- **Be patient.** You can't hurry creativity, so take time to ponder your ideas. Sit back and take time to think things over. That's usually how the best ideas bloom.

- **Evaluate the results.** At the end of the process, ask yourself: Has my vision been realized? Learn from what works and what fails so you can move on to your next project.

Creativity isn't just a process. It's a value. If you value success, get creative!

MACKAY'S MORAL

It only takes a little spark to ignite a great fire.

IMAGINATION IS THE FUEL
FOR SUCCESS

Take a close look at the back of a dollar bill. On the left side is a pyramid, with an eye at the top. Over the pyramid is the Latin inscription "annuit coeptis." It means: "Providence has favored our undertakings."

The pyramid symbolizes the strength of the union of the states. The top of the pyramid is unfinished, meaning there is still work to be done to make our system even better. The eye stands for the all-seeing God, Supreme Builder of the Universe. Benjamin Franklin chose this motto because he believed imagination was the singular characteristic of the people he helped to forge into a new nation. I think Ben Franklin would be pleasantly surprised where imagination got this great nation.

Earl Nightingale, one of the pioneers of the motivational movement, said, "The most interesting people are the people with the most interesting pictures in their minds." I'm always fascinated listening to people who see the world through a different lens. Most of us have ideas of what we'd like to change, but not necessarily the vision to make it happen. People who can clear the negative clutter from problems will always be successful.

The famous inventor Thomas Edison used to say his deafness was his greatest blessing, because it saved him from having to listen to reasons why things couldn't be done.

Curtis Carlson, founder of the Carlson Companies and one of my mentors, spent his life building and expanding. When asked what personal qualities contributed to the building of his successful empire, Curt responded, "I think my success is the result of my ability to see and to imagine how things can be. I'm not distracted by how things are."

It's never too late to develop your imagination, although I believe that the longer you suppress it, the more challenging it will be. Consider this lesson that was shared by Gordon McKenzie, a well-known creative force at Hallmark Cards.

McKenzie often visited schools to talk about his work. He usually introduced himself as an artist, and then would ask the students, "How many of you are artists?"

In kindergarten and first grade, almost every hand was enthusiastically raised. In second-grade classrooms, about three-fourths of the children would raise their hands, but not as eagerly. Just a few third-graders admitted their artistic talent. By the time he interviewed the sixth-graders, he said not one of them raised a hand. They thought being an artist was "uncool." (My guess is that Curt Carlson was one of those kids who didn't mind being "uncool.")

So if we want to cultivate creativity and imagination, a good place to start is with children. Children don't recognize limits on possibilities and are open to trying all kinds of solutions. They look through that different lens, that is, until we train them to focus on the practical. We would do well to learn from them that there is rarely just one way to get a job done.

A friend shared a story from the NewsOK website about two parents working on their Christmas cards with their six-year-old son. The son's job was to lick the stamps (back before self-adhesive stamps were available). But the little boy balked because he didn't like the taste of the glue on the stamps. His parents prevailed and, reluctantly, he went to his room to finish his assignment.

Before long, he emerged from his room with a big smile on his face and handed his father the pile. Every envelope was stamped. His stunned father said, "But I thought you didn't like the way the stamps tasted when you licked them!"

"Yeah, that was yucky," the son replied. "So I just licked the envelopes and then stuck the stamps on."

Of course, I love a good story about envelopes!

From Napoleon Hill's famous book *Law of Success* comes this summarizing thought: "Just as the oak tree develops from the germ that lies in the acorn, and the bird develops from the germ that lies asleep in the egg, so will your material achievements grow out of the organized plans that you create in your imagination. First comes the thought; then organization of that thought into ideas and plans; then transformation of those plans into reality. The beginning, as you will observe, is in your imagination."

MACKAY'S MORAL

The only person who can put limits on your imagination is you.

8

CUSTOMER SERVICE

WARNING—
CUSTOMERS ARE PERISHABLE

A man who had lived an exemplary life died and was given a preview of heaven and hell. In heaven, people were peaceful and serene and smiling. In hell he was given a stretch limo, the best food and drink, and an endless list of parties. He chose hell.

As soon as he walked through the gates, the devil began flogging him with a whip and he was thrown into a fiery chasm. "Wait!" he said. "Yesterday I was treated like a king, and now this. Why?"

"Ah," said the devil. "Yesterday you were a prospect. Today you're a customer."

Unfortunately, the same thing happens in many organizations. They wine and dine you to entice you, only to lose track of you and seem disinterested after you make the decision to buy.

There's one thing no business has enough of: customers. Take care of the customers you've got, and they'll take care of you.

There's one thing no business has enough of: customers. Take care of the customers you've got, and they'll take care of you.

That's why I preach, "The sale *begins* when the customer says yes." Good salespeople make sure the job gets done on time—and done right. They must have a fanatical attention to detail!

Companies and sales reps that understand this mentality do extremely well. They're at the head of the class. They understand the 80/20 rule—that 80 percent of their business comes from 20 percent of their customers. And trust me, it's trending toward 90/10.

That's why you have to cultivate the people who have done business with you in the past. A large part of your sales strategy should be based on expanding your share of your existing customers' business.

Those are all great thoughts, but you are really looking for the "how." Let me share some of the lessons I have learned about customer loyalty in my 50-plus years in business.

Pricing should not be the primary issue. A business built on price alone will only be a business as long as no other business offers a lower price. Price is important, but it's just one feature of a sale. Don't price yourself out of the market, but don't price yourself out of business.

Quality is important, but alone it's not enough. Sometimes, good enough is all the customer wants, not the top-of-the-line product you are hawking. You have to listen very carefully to your customers to determine what's most important to them.

Service alone won't guarantee a repeat customer. Great service is, in my estimation, probably more important than either price or quality. But without a combination of the three, your customers will be shopping around before your next courtesy call. Give them the total package.

How a customer complaint is handled is what truly determines your future relationship. You've aced the price, quality, and service. But the day that something goes wrong is the real test. The shipping department laid your order aside for an extra day, when it was promised yesterday. Oops, the customer got 1,000 widgets instead of 2,000. You quoted last month's lower price, but accounting didn't look at your text message typed in bold, capital letters highlighted in yellow. Then comes the phone call. Your response must be immediate and more than fair. When someone is counting on you, it's often because someone is counting on them. So it's not just you who looks bad! Fix it quickly and fix it well. It may cost you big time, but it will pay off in the future.

No matter how many people there are in this world, there will always be a finite number of customers. I don't care whether you are selling computers, cars, phones, or even envelopes. There are just so many people you can sell to. Develop relationships with as many as you can realistically service. Put yourself in the customer's role: What if you had to go to a different grocery store every time you shopped? Would you save any time if you had to switch suppliers every time your company needed print cartridges? What if you had to take your precious little red Corvette to a new mechanic each time it needed a tune-up?

I once figured it cost my company around $5,000 to put a new customer on the books. I'm not willing to let that kind of investment go bad.

MACKAY'S MORAL

A wise old salesman once told me, "A cup of water can keep you going for a day. Find a well and you can go back to it year after year after year."

TAKING CARE OF CUSTOMERS IS TAKING CARE OF BUSINESS

"Customer service in America stinks."

That's what my friend Tom Peters, author of the blockbuster book, *In Search of Excellence*, said many years ago. It must still be true because every time I write about poor customer service, I get more Amens than a Billy Graham sermon. That's why I want to touch on customer service from a different perspective.

It's unbelievable to me how many business owners remain ignorant of the devastating effects of lousy service. And they wonder why business is suffering and the cash register isn't ringing?

The Research Institute of America conducted a study for the White House Office of Consumer Affairs, which found:

- Only 4 percent of unhappy customers bother to complain. For every complaint we hear, 24 others go uncommunicated to the company— but not to other potential customers.

- 90 percent who are dissatisfied with the service they receive will not come back or buy again.

- To make matters worse, each of those unhappy customers will tell his or her story to at least nine other people. These days, if those customers are posting their complaints on social media or websites that review businesses, they're actually telling their story to thousands, if not millions, of potential customers.

- Of the customers who register a complaint, between 54 percent and 70 percent will do business again with the organization if their complaint is resolved. That figure goes up to 95 percent if the customer feels that the complaint was resolved quickly.

- Sixty-eight percent of customers who quit doing business with an organization do so because of company indifference. It takes 12 positive incidents to make up for one negative incident in the eyes of customers.

When I started out in sales, a salty old veteran told me, "Harvey, never make promises in business. They'll ruin you every time."

That might be good advice, but only up to a point. That point is reached when you go to contract because in a contract, you make commitments, which are the same as promises. You vouch for planned delivery dates, not random drop-off times. These are not tossed-off verbal guarantees but well-researched commitments.

Nothing is more important than customer service. No customer service, and pretty soon, no customers.

Nothing is more important than customer service. No customer service, and pretty soon, no customers.

The key is to latch on to your customers and hold them fast. Don't just meet their needs. Anticipate them. Don't wait for them to tell you there's a problem. Go out and ask them if there's a problem. They are your most important focus group. Every word of personal feedback they give you is worth a million faceless questionnaires.

With business operating at digital speed, the margin for negligence is disappearing. Broken promises, missed deadlines, inadequate customer service and support—give in to any of these and you're finished.

And as customers become more knowledgeable, customer service becomes more difficult. A while back there was a series of articles in *Fortune* magazine focusing on customer satisfaction and why Americans are so hard to please.

A researcher at J.D. Powers & Associates, a company that studies customer satisfaction in the auto industry, computers, airlines, and phone service, stated: "What makes customer satisfaction so difficult to achieve is that you constantly raise the bar and extend the finish line. You never stop. As your customers get better treatment, they demand better treatment."

When I speak on customer service I usually tell a story that I read many years ago in *USA TODAY*. A man walked into a bank in Spokane, Washington, to cash a $100 check. The bank teller refused to validate his parking ticket, saying he had to make a deposit. The customer asked to see a manager, who also refused to stamp the parking ticket. At that point the customer proceeded to withdraw $1 million from his account and walked across the street to a competitor and opened a new account. The next day, he went back to the same bank teller and withdrew another $1 million.

That's an expensive lesson to learn. So is losing any customer.

MACKAY'S MORAL

Disappoint customers and they'll disappear.

CREATE A SERVICE CULTURE

When I went into business many years ago, I told people I owned an envelope company. I had business cards printed that identified me as an "envelope salesman." I described myself as an entrepreneur.

All of those facts are still true, but incomplete. What I and our company really do is provide customer service.

Well sure, Harvey, you say. But isn't that just a part of the whole operation?

Absolutely, positively, irrefutably, NO. I am in the service business, regardless of the product I make and sell. If my service is lacking, my business will be sent packing.

To validate my thinking, I visited with John Tschohl, president of the Service Quality Institute. John has spent more than 35 years focused on customer service. He has written hundreds of articles, as well as seven books on the topic. You've probably heard him interviewed on television or radio. He has been called the "guru of customer service" by *USA TODAY, Time,* and *Entrepreneur* magazines.

Even the most successful companies are in constant competition for business. What sets them apart often boils down to one factor: outstanding customer service. John offered up some stellar advice for creating a service culture, no matter what business you're in.

First, you've got to understand you're in the service business. "Most companies think they are in manufacturing and retail; airlines don't know they are in the service business," he said. "Southwest Airlines is successful because they understand they're a customer service company—they just happen to be an airline."

Second, you have to look at all the policies, procedures, and systems that you've got in place "that make life miserable for customers. You could have the nicest people in the world, but you could have stupid hours, stupid rules, stupid procedures, that just burn the customer." When you make it that difficult for customers to deal with you, they find someone else who is more accommodating.

Third, you have to have empowerment. "Every single person has to be able to make fast and power decisions on the spot, and it better be in favor of the customer," John said.

Fourth, you have to be more careful about whom you hire. "The service leaders hire one person out of 50 interviewed, sometimes one out of 100, but they're very, very, very careful," he said. "Look for the cream, the A players, instead of bringing on B and C players."

Fifth, educate and train the entire staff on the art of customer service with something new and fresh every four to six months. "Let's say you want to create the service culture. No matter if you have a hundred or a thousand or a hundred thousand employees, you better have something new and fresh, so it's constantly in front of them," John said. "So when they wake up every day, and they go to work, they say, 'Fantastic, I'm taking care of customers!'"

Finally, measure the results financially so that you know the impact it's making on revenue, sales, profit, and market share.

Everything you do, according to John, should be built around the concept of creating an incredible customer experience. He cites Amazon as one of his favorite role models. "At Amazon, they've got technology, speed, price. They've got everything. If I'm on their website and I want them to call me, they're going to call me back in one second. That's speed. When you place an order, you can do it 24 hours a day, seven days a week. And 60 seconds later, you get a confirmation."

I realize Amazon is in a class by itself, and most businesses aren't ever going to achieve the growth or profits of that gargantuan company. But John's advice can be translated to companies of any size. A one-person shop can provide great service because they often have personal contact with their customers. Bigger companies have more resources available, which should enhance the service experience.

Perhaps the simplest way of creating a service culture is a variation of the golden rule: Treat your customers as you wish to be treated. Make your customers excited that you're in business. Make them grateful that they have the opportunity to buy your services or products. Make them feel like they are your most important client. Make your service so outstanding that they wouldn't think of doing business with anyone else.

And then find a way to make your service even better!

MACKAY'S MORAL

Customer service is not a department, it's everyone's job.

The art of the apology

Have you heard the colossal customer service bungle about the "bedbug letter"?

A guest in a hotel finds himself attacked by bedbugs during his stay. He writes an angry letter to the president of the hotel company. Within days, the president sends the guest a heartfelt apology which reads in part: "I can assure you that such an event has never occurred before in our hotel. I promise you it will never happen again."

Sounds good, except for one small detail: included with the apology is the guest's original letter. Scrawled across the top is the message: "Send this idiot the bedbug letter."

So it begs the question, who is sorry now?

There are several lessons to be learned from this situation.

Remedial customer service may start with an apology.

Never, ever mess up an apology.

The apology is almost always the start, not the end, of finishing things.

If you think being sorry solves a problem, you will really be sorry.

Finally, the cost of the fix is nearly always greater than doing things right the first time.

Start with the premise that everyone makes mistakes. It's human nature. What happens next is what demonstrates the true level of regret. The hotel president likely lost that customer forever. Unfortunately, it doesn't stop there. That customer tells family, friends, and anyone who will listen about his experiences—both with the bugs and the insulting letter. Reputations are ruined in an instant.

Businesses have long understood that bad customer experiences will be reported to family and friends nine times more than good experiences. Misery loves company, I guess.

Even the most sincere apology has a limited effect. But if it helps a little, it's worth the effort. So don't blow what could be your only opportunity.

We see an apology from some thoughtless public figure weekly: "If I offended anyone, I apologize." "My words were taken out of context." "I didn't realize that my actions would cause such a stir." All pretty pathetic attempts at sounding sorry, in my opinion.

Train your brain to think before you speak, act, or tweet. Self-restraint is not old-fashioned. Remember that your private conversations or anonymous postings may be anything but private and anonymous.

The apology is just the beginning. It is critical to get it right. So take steps to be sure you don't disappoint a second time. The shallow "if I offended anyone" indicates that you are only sorry because you were forced into the apology. I'm curious: Does anyone take those similarly phrased apologies seriously? Or do they sound like something your mother may have made you say when you were a child?

In business situations, apologies are generally related to poor service or defective products or missed deadlines. Those apologies must go beyond words.

First, admit your mistake. Don't gloss over the error or the effect it had on your customer. Get to the point and own the situation. You will not win the blame game.

Next, offer a solution that will demonstrate your sincere desire to make things right. Even if the customer had some responsibility, the cost of fixing one mistake is much lower than trying to repair a reputation after you've been panned on Facebook, Twitter, or Angie's List.

Third, express your intention to make sure the same mistake never happens again. Offer the customer an opportunity to make suggestions, and be prepared to deal with critical feedback. Be sure to thank him or her for the input.

Finally, learn from the experience and use the lesson to train your staff. Make sure they understand that even minor mistakes and disappointments can cause major damage to your company's good name.

So my ideal apology might read: "We are so sorry for messing up what could be our only opportunity to serve you. Your disappointment in us is completely justified. We will fix this problem immediately and will not consider the case closed until you are completely satisfied. Here is the name, email, and phone number of the person you can contact 24 hours a day to question, complain, or check the progress of your situation." Then insert the name of the president of the company. That should let them know that you're serious.

MACKAY'S MORAL

Saying you're sorry and showing you're sorry are not the same thing.

9

HIRING/FIRING/ JOBS

Hire a professional

A woman received a phone call at work that her daughter was very sick with a fever. She left the office and stopped by the pharmacy to get some medication, but when she got back to her car, she discovered that she'd locked her keys inside.

Desperate, she started to pray: "Dear God, please help me get back in my car so I can help my daughter."

Just then a man pulled up on a motorcycle. He had a long beard and his arms were covered with tattoos. He asked what the matter was, and the tearful mother told him.

"Don't worry," the biker said. "I can get inside the car." He went into the drugstore and came out with a coat hanger. In minutes, he had the door open.

"Oh, thank you!" the woman cried. "I prayed for someone to help me, and God sent me the kindest man in the world!"

Embarrassed, the man took a step backward. "I'm not actually a good person, ma'am. In fact, I just got out of prison last week for stealing cars."

The woman looked up toward heaven. "Thank you, God, for sending me a professional!"

Whenever I need to get something done, and I realize I don't have the skills for the job, I hire a professional. Maybe you need help designing a marketing piece or a website. Or you are writing a book and need a professional editor. How about public speaking or planning a special event? You will save yourself many headaches and mistakes if you hire a true professional.

After all, you want the best results possible.

And most of the time, the payoff far exceeds the expense.

Professionals are knowledgeable, experienced, focused, and most importantly, they are cool under pressure and used to dealing with the unexpected. They are not infallible and they still make mistakes, but they are better equipped at dealing with them.

We all have specific skills, but we can't know everything. There is no glory in trying to fix a problem if your efforts only make matters worse. You think you will save time and money? It's far less expensive to swallow your pride than to choke on arrogance.

If I want to learn a new skill, I hire a professional coach to teach it to me. I want to practice the right concepts, so I won't get it wrong. Practice makes perfect ... not true. You have to add one word ... *perfect* practice makes perfect.

Practice makes perfect ... not true. You have to add one word ... perfect practice makes perfect.

Legendary Dallas Cowboys Coach Tom Landry explains, "A coach is someone who tells you what you don't want to hear, who has you see what you don't want to see, so you can be who you have always known you could be."

Over my lifetime, I've had numerous professional coaches to help me develop whatever natural talent I may have. I understand that I will never be as good as the coaches I've hired, but I can surely improve on my limited abilities. So I go to the people who know what they are doing.

I've hired professional coaches for public speaking, writing, ideas/creativity, foreign languages, running marathons, golf, tennis, water and downhill skiing, swimming, dancing, bowling, boxing, scuba diving, ice skating, basketball, and many others.

I'm not spending a single penny; I'm making an investment in myself. And, believe me, it comes back ten-fold.

Many times over the years when I've purchased a new electronic gadget, I've hired the person who sold me the device and paid him to come to my office to teach me how to use it. Technology can be difficult for me, so I hire a pro to teach me and take copious notes. Does that seem frivolous? Not to me. The sooner I can be up and running, the more efficiently I can work.

The old saying "time is money" is so true. Why waste your time and money when so much help is available to enable you to save both time and money in the long run?

I've been on the other side of the equation, too. I've been honored to be asked to be a mentor, usually not paid, to help aspiring salespeople and entrepreneurs hone their skills. It's so rewarding to pass along professional knowledge and experiences. If I can steer someone away from making a monumental mistake, I'm satisfied. I want to demonstrate the highest level of professionalism so that others understand the importance of seeking the best advice.

MACKAY'S MORAL

Admitting your own weaknesses is a sign of strength.

MAKE A BAD HIRE
AND YOUR PLANS COULD BACKFIRE

If there is anything more scarce, more unique, more rare than ability ... it's the ability to recognize ability.

For example, you are considering a person for a software position at your company. You interview her for six months and give her every test known to mankind. You would think that you would know the candidate well, but this is not necessarily true. Hire the person and you will know more in the first 30 days watching her on the firing line than you learned during the previous six months of interviews.

It is extremely difficult to pick good people, but if you have a system and commit yourself to it, the chances will go up dramatically that you will succeed. And it is essential to hire and retain good people. You cannot build a business that has a revolving door.

When I started in business at Mackay Envelope Company (which is now MackayMitchell Envelope Company), I came up with an eight-point plan to ensure the highest probability of success in hiring key employees. These concepts have worked very well for me, and we have continually led our industry in employee loyalty and longevity. I hope you get one or two good ideas from my system:

1. **Multiple interviews.** Have six to eight interviews with a candidate and involve others in the interview process—coworkers, friends, and colleagues. The more people you have interview the candidate, the better.

2. **Full disclosure.** When a candidate becomes a finalist at our company, we allow them to talk to anybody on our payroll. We don't have a company point of view. Everyone can express him- or herself individually. We want the candidate to have 100 percent full disclosure of how any of our people feel. We have no hidden agenda or small print under the small print.

3. **Interview in different environments.** I want to check out candidates away from the office to see how they handle themselves in different social and casual circumstances. We might play golf, tennis, attend a concert or play, have breakfast, lunch, or dinner. Believe me, you'll have a better feel, touch, and pulse of that candidate.

4. **Interview the candidate using the telephone, email, and online conferencing.** Today, everyone must be good in all forms of communication, which I believe can be awesome weapons. This is doubly important for the people who use these tools for their jobs.

5. **Interview the spouse and family.** A lot of people do not agree with me on this, but I feel spouses and family members need to realize we care about them, as well. Caring is contagious ... help spread it around. We want candidates to know that when we make the decision to bring them on board, we consider it the single biggest decision MackayMitchell Envelope Company can make. Remember, anyone can buy an envelope machine, but it takes talent to hire the right person.

6. **Use industrial-organizational psychologists.** For hiring key employees, a valuable tool is using psychologists. They don't make decisions for you; all they do is help you make the decision. But if you have some specific concerns, they can laser in on the problem.

7. **The Acid Test of Hiring.** Let's say I'm hiring a sales person. Approximately 10 to 15 minutes into the interview I ask myself, "How would I feel if this person were working for my competitor?" If I'm not worried, that's the end of the interview.

8. **Agreements prevent disagreements.** I strongly believe in written contracts. If you are willing to fight your guts out for an agreement, you won't have a disagreement.

There is one overriding philosophy that you have to keep in mind for every person you hire. Never compromise your standards.

MACKAY'S MORAL

The single greatest mistake a manager can make is to make a bad hire.

FIRING IS LIKE PUBLIC SPEAKING; FEW LIKE TO DO IT

In the last chapter I outlined an eight-step plan to improve your hiring techniques. Now let me switch gears for a moment and move to the other side of the ledger: firing.

Anyone who thinks he is indispensable should stick a finger in a bowl of water and notice the hole it leaves when he pulls it out.

A substantive, in-depth survey was done a couple years ago that asked 1,000 executives, "What's the most difficult task you have to do on your job?" Of course, the answer that was head and shoulders above the rest was firing someone. To terminate another person is the most difficult task any of these executives have, and there are a myriad of reasons why:

Their business is going well and they are making money.

It's easy to procrastinate.

They might have a personal relationship with this person, which would make it very difficult to terminate him or her.

They might be in the comfort zone.

This reminds me of the story of the worker who was asked, "Why did the foreman fire you?"

"Well, you know, the foreman is the person who stands around and watches other people work."

"But why did he fire you?"

"He was jealous. A lot of other people thought that I was the foreman."

Jack Kent Cooke, former owner of the Washington Redskins, said: "Hiring and firing people is the most unpleasant part of being an employer, but it is a major part of the responsibility a proprietor has to himself, his organization, the persons who are dependent on that organization for their living, and those who support it."

Another interesting statistic from that executive study: 92 percent of the executives said, "I should have done it sooner."

None of them ever said, "Gosh, I wish I had Mary or Paul back on the payroll."

Here is one more point from the study. Some of you might not agree with me, but no one can talk me out of it, at least from my experience. If you ever have to fire another person, and he or she is shocked or surprised … you are a poor manager. You see, you have to work with these people.

You have to be a coach. You have to help them accomplish their short-term and long-term goals, their dreams, their hopes, and their vision.... But, of course, sometimes it just doesn't work out.

And if it doesn't, then that person will have to jump to another lily pad. And almost always, you're doing that person a real favor because he or she may be more successful in a different environment.

Do you know where the term firing came from?

It started with family clans in early civilizations. When they wanted to get rid of their unwanted people without killing them, they used to burn their houses down—hence the expression "to get fired."

We're a little more civilized now, and I can name many successful people who were fired, and it turned out for the best.

Ronald Reagan was elected president of the United States after he was fired by Warner Brothers (with a few other jobs in between). Lee Iacocca was booted out of the presidency of Ford Motor Company by Henry Ford before he revived the dying Chrysler Corporation. Television host Sally Jessy Raphael, by her own count, was handed the pink slip no fewer than 18 times. Luciano Pavarotti was fired from the Lyric Opera of Chicago in 1989. Even Fred Astaire, Burt Reynolds, and Clint Eastwood all flunked screen tests.

Fortunately, these people all found bigger and better jobs where they could showcase their talents. Getting pushed out the door was a step in the right direction.

MACKAY'S MORAL

It's not the people you fire who make your life miserable; it's the people you don't fire who make your life miserable.

Employee retention:
A cause for reflection

Employee retention is a hot business topic today. No longer do people stay at the same company for 25 years and collect the gold watch like in years past.

In fact, according to the U.S. Bureau of Labor statistics, the average worker will have 12 jobs from age 18 to 48. A shocking statistic. That alone should tell managers that all the time they put into hiring, training, and promoting may just be preparation for the employee's next job—and chances are it will be somewhere else.

Employees have more bargaining power than ever before. Unemployment is relatively low, and social media makes a company's employee retention information and job satisfaction public knowledge.

Factor in that a recent Gallup poll shows that only 31 percent of employees are engaged at work, 51 percent are disengaged, and 17.5 percent are actively disengaged. Translation: less than one-third of employees are excited about their jobs. Glassdoor, a website where employees and former employees anonymously review companies and their management, says that the average employee gives their company a C plus (3.1 out of 5) when asked whether they would recommend their company to a friend. In other words, companies need to do a better job retaining their valuable employees.

Then there is the collateral damage. Customers have an uncanny talent for picking up on dissatisfaction, and that can damage the bottom line. Can your company afford that?

Why do people leave companies in the first place? There are many reasons: changes in benefits, bosses, and job responsibilities, difficult coworkers, unethical practices, poor leadership, lack of challenges, and many more.

I happen to believe that employees leave managers; they don't leave companies.

I happen to believe that employees leave managers; they don't leave companies.

Taking action when your employees are seriously dissatisfied with your organization's policies or decisions is a test of your leadership. A face-to-face discussion about grievances can clear the air, but you have to be careful to prevent it from turning into an explosive gripe session. A productive meeting needs careful planning, so consider these suggestions:

Prepare to hear some painful conversation. Be ready to listen without becoming defensive or arguing back.

Limit the size. A group of 10 to 15 employees is large enough so people don't feel exposed and singled out, but still small enough so everyone can participate.

Assure privacy. Meet in a conference room where you won't be overheard, not the lunchroom or break area where other employees might wander in and out.

Ask for input. State the problem as you've heard it and ask for everyone's opinions and feedback. Promise that you won't punish anyone for speaking out, and stick to your word. Ask participants to prioritize the list so that the most important issues can be addressed first.

Respond honestly. Address each complaint. If you believe any issues are invalid, explain why, but be willing to listen to other points of view. Specify what you will do in response to the valid complaints.

Follow up promptly. If you can't resolve a problem immediately, promise that you will respond in a short, specific time.

Thank the group. Express your sincere appreciation for their courage and honesty in bringing each issue to your attention. Re-emphasize your mutual goal of working together productively and efficiently so employees know you value their opinions.

That's a good start, but keeping good employees is a long-term proposition.

Retention depends on more than bonuses and rewards. The best strategies engage employees on the job with equitable and generous compensation and benefits. Reliable, long-term retention depends on actions that managers should be practicing every day.

Coach employees on how to influence, motivate, and persuade people. They'll be able to accomplish more, which will lead to greater job satisfaction, if they can motivate others.

Help them develop their leadership skills. When employees see a path to advancement, they won't have to look elsewhere for better opportunities. Providing opportunities for leadership shows they can have a future with your organization.

Give constant and immediate feedback. Tell employees what they're doing right, and how they can improve. They'll see that you are paying attention and are committed to their success.

Encourage workers to suggest ideas and innovations, and take them seriously when they follow up. Show that you value their experience and skills.

Recognize their contributions. Praise employees for their efforts, share credit as widely as possible, and give their achievements the attention they deserve.

MACKAY'S MORAL

Solving employee turnover is easier when employees own a piece of the pie.

Getting a job is a job

Getting a job is a full-time job. Here are 10 things you should do to improve your job situation:

1. **Get a routine and stick to it.** Getting a job is not a nine-to-five job. It's a 16-hour a day proposition from the moment you get up until you go to sleep. With that kind of workload, you need a daily schedule to establish that routine and organize your time.

2. **Get back in shape.** Companies have always hired according to subtle, hidden values. Take huge pains with your wardrobe, hairstyling, and makeup. And not just at interviews, either. Looking good is the rule every time you poke your nose outside the door. In fact, in this age of video chats and teleconferencing, you need to look good even if you don't step outside. For that matter, be sure that your home is clean and organized, and have a well-arranged room from which you might perform video interviews. Similarly, make sure your LinkedIn, Facebook, and other social media profiles project the right image for when human resources departments check them. Appearance has always been 30 percent nature and 70 percent cunning artifice, so we can all be at least 7s if we try.

3. **Read.** Start with online job boards. The Internet gives you the classifieds, which are the meat and potatoes of your job search. The *Wall Street Journal* is your link to the state of the national economy and the job market. It would be prudent to check the business section of *USA TODAY*, as it often leads in identifying new trends. Also, it's not uncommon for an interviewer to ask the "friendly" and "casual" question: "What have you been reading lately?" Have a good answer.

4. **Make those calls.** Keeping your network alive means casting a wide net. Dive into your LinkedIn connections, professional networks, address books, and lists of contacts and give yourself a quota of, say, five contacts a day. Be brief. Your agenda is obvious: What do you know that I don't that might provide me any leads? It will also help if you can carry your own weight and provide the persons you're calling with some information that may be of value to them.

5. **Do your homework.** Stay on top of new developments in your field. Now is the time to take those courses you never had time for... and be sure you find a way to mention them during your interviews.

6. **Know the company you keep.** Before you interview, check with anyone you know who knows about the company—employees, customers, bankers, vendors, and others. You're looking for two things: First, you want clues about the company's reputation. Is it a leader in its industry? An also-ran? How does it compete? Does the company emphasize price? Quality? Service? Innovation? Second, you want to know the company's values and style. Check the company's website to see where they are focusing their energy and what they value. If you can, find out who will be interviewing you and check their online profiles. You can be sure they'll be checking yours as well.

7. **Thank you. Thank you. Thank you.** Did you have a little chat with the receptionist or with an assistant while you were waiting for one of your interviews today? Write down that name and send a thank-you note or an email recalling the conversation. It'll help differentiate you from the pack when you call that firm. It won't hurt your chances of having those calls put through, either. And, of course, the interviewer and anyone else you may have met at the company are musts on your thank-you list.

8. **Keep notes.** You need a system for keeping track of people. When I started in business, I kept a well-worn business card file that I thumbed through on a daily basis. Then the backs of the cards were so covered with smudges and chicken scratching that they became unreadable. I developed a system on paper where I could make regular notations to my customer files. That evolved into the Mackay 66, a 66-item profile I keep on my key customers, vendors, and so on. These days, there is a wide array of apps and software that can help you. You can start with your email address book and your LinkedIn, Facebook, Twitter, Instagram, and other social media connections and build from there.

9. **Volunteer.** Get involved in a cause that means something to you. First, you're keeping actively busy during an emotional downturn in your life, which is good for the head. Second, you're improving your job-hunting skills. Volunteering involves marketing, selling, time management, public speaking, fundraising, creativity, and more. Third, depending on the organization and the role you take, volunteering can put you in contact with some of the most important

people in your community. They'll see you do your stuff. Finally, doing something good for others helps shape your attitude and keeps your own situation in perspective.

10. **Get ready for tomorrow.** Clothes in shape? Appointments confirmed? Schedule set? Sign off. You've had a busy day.

MACKAY'S MORAL

When you're unemployed, you have to work all the time.

HOW DO YOU GET BETTER AT YOUR JOB?

When I am hired to speak to a company or association, I typically talk ahead of time with six to eight people who will be in the audience to get a better sense of the group. I ask them a series of questions about creative selling, teamwork, negotiations, how they get close to their customers, and so on. Then I surprise them and ask what they do to get better at their jobs?

Over the years some of the typical answers I've received include going back to school to learn new skills or get another degree, joining trade organizations and attending events, networking, listening to speakers, reading everything they can get their hands on, being more available, working harder and smarter, improving people skills, and many more.

These are all great ideas, but I'd like to add to the list and share some of my ideas on what you can do to get better at your job.

Improve your time management. Most people fail because they let time manage them rather than managing their time. Time becomes a crook. Often it's the people who make the worst use of their time who complain there is never enough of it.

Get organized. This will not only improve your productivity, but it will streamline your life, lower your stress, and save you money. The *Wall Street Journal* reported that the average U.S. executive wastes six weeks per year retrieving misplaced information from messy desks and files. (I'm still working on this.)

Stay positive. Positive thinking is more than just a tagline; it changes the way we behave. And I firmly believe that when I'm positive, it not only makes me better, but it also makes those around me better. Positive thinking turns obstacles into opportunities.

Write down your goals. Goals not only give you a reason to get up in the morning; they are an incentive to keep you going all day. Goals tend to tap the deeper resources and draw the best out of life. Achieving goals produces significant accomplishments.

Learn to compromise. When you observe the politics in Washington, compromise appears to be a lost art. Maybe that's because it often is looked upon as weakness. Nothing could be further from the truth. Business involves constant compromise—negotiating contracts, hiring, closing sales, and so on.

Exercise your mind and body. Taking care of business starts with taking care of yourself. Exercise makes me feel better and gives me energy to work more productively. My philosophy is that exercise doesn't take time; it makes time.

Develop your confidence. Confidence doesn't come naturally to most people. Even the most successful people have struggled with it in their careers. The good news is that you can develop confidence just like any muscle or character trait. Some tips: improve your skills, keep track of your success, practice being assertive, and step out of your comfort zone.

Improve your relationship with your boss. A good relationship with your boss is the foundation of a successful career. Your boss is the person most likely to recognize your contributions and achievements and potentially recommend you for promotions. Strive for a positive work environment.

Surround yourself with mentors and coaches. You can't do it all by yourself. Seek out the very best help you can find to take your game to the next level. On the flip side, don't shy away from mentoring younger workers because business is a team sport.

Practice public speaking. Most people dread public speaking, but there are few skills that are more important. Public speaking improves your confidence and communication skills and helps you think better on your feet. How you say things can be as important as what you say. Join Toastmasters International, one of the best-kept secrets in the world. (I did.)

Learn to love feedback. You can learn from anyone if you are open to accepting feedback from not only your manager but from colleagues and customers. If you really believe in yourself, you'll be open to criticism, learn from it, and improve your performance.

The main thing is that you keep working on you. Life is like riding a bicycle. You don't fall off unless you stop pedaling.

MACKAY'S MORAL

Improvement begins with I.

10

HUMOR/LAUGHTER

LAUGHTER: THE NATURAL HIGH

Can you identify this description of a physical reaction?

- The neural circuits in your brain begin to reverberate;
- Chemical and electrical impulses start flowing rapidly through your body;
- The pituitary gland is stimulated, and hormones and endorphins race through your blood;
- Your body temperature rises half a degree;
- Your pulse rate and blood pressure increase;
- Your arteries and thoracic muscles contract, your vocal cords quiver, and your face contorts;
- Pressure builds in your lungs, your lower jaw becomes uncontrollable, and breath bursts from your mouth at nearly 70 miles per hour.

Okay, all you *Grey's Anatomy* fans, what just happened? Should we call an ambulance?

Better to call a friend and share the joke with them. You just laughed!

Starting your day with a good laugh, or at least a big smile, is as beneficial to your health as it is to your mood. Scientific studies at Northwestern University and Fordham University concluded that laughter benefits the heart, lungs, stomach, and other organs. It relaxes tensions, changes attitude, and increases the body's natural painkillers. It has no harmful side effects. Why don't we do it more?

We used to, at least when we were little kids. Children laugh an average of 150 to 450 times a day, depending which study you believe, but all the research says adults laugh a paltry 15 times a day. That's pathetic. Aren't we supposed to work hard so that we can enjoy life?

Laughing isn't hard work, and hard work isn't funny. But it is possible—even desirable—to merge the two. There is no place that needs humor more than the workplace. Considering the number of hours you spend there, and the huge effect it has on your life, wouldn't you like it to be just a little more fun?

Marty Grunder, who owns a very successful landscaping business in Miamisburg, Ohio, shared his formula for recruiting interesting (yet competent) people. He told me about the following ad he had run: "RECEPTIONIST/Rude, lazy, disorganized slob needed to answer phones for national award-winning company. Ideal candidate must talk fast, not listen well, read magazines a lot, and chew gum loudly. Inability to work in a fast-paced environment a must. Sense of humor required...." Marty got 42 resumes from that tongue-in-cheek ad. I'd be willing to bet applicants would pay *him* to let them work there. I'd also wager they'll work hard and love the job.

Where do you start to lighten up? First, you have to be able to laugh at yourself. The people who can laugh at themselves will never run out of things to laugh at. Telling a funny story about your foibles or a common dilemma at your office is fine; poking fun at others is risky at best. This is a good time to remember the Golden Rule. Keep it friendly.

Humor builds positive relationships and improves morale. With so many projects dependent on teamwork to be successful, open communication is essential. Laughter is the ultimate icebreaker and bridge-builder. Have you ever noticed how many brainstorming sessions contain a larger than usual amount of chuckles? Humor and creativity are closely linked. I don't know of any companies that deny the importance of creativity. I surely wouldn't want to work for one.

To me, the responsibility of the NASA launch teams seems huge. They are working on multi-billion dollar projects, sending courageous astronauts into the great unknown, their every move monitored around the world. In short, it IS rocket science. Most folks don't connect astrophysics with raucous laughter. But have you ever listened to the conversations between mission control and the astronauts in orbit? They're hysterical! The music that wakes the astronauts up in the morning—"Fly Me to the Moon," "Oh What a Beautiful Morning," "Up, Up and Away," "Leaving on a Jet Plane" ... somebody knows how to mix business with pleasure.

You may also recall Alan Shepard's famous golf game—on the moon. I've had trouble shipping my clubs to Phoenix. These super brains decided to give the folks watching at home a good laugh. They still had a long, scary flight home, but they understood how to take the edge off. Maybe we should all sign up for a rollicking week at space camp!

MACKAY'S MORAL

Take your work seriously, but don't take yourself too seriously.

A SENSE OF HUMOR IS NO JOKE

There is an Apache legend that the creator gave human beings the ability to talk and to run, and to look at things. But in addition, the legend says he was not satisfied until he also gave them the ability to laugh. After giving humans the ability to laugh, the creator said, "Now you are fit to live."

A good sense of humor helps to overlook the unbecoming, understand the unconventional, tolerate the unpleasant, overcome the unexpected, and outlast the unbearable.

"A sense of humor is the one thing no one will admit not having," said none other than Mark Twain.

Life is too short to be serious all the time. How dull our existence would be without the potential to see the lighter side of situations. And how hopeless, too! Humor often represents hope, that the worst is behind us and better things are coming.

True, not all things are funny. Knowing how and when to apply a filter is critical. And it's usually better when the joke is on you, so your obvious amusement signals permission to see the humor in a situation.

"If I were given the opportunity to present a gift to the next generation, it would be the ability for each individual to learn to laugh at himself," said Charles Schulz, creator of the long-running "Peanuts" comic strip.

I value a sense of humor very highly when I am hiring people, especially for sales and customer service jobs. My employees know I love a good laugh. For years I started every sales meeting with a funny story or joke and asked other managers to do the same. I wasn't looking for the next Tina Fey or Jimmy Fallon. I just wanted to loosen up the group and put them in a good mood.

The same attitude is important for anyone who comes into contact with customers. If you've ever flown on a Southwest Airlines flight, you might have heard the safety instructions delivered in a variety of amusing ways. The message is quite serious, but their approach serves a number of purposes: encouraging people to actually listen to what's being said, putting passengers in a more relaxed mood after the stress of airport hassles, and letting folks know that the flight attendants are enjoying their work and want you to enjoy your trip.

Do you watch the Super Bowl? Or more specifically, do you watch the commercials? At a cool $5 million for a 30-second spot, the price tag is enough to make a business cry. But year in and year out, the ads command almost as much attention as the game itself—because they make people laugh. And then talk about them the next day. And buy those products. Beer isn't inherently funny, nor are tortilla chips or car insurance, but somehow humor makes those items more memorable.

Some of the funniest people I know are also among the quietest. You have to listen closely to what they say, because the quips sneak out when you least expect them. For example, a woman approached President Calvin Coolidge, aptly nicknamed "Silent Cal," at a dinner and said, "Mr. President, I have a bet with my friend that I can get you to say more than two words." Coolidge replied, "You lose!"

You may think you have to be born funny, but I disagree. Finding the humor in everyday life is easy if you just look for it. People who take themselves too seriously are a constant source of amusement for me. Take this young job-seeker, for example:

At the end of a job interview, the human resources person asked a young engineer fresh out of a top university, "And what starting salary were you looking for?"

The engineer said optimistically, "In the neighborhood of $125,000 a year, depending on the benefits package."

The interviewer said, "Well, what would you say to a package of five weeks vacation, 14 paid holidays, full medical and dental, company matching retirement fund to 50 percent of salary, and a company car leased every two years, say, a red Corvette?"

The engineer sat up straight and said, "Wow! Are you kidding?"

And the interviewer replied, "Yeah, but you started it."

MACKAY'S MORAL

Life isn't always funny, but a sense of humor always helps.

HUMOR WORKS AT WORK

Life is funny, the saying goes. And when it isn't funny, sometimes a sense of humor is what gets us through the tough times. Humor plays a special role at work. As critical as it is to take your work seriously, it is equally important to NOT take yourself too seriously.

Many years ago, a *Fortune* magazine article talked about how executives should be funnier. I remember it well, because one of my biggest pet peeves is people who cannot laugh at themselves. The wonderful example the magazine used involved auto executive Eugene Cafiero.

When he was president of Chrysler, Cafiero went to England to meet with troubled employees at the company's plant there. Conflict between management and union employees was tense. As Cafiero entered the plant he was confronted by a man who loudly said, "I'm Eddie McClusky, and I'm a communist."

The composed Chrysler executive extended his hand and replied, "How do you do. I'm Eugene Cafiero, and I'm a Presbyterian." The subsequent laughter squelched this potentially explosive confrontation.

I like to say if you can't take a joke, then you'll have to take the medicine. That can be a bitter pill to swallow.

Think about your coworkers who you most enjoy working with: They typically have a good perspective on the importance of specific projects, get work finished on time, offer to help out when it's crunch time, and keep a smile on their faces through it all. And they often manage to put a smile on your face too.

Humor can make unpleasant tasks more palatable. It can diffuse difficult situations and improve already good relations.

Humor can make unpleasant tasks more palatable. It can diffuse difficult situations and improve already good relations.

I have a friend in a business that you would usually not associate with humor—he's a funeral director. He doesn't joke around about the seriousness of his work, but he does encourage his clients to allow themselves to laugh and share humorous memories about their loved ones. He says it helps break the tension and brings comfort to a trying situation.

There is plenty of evidence to support the benefits of humor at work. In a new study, researchers from Harvard's Business School found that cracking jokes at work shows your employer an increased perception of confidence and competence. The study shows the most effective joke-tellers are more likely to be chosen as group leaders.

Just make sure the jokes in the office are appropriate. Researchers found inappropriate jokes lead to a perception of low competence. In other words, save the locker room banter and personal insults. Those are never funny anyway.

The most difficult part of using humor at work is knowing where to draw the line. You can joke with a customer, but never about a customer. You can tease your coworkers, or even your boss, but when it gets personal or hurtful, you are in dangerous territory. Refer to the Golden Rule if you are wondering whether your remarks are appropriate: Do unto others as you would have them do unto you. If you have to ask someone, you already have your answer. No joke is funny if you are the only one laughing.

Here's a great take on how one company used humor—as an April Fool's joke—to deal with requests for taking a day off:

- There are 365 days per year available for work.
- There are 52 weeks per year in which you already have two days off per week, leaving 261 days available for work.
- Since you spend 16 hours each day away from work, you have used up 170 days, leaving only 91 days available.
- You spend 30 minutes each day on coffee breaks; that accounts for 23 days each year, leaving only 68 days available.
- With a one-hour lunch period each day, you have used up another 46 days, leaving only 22 days available for work.
- You normally spend two days per year on sick leave. This leaves you only 20 days available for work.
- We offer five holidays per year, so your available working time is down to 15 days.
- We generously give you 14 days of vacation per year, which leaves one day available for work and no way are you going to take it.

MACKAY'S MORAL

Humor is more than funny business.

11

IDEAS/INNOVATION

IDEAS WITHOUT ACTION
ARE WORTHLESS

Anybody who is past third grade knows that Sir Isaac Newton formulated the Law of Gravity. Back in 1684, Isaac was sitting under an apple tree and saw an apple fall (or it bonked him on the head, depending on your source).

His main goal that day was to take a little rest, but watching this everyday autumn event, he hit on something really big, aka the Law of Gravity: the gravitational attraction between two bodies is directly proportional to the product of the masses of the two bodies and inversely proportional to the square of the distance between them.

Wait a minute! Wasn't he just loafing around—nothing in particular on his mind, except to take it easy?

I've never had an idea quite like that, but some of my really inspired thoughts came to me not while I was sitting at my desk, but in an unusual assortment of venues—watching a football game, lining up a putt, looking out the window of an airplane. I do some of my best thinking at 30,000 feet. The few minutes away from your daily grind can be a tremendous source of inspiration. The trick is putting those ideas into action.

Another fellow, who lived a few years before Newton, sat watching a great swinging lamp as a form of meditation. Then Galileo hit on the idea of a pendulum swinging as a means of accurately measuring the passage of time. (Impress your friends with this tidbit: it's called isochronism.) The tick-tock of your grandfather clock started centuries ago.

Finding a better way to get things done has proven to be a great source of good ideas.

We've all heard about the genesis of the Post-it Note, developed as a non-skid bookmark by a 3M scientist to use in his choir book at church. The rest of us said a loud "alleluia" when he shared that gem with the world.

Do you remember life before Velcro? Sneakers haven't been the same since that bright idea. It all started with a walk in the woods and the natural aftermath, burrs stuck to clothing. The next thing you know, George de Mestral had patented the next best thing to the magnet. Was he looking for a better way to keep his kids' shoes on? No. The idea was just too good to waste.

Ole Evinrude was tired of having his ice cream melt in his rowboat before he reached his island picnic spot. We can thank Ole for dreaming up the outboard motor. Thoughts like that inspired whole industries, like water skiing, fishing, and boating in its many manifestations.

Sometimes, ideas just naturally follow from things we already know.

Roy Speer and Lowell Paxson used their three observations about modern lifestyles to build a business worth hundreds of millions (billions) of dollars in annual revenues. First, they noted that people like to shop; second, that people like to watch TV; and third, that people like to shop or watch TV anytime they wish. Their Home Shopping Network is seen around the world 24 hours a day. It has been so successful that at least six other shopping networks have followed HSN's lead, and infomercials dominate late-night television.

It's the incredibly practical inventions, borne of the occasional stroke of genius coupled with an action plan, that make us ask, "Why didn't I think of that?" Imagination is great, but by itself, it's not much more than a pleasant pastime. But give your thoughts some wings, and there's no telling how far you can fly with it. And often, you are working from the ground up.

A case in point is Will Parrish, a lawyer and conservation specialist. Familiar with rising energy costs and well aware that fossil fuel resources are diminishing, he was always on the lookout for alternative sources of energy. On a trip to India, he ate a meal which had been heated by, of all things, flaming cow dung. Instead of being disgusted, he was inspired. He formed National Energy Associates. The company burns 900 tons of cow cookies a day and produces enough megawatts to light 20,000 homes. *Fortune* magazine has called him the world's true "entre-manure."

MACKAY'S MORAL

If you keep thinking what you've always thought, you'll keep getting what you've always got.

BIG INNOVATIONS
START WITH LITTLE IDEAS

Way back about 200 B.C., Hannibal, the great Carthaginian general, came up with a good definition for creativity: "We must either find a way or make a way." You remember Hannibal—he led 90,000 infantry, 12,000 cavalry, and 40 elephants across the Pyrenees Mountains and on through the Alps. He really had to find a way.

Sometimes it might feel like you are leading thousands of coworkers and large mammals over rough terrain ... and that's when your most innovative, creative ideas are essential. Unfortunately, it's also the time when the creative juices seem to flow the slowest.

Being able to think on your feet is a huge asset for any employee or manager. When Mark Twain was asked to name the greatest of all inventors, he replied with one word: "Accident." I might add a few more: Necessity. Emergency. Keeping your company solvent.

I can't teach you in a few short minutes how to think on your feet. I can tell you, however, that there are a couple of questions that might get you started thinking in a different way. Faced with a new challenge, ask what needs to ultimately be accomplished. Creating a new product? Re-marketing an old one? Selling a new account? Trying to retain a longstanding customer?

We hear so much about "thinking outside the box." Maybe it's time to trash the box altogether, and never crawl back in. One study showed that out of 61 basic inventions, only 16 (around 25 percent) were discovered in big companies. Some examples of inventions discovered outside big companies: an undertaker invented the dial telephone; a sculptor came up with the ballpoint pen. Further evidence comes from a study by economist Burton Klein, who looked at 50 major innovations developed in the American economy over the last several decades of the 20th century. None of those innovations came from a company that was an industry leader at the time.

The entrepreneur *finds* a need and fills it. The innovator *anticipates or creates* a need and fills it. Forget about putting together a "to-do" list. Instead, come up with a "to create" list. Look for the new possibilities; redesign existing ones—even when they are working right now. Tomorrow could be a different story. How can you breathe fresh air into a stale market?

The entrepreneur finds *a need and fills it. The innovator* anticipates or creates *a need and fills it. Forget about putting together a "to-do" list. Instead, come up with a "to create" list.*

Innovative thinking can save your corporate skin, as witnessed in the tale of the dachshund and the leopard:

A man goes on safari in Africa and takes his pet dachshund with him. The dog starts chasing butterflies through the fields, and before long, gets lost. He wanders around, trying to find his way back to camp, and notices a leopard heading his way, looking at his potential lunch.

The dachshund smells trouble. Noticing some bones on the ground nearby, he starts to chew on them with the leopard still approaching. Just as the leopard is about to pounce, the dachshund exclaims loudly, "Gee, that was a delicious leopard. I wonder if there are any more around here?"

The terrified leopard retreats to some nearby bushes. "That was close," he thinks. "That dachshund nearly had me!"

Clearly, the dachshund is following Peter Drucker's advice: "Don't try to innovate for the future. Innovate for the present!"

Truer words were never spoken. What are the most talked-about cars at the Detroit auto show? The concept cars. Will they actually be available for sale? Maybe, maybe not. But the ideas generated from them will be in your next ride.

The innovative worker doesn't go to work because she is inspired, but gains inspiration because she is working. The great composers are marvelous examples of that: given eight notes in a couple octaves, can you begin to count the number of songs they've created? Or the various harmonies? They really didn't have anything new to work with; they just found a new way to use what they had.

The Hewlett-Packard Company was famously founded in a one-car garage by William Hewlett and Dave Packard. It has become one of the world's most innovative and successful technology companies, but it never lost sight of its founders' original vision. According to legend, these rules on innovation were posted in the garage:

- Believe you can change the world.
- Work quickly, keep the tools unlocked, work whenever.
- Know when to work alone and when to work together.
- Share—tools, ideas. Trust your colleagues.

- No politics. No bureaucracy. (These are ridiculous in a garage.)
- The customer defines a job well done.
- Radical ideas are not bad ideas.
- Invent different ways of working.
- Make a contribution every day. If it doesn't contribute, it doesn't leave the garage.
- Believe that together we can do anything.
- Invent.

Feel free to borrow these rules until you develop a set of your own. And then post them where you will see them every day. Be innovative!

MACKAY'S MORAL

Maybe you can't change the whole world, but you can change your world.

Spark innovation in your company

One of the hottest words in business is innovation. The word, and its significance, never actually went away, of course, but it was heard less often during the booming 1990s. Now, companies like the Ford Motor Company are basing their entire advertising on the concept of innovation.

Innovation is not a one-time event. It is a dynamic process that we must do every day. Truly innovative companies allow employees to take risks, large and small, to build a better mousetrap.

Innovation is not a one-time event. It is a dynamic process that we must do every day. Truly innovative companies allow employees to take risks, large and small, to build a better mousetrap.

Whether you're the CEO of your company or a front-line employee, you can't afford to take innovation for granted. Take an active role in inspiring new products and services with these strategies:

- **Start close to home.** You don't have to design a brand-new product or come up with a revolutionary idea that's never been seen before. Improve on what already works, or apply it to a different problem. Can you add features, make it faster, or deliver more value? Listen to your customers. Are they asking for changes that you hadn't thought about?

- **Stimulate the right people.** Recruit employees who are talented, but frustrated with the status quo. Their energy will produce some outside-the-box thinking that will spark new ideas.

- **Cross-pollinate.** If only engineers are working on a project, they'll tend to see engineering problems and find engineering solutions. Get as many people and departments actively involved as you can manage. Innovation thrives in an environment of different perspectives. Bring in people with different experiences to open up possibilities. Ask those who use the products what they would change if they could.

- **Tolerate risk.** Expect some failures, and treat them as learning experiences. Be open to the possibility that a "mistake" may turn out to be a great idea.

- **Don't just follow the money.** Revenue is your ultimate goal, but other factors should guide your decisions as well. Innovation should produce value to customers, employees, the community, and your other stake-holders. Focus on delivering value and the revenues will follow.

- **Start the clock.** A deadline creates urgency and excitement. While innovation in general should be ongoing, it's reasonable to set a firm timeline for results on specific projects. "Perfect" solutions may be elusive, but improvements that are workable are an important first step. Implement them while they're still fresh to keep enthusiasm alive.

- **Reward your team.** Share the financial benefits, but don't forget to show your appreciation in other ways. Praise your employees for their creativity and commitment to the project. Celebrate their success and willingness to take chances.

- **Encourage ongoing innovation.** Create a culture of innovation where employees know their ideas are welcome and valued. Provide continual learning about your products, services, customers, technologies, competitors, and industry. A well-informed and educated workforce is more likely to recognize opportunities for innovation.

Richard C. Notebaert, former CEO of Ameritech and Qwest International, illustrated how lack of innovation has been an issue for thousands of years: "In a museum at Princeton University, there is a toy from a pre-Columbian civilization. It's a pull-toy complete with wheels. Now the question is, if the craftsmen of the day were able to conceive of and construct wheels for an amusement—a toy—why didn't they take that technology a step further and design carts and wagons? Why didn't they develop tools that would ease their burdens? Many scholars conclude they just never thought of it."

MACKAY'S MORAL

Charge up your work environment! A tiny spark can produce electric results.

12

LEADERSHIP

ATTENTION: LEADERSHIP LESSONS FROM THE MARINES

Follow the leader—it's a game we learned as little kids. As I recall, we would follow whoever was in front of the line all over the neighborhood, through puddles and over fences. When it was finally your turn to be the leader, you tried to prove your worthiness, at least until everyone got tired of the game and found something else to do.

Not much changed, except maybe the geography, as we grew up and went into business. Leadership became a major factor in our success: could we convince our employees and associates that we had the right stuff to lead a company? Or would they get tired of the game and find other jobs?

Some people are born leaders; they just know what needs to be done and how to motivate others to do it. However, if you don't fall in that category, I have good news for you: Leadership can be learned!

A phenomenal lesson comes from our brave military, specifically the Marines, where good leadership can mean the difference between life and death. These 11 principles of leadership are found in the *Guidebook for Marines*, published by the U.S. Marine Corps. The first sentence—listed in bold—is from the guide, and I've added my thoughts to each. Feel free to substitute employees for Marines to make it suit your situation. Study them, and hone your leadership skills.

1. **Know yourself and seek improvement.** Be honest when you evaluate yourself. Seek the honest opinions of your friends or superiors to learn how to improve. Have a definite goal and a specific plan to achieve it.

2. **Be technically and tactically proficient.** Know your job, and work to broaden your knowledge.

3. **Know your Marines and look out for their welfare.** Know their problems, and make sure that they receive all appropriate help that they need. Encourage their individual development.

4. **Keep your Marines informed.** Make sure that people know that they can always look to you for the truth. Provide information so that subordinates feel like part of the team and could carry on without your personal supervision if necessary.

5. **Set the example.** How you conduct yourself says more than any instructions you may give. Set high personal standards and expect the same from your staff.

6. **Ensure the task is understood, supervised, and accomplished.** Employees must understand what is expected of them in order to complete a job or assignment. Follow through to make sure the job gets done.

7. **Train your Marines as a team.** Employees should understand that the contribution that each one makes is critical to the entire effort.

8. **Make sound and timely decisions.** Learn to think on your feet, to evaluate a situation and decide on a course of action in a reasonable amount of time. If you realize you have made a bad decision, correct it as quickly as possible.

9. **Develop a sense of responsibility among your subordinates.** Delegate authority to give your subordinates the opportunity for professional development.

10. **Employ your command in accordance with its capabilities.** Set goals that are achievable and make sure you are realistic about the tasks at hand. At the same time, don't underestimate your staff either.

11. **Seek responsibility and take responsibility for your actions.** If you wish to lead, you must be willing to assume responsibility for your actions as well as those of the people who report to you. If your subordinates fail, determine whether the fault lies with you.

That set of lessons is a mini-MBA in management. Making it work demands that you are brutally honest with yourself about your abilities and strengths as well as your weaknesses.

To help you evaluate yourself, here's the list of the 14 basic leadership traits identified by the Marines to help leaders earn the respect, confidence, and cooperation of other Marines: justice, judgment, dependability, initiative, decisiveness, tact, integrity, enthusiasm, bearing, unselfishness, courage, knowledge, loyalty, and endurance. Each of these traits is so important that the Marine Corps has developed an acronym to help remember them all: J. J. DID TIE BUCKLE (taken from the first letter of each trait).

Consider these lessons one more reason to be grateful for our brave men and women in uniform. Not only are they protecting our right to do business, but they are setting a fine example of how to get the job done.

MACKAY'S MORAL

Good commanders look after their troops, and good troops look after their commanders.

GOOD LEADERS BRING OUT THE BEST IN EMPLOYEES

One of the greatest privileges we have in America is selecting our own leaders. While we have widely varied opinions of who should win, the fundamental characteristics of good leadership remain constant.

A sociology professor from one of the country's major universities spent his life studying leadership by tracing the careers of 5,000 former students. When he was asked how you spot a leader, he said, "I have come to the conclusion that the only way one can determine a leader is to look at the person and see if anybody is following."

Leadership is a difficult skill to measure. But it is certainly easy to determine when leadership is not present in an organization.

In four years of executive seminars conducted by Santa Clara University and the Tom Peters Group/Learning Systems, more than 5,200 senior managers were asked to describe the characteristics they most admire in a leader. Here are the top 10 characteristics, as reported in *Management Review* magazine: honest, competent, forward-looking, inspiring, intelligent, fair-minded, broad-minded, courageous, straightforward, and imaginative.

Three of these characteristics are particularly significant in my opinion: forward-looking, inspiring, and courageous. All the others are necessary ingredients not only for an effective leader but also for every employee.

Chinese philosopher Lao Tzu said, "Fail to honor people, they fail to honor you. But of a good leader, who talks little, when his work is done, his aim fulfilled, they will all say, 'We did this ourselves.'" He made that observation over 2,000 years ago. Some things never change.

Good leaders really listen to the people who work for them. Good leaders pay attention to what people are telling them and take it very seriously. Good leaders use their power to implement ideas that workers bring forth, and then are quick to give credit to the person who had the idea. Then comes the action that really sets good leaders apart. They are willing to accept the blame and criticism when mistakes are made. They don't abandon their employees.

Good leaders really listen to the people who work for them. Good leaders pay attention to what people are telling them and take it very seriously.

The late Warren Bennis spent much of his life researching leadership and wrote several books on the subject of what makes leaders. Warren was a Distinguished Professor of Business Administration and the founding chairman of The Leadership Institute at the University of Southern California, which I had the honor of serving on the board. In 2007, *Businessweek* magazine called him one of the 10 business school professors who have had the greatest influence on business thinking.

Bennis traveled around the country spending time with 90 of the most effective and successful leaders in the nation—60 from corporations and 30 from the public sector. His goal was to find these leaders' common traits. At first, he had trouble pinpointing any common traits, for the leaders were more diverse than he had expected.

But he later wrote: "I was finally able to come to conclusions, of which perhaps the most important is the distinction between leaders and managers. Leaders are people who do the right thing; managers are people who do things right.

"Both roles are crucial, but they differ profoundly. I often observe people in top positions doing the wrong thing well," he wrote in his book *Why Leaders Can't Lead.*

I tend to think of the differences between leaders and managers as the difference between those who master the context within which they operate and those who surrender to it. There are other differences, as well, and they are enormous and crucial. Bennis details them in his book, *On Becoming a Leader*, and they include:

- The manager administers; the leader innovates.
- The manager is a copy; the leader is an original.
- The manager maintains; the leader develops.
- The manager focuses on systems and structure; the leader focuses on people.
- The manager relies on control; the leader inspires trust.
- The manager has a short-range view; the leader has a long-range perspective.
- The manager asks how and when; the leader asks what and why.
- The manager has his eye always on the bottom line; the leader has his eye on the horizon.

- The manager imitates; the leader originates.
- The manager accepts the status quo; the leader challenges it.
- The manager is the classic good soldier; the leader is his own person.

MACKAY'S MORAL

Good leaders develop more than good employees, they develop more good leaders.

REAL LEADERSHIP OFTEN DEFIES THE RULES

Leading an organization, whether public, private or non-profit, requires making tough decisions. It's just part of the job, whether it's in the job description or not, because as they say, it's lonely at the top.

Business school classes in leadership offer sound advice based on solid research and practical experience. In theory, it all works beautifully. You make the rules, you set the example, you toe the mark. Everyone follows your lead. Leadership training is important, even if it doesn't prepare you for every scenario.

But in practice, results aren't always so predictable. Sure, personality matters. Some people are better leaders than others. And unexpected situations arise that defy all logic. Trust me, I've been in business long enough to say I've seen it all—until I see the next crazy event.

To become the best leader you can be, you must take advantage of every opportunity to learn and improve. Learning from others' mistakes and experiences can save you plenty of misery and embarrassment.

But even more important, in my view, is setting standards for what you will and will not do, and what you will and will not tolerate. Take the time to determine what values are important to you and your organization. Make sure everyone you lead understands what is expected. Then practice what you preach.

One of my favorite examples of well-defined leadership is attributed to Kent Keith, which he titled his "Paradoxical Commandments of Leadership." I've added my thoughts to these "ten commandments," and hope they help you prepare your value statement.

1. **People are illogical, unreasonable, and self-centered. Love them anyway.** I've learned that coworkers and customers do not always respond as I would hope. But if I want to keep them as colleagues and customers, I need to cut them some slack.

2. **If you do good, people will accuse you of selfish ulterior motives. Do good anyway.** If you are doing well, then you should be doing good. The good you do will outweigh the criticism you endure. In truth, it would be more selfish to abandon your good works in order to avoid conflict.

3. **If you are successful, you win false friends and true enemies. Succeed anyway.** There will always be those who will want to

jump on your bandwagon or be jealous of your good fortune. That shouldn't prevent you from doing the best you can do.

4. **The good you do today will be forgotten tomorrow. Do good anyway.** Do good because it's the right thing to do, not because you are looking for lifetime recognition. Remember, virtue is its own reward.

5. **Honesty and frankness make you vulnerable. Be honest and frank anyway.** I maintain that lying and cheating make you more vulnerable. Being honest and frank translates into trust, which is the most important five-letter word in business.

6. **The biggest men with the biggest ideas can be shot down by the smallest men with the smallest minds. Think big anyway.** Small people with small minds rarely accomplish big things, and they are not leaders. Take some risks, and trust your judgment.

7. **People favor underdogs, but follow only top dogs. Fight for a few underdogs anyway.** Top dogs were underdogs once, too. Great leaders mentor their replacements because they know they won't be the top dogs forever. They also have a knack for recognizing talent.

8. **What you spend years building may be destroyed overnight. Build anyway.** You can't predict the future, but you can be prepared to face problems with careful planning.

9. **People really need help but may attack you if you do help them. Help people anyway.** A helping hand might get slapped away. But if you stand by and do nothing when you have the capacity to be helpful, shame on you. That's not leadership, that's cowardice.

10. **Give the world the best you have and you'll get kicked in the teeth. Give the world the best you have anyway.** Put a smile on your face and give your detractors a big toothy target. You never have to apologize for doing your best. You should apologize if you do less than your best.

A well-defined purpose is central to effective leadership. It doesn't just happen. You have to know why you are doing what you are doing. Otherwise, how will you know where you are going?

MACKAY'S MORAL

When you lead with a purpose, people have a reason to follow you.

13

NEGOTIATION

Successful negotiations start with stellar preparation

One of the many glitches in the human makeup is the difference in our abilities when it comes to performing for others as compared to how we perform for ourselves. It always baffles me to read about the psychiatrist who has helped so many of his patients rebuild their lives but whose own personal life is in turmoil. How about the financial adviser who never picked a stock right for himself but managed to build a tidy pile for his clients?

Not many of us are able to do things for ourselves the same way we do them for others. That translates into whether we're better at our jobs or better at our personal affairs. Even people who make their livings negotiating can really mess up in the use of their professional skills in their own personal interests. Not every real estate expert who spends her career negotiating commercial retail leases is an expert when it comes to negotiating her own compensation. The insurance company adjuster who knocks heads all day long negotiating settlements with personal injury lawyers still may be a patsy in settling his own salary differences with his employer.

Unfortunately, there's no way we can escape having to represent our own interests, whether we're good at it or not. So we might as well try to learn how to be good at it. Whether or not you've ever negotiated anything else in your life, when it comes to getting a job, asking for a promotion or a raise, or even hanging onto the job you have, at some time your ability to negotiate on your own is going to be tested.

Whatever you're negotiating for, including a job, you'll do best if you forget the flowery speeches and concentrate on knowing the other side's strengths and weaknesses. In other words, do your homework!

Whatever you're negotiating for, including a job, you'll do best if you forget the flowery speeches and concentrate on knowing the other side's strengths and weaknesses. In other words, do your homework!

- **You need superior information.** That's why car dealers win in negotiations. They know exactly how much they paid for the car they're trying to sell, and also how much your trade-in is worth. Few ordinary car buyers take the time to learn those two critical numbers. And even when they think they do, the dealer throws in variables like options and financing charges that help disguise the dealership's true profit margin. The result is that only the most sophisticated customers know how to cut a deal without cutting their own throats. The true pro has customers believing they have stolen the car.

- **Don't make decisions for other people.** When you let them decide, you *make* them decide.

- **Stay calm.** If you're tight in the batter's box, you can't hit. The high average hitters always keep a quiet bat until it's time to swing. Pounding the table only works in the movies.

- **Anticipate questions.** Know the answer to every question you might be asked before you sit down at the table and you won't have to appear as if you are negotiating.

- **Be a spin-doctor.** Finesse questions. For example, if you are asked, "What do you need for a salary?" reply with, "Do you have a salary range established for the position?"

- **Silence is golden.** Do as little negotiating as possible. Make your employer make the first offer ... it could be a pleasant surprise. On the other hand, if you make the first offer and suggest a number lower than the employer was about to offer you, you're giving them a pleasant surprise.

- **Evaluate the employer.** What do you know about their needs? Is this a tough position to fill? Do they have the reputation for being high payers or low payers? Are they noted for high or low turnover? Do they tend to provide a fast track or a slow track for their employees?

- **Evaluate yourself.** What bargaining advantage do you hold? Top grades? Great potential? Superior past performance? First-rate credentials and experience? Proven skills? Proven loyalty? Will it matter to the company if they don't hire you and hire someone else instead? Is your potential to perform of such value to them that they wouldn't want it to go to the competitor? Can you prove it?

MACKAY'S MORAL

The smartest thing you can do in a negotiation, often, is keep your mouth shut.

NEGOTIATING 101: 50 YEARS OF EXPERIENCE

If you ask me what one skill has made the biggest difference in my career, I would answer you, hands down, negotiating. It applies to selling, purchasing, hiring, firing, expanding, downsizing, and every other phase of business you can name. It's part of the game that I am particularly fond of, and it's not just to see how much I can get the other person to give. I like to learn from the varied strategies that other people use.

Here are some of the lessons I have learned over a lifetime:

1. You can't negotiate anything unless you absolutely know the market. Only then you will be able to recognize a good deal when you see it.

2. If you can't say yes, it's no. Don't sugarcoat it. Don't talk yourself into yes just to seem like a nice guy. No one ever went broke because he or she said "NO" too often.

3. The single biggest tool in any negotiation is the willingness to get up and walk away from the table without a deal.

4. It's not how much it's worth! It's how much people *think it's worth*.

5. Many people listen … very few actually hear. You can't learn anything if you are doing all the talking.

6. In any negotiation, the given reason is seldom the real reason. Find out the real reason and your probability of success goes up dramatically.

7. No one ever choked to death swallowing his or her own pride.

8. In the long run, instincts are no match for information.

9. There's no more certain recipe for disaster than a decision based on emotion. Or another way of saying this is: Make decisions with your heart and you'll end up with heart disease.

10. A dream is always a bargain no matter what you pay for it. If it's something you've always wanted, and this is your big chance to get it, go for it and make it work.

11. The most important term in any contract isn't "in" the contract. It's dealing with people who are honest. As the old adage goes: You lie down with dogs … and you get up with fleas.

12. There is no such thing as a "final offer."

13. Try to let the other person speak first.

14. Never give an ultimatum unless you mean it.

15. You cannot get dealt a straight flush unless you are in the game.

16. Smile and say no, no, no, no, no … until your tongue bleeds.

17. Agreements prevent disagreements. You have to fight your guts out for an agreement and then you won't have a disagreement.

18. If you *can afford* to buy your way out of a problem, you don't have a problem.

19. More deals result from whom you know than what you know. And it's not just whom you know but how you get to know them.

20. The walls have ears. Don't discuss any business where others can overhear it. Almost as many deals have gone down in elevators as elevators have gone down.

21. People don't plan to fail, they fail to plan. Top negotiators debrief themselves. They keep a book on themselves and their opponents. You never know when that information may be gold.

22. Your day usually goes the way the corners of your mouth turn. Your attitude determines your altitude.

23. People go around all their lives saying: What should I buy? What should I sell? Wrong question: *When* should I buy? *When* should I sell? Timing is everything.

MACKAY'S MORAL

When a person with money meets a person with experience, the person with the experience ends up with the money and the person with the money ends up with the experience.

Everything's negotiable— and here's how to do it

During the Civil War, President Abraham Lincoln was urged by a friend to give up Forts Sumter and Pickens and all government property in the Southern states. In reply, Lincoln said, "Do you remember the fable of the lion and the woodsman's daughter? Aesop writes that a lion was very much in love with a woodsman's daughter. The fair maid referred him to her father. And the lion went to the father and asked for her hand.

"The father replied: 'Your teeth are too long.'"

The lion went to a dentist and had them extracted. Returning, he asked again for his bride.

"'No,' said the woodsman. 'Your claws are too long.'"

Going to the doctor, he had the claws removed. Then he returned to claim his bride, and the woodsman, seeing that he was unarmed, beat out his brains.

"'May it not be so with me,'" concluded Lincoln, "'if I give up all that is asked?'"

I learned a long time ago that you can't give anything away in negotiations without receiving something in return. I also know that the most important term in any contract isn't the contract. It's dealing with people who are honest.

Before you start any negotiation, look beyond the title and make sure that the person you're dealing with is in a position of authority to sign off on the agreement.

Before you start any negotiation, look beyond the title and make sure that the person you're dealing with is in a position of authority to sign off on the agreement.

No matter what industry you're in, or how far you go in your career, the ability to effectively negotiate can make the difference between success and mediocrity. It doesn't matter whether it's a multimillion-dollar contract, a job offer, or a house sale. The rules of good negotiating are the same.

- **Know what you want.** Don't go to the table without a clear, realistic idea of what you want to achieve. It will help you negotiate with confidence.

- **Ask for what you want.** Don't be afraid to make the first offer. You'll set the tone for the discussion, and studies suggest that the negotiator who goes first usually comes closer to getting what he or she wants. While I often counsel people to let the other person go first, someone has to start the process. I have found that either way, I need to be clear about my expectations or I will be disappointed.

- **Understand what your adversary wants.** A successful negotiation should satisfy both sides. Instead of trying to crush your competition, find out what he or she hopes to get, and try to work together toward a solution that works for you both.

- **Don't concede unilaterally.** Usually one side or the other has to give something up. If you offer something, be sure to get a comparable concession from the other person. Giving away something for nothing will be taken as a weakness to be exploited. The playing field needs to be level. You don't have to accept being bullied.

- **Don't rush.** Time can be your friend if you're willing to wait for the right deal. If the other side senses a deadline, he or she may be motivated to hold out until the last minute, or try to force you into accepting unreasonable terms. Be patient and let the time pressure work against the other side.

- **Be ready to walk away.** This can take a certain amount of courage, but it's necessary to avoid being backed into an agreement you don't want. If possible, keep an ally in reserve—someone with the power to approve or reject the deal. This can give you an out if you need to turn down a deal, or motivate the other side to make the best offer possible.

- **Listen.** Sometimes what the other side says is not the same as what they want. They say the price is too high, but their most important demand is quality, which almost always costs a little (or a lot) more. Pay attention for cues that will help you direct your response to a better outcome for all.

Financier J.P. Morgan once wanted to buy a large Minnesota ore mine from John D. Rockefeller. So Rockefeller sent his son, John D. Jr. to talk to Morgan.

Morgan asked, "Well, what's your price?"

He was unprepared for the response. Junior said, "Mr. Morgan, I think there must be some mistake. I did not come here to sell; I understood you wanted to buy."

MACKAY'S MORAL

There is no such thing as a final offer.

14

NETWORKING

DIG YOUR WELL
BEFORE YOU'RE THIRSTY

If I had to name the single characteristic shared by all the truly successful people I've met over a lifetime, I'd say it is the ability to create and nurture a network of contacts.

Although I never met David Rockefeller, he certainly would have fit in this category. When he passed away in March 2017 at the age of 101, *Bloomberg News* revealed that he had an "electronic Rolodex" of 150,000 people. The *Wall Street Journal* recently reported it was 200,000. He was a master networker during his 24 years as the head of Chase Manhattan Bank and 60 years of being involved with the Council on Foreign Relations.

In my corporate speeches, I often ask the question: What is one of the most important words in the English language? I add that if all of us understood this word just a little bit better, we'd be way more successful than we already are. That word is "Rolodex," which of course is now referred to as a contact management system or a customer relationship management (CRM) system. Call it what you will. It all boils down to how you connect with the people you know.

My father, Jack Mackay, who for 35 years headed the Associated Press in St. Paul, Minnesota, shared his secret with me when I was 18. He said, "Harvey, every single person you meet the rest of your life should go in your Rolodex file. Write a little bit about that person on the bottom or the back of the card. And now, here's the key—find a creative way to keep in touch."

That's what I've been doing ever since. I now have nearly 20,000 names in my CRM system, a far cry from David Rockefeller's 150,000-person electronic Rolodex, but still crucial to my career.

My Rolodex was instrumental in launching my publishing career. Let me explain. In 1988, there were roughly two million "wannabes," people who wrote manuscripts. Approximately 200,000 different titles were published. Of those only a small percentage were business books. If you were a first-time, unknown author like me and you wrote a business book, you wanted to get it published. All the major publishers would print 10,000 hardcover books. That's it. Tom Peters, *In Search of Excellence*, 10,000 copies; Ken Blanchard, *The One-Minute Manager*, 7,500 books.

This is why it was so tough to get started. There were 5,000 bookstores back in the 1980s and 1990s, which meant an average of only two books per store if they printed 10,000 copies.

I had written a book titled *Swim with the Sharks Without Being Eaten Alive*. I wanted the publisher to print a lot of books so they would promote it and not run out of books. I scheduled a summit meeting with William Morrow and Company—the CEO, president, and VP of National Sales. About 45 minutes into the meeting I asked for the order. I said, "I would like you to seriously consider printing 100,000 hardcover copies of *Swim with the Sharks*. We were on the 37th floor, and they basically told me to jump. The VP of National Sales closed his notebook and said, "Thank you very much, Mr. Mackay. Obviously, we're not going to get together." Then he basically screamed, "Who are you, coming in here asking for 100,000 copies? We only print 10,000 copies for any first-time unknown author."

I'd brought in two humongous briefcases and took them out. Inside were two huge Rolodex files, 6,500 names at the time. I started to go through them: "Pillsbury, 18,000 employees. We do business with them. Maybe they'll read the book and pass it along. General Mills, 23,000 employees; Cargill; 3M; here's American Express." I went to the second Rolodex file. "We do business in six countries, France, Germany, Spain … maybe it'll be an international bestseller."

Three weeks and three meetings later, they published 100,000 hardcover copies of *Swim with the Sharks*. And it became a *New York Times* #1 bestseller.

Did I know when I was 18 where my contacts were going to come from? Do any of you know where your contacts will come from 5, 10, or 15 years from now?

Our lives basically change in two ways—the people we meet and the books we read. Trust me; the people you meet every day are extremely important in building your network.

Our lives basically change in two ways—the people we meet and the books we read. Trust me; the people you meet every day are extremely important in building your network.

In my entire career I have never once heard a successful person say he or she regretted putting time and energy into keeping a CRM system, even if it was an old-fashioned Rolodex file.

MACKAY'S MORAL

When you work on your network, your network works for you.

HOW DOES YOUR NETWORKING REPORT CARD STACK UP?

For years I've had a plaque on the wall of my office that reads: "Pray for a good harvest ... but keep on hoeing!" I looked at that so many times over the years that it's permanently burned into my memory.

Some people still use the old physical Rolodex file, but most people today have all their contact information in their CRM system. From force of habit, I still refer to my CRM system as my Rolodex file.

If you want your CRM system to produce a fruitful harvest, you have to be persistent, and you have to keep on hoeing. Remember:

- **It's a chronicle of your life.** As the world changes, one thing will remain constant—the relationships you develop over a lifetime.
- **Guard it with your life.** For me, my CRM system is still one of my most prized possessions.
- **Consider it an investment.** We all start out in life with the same amount of time each day. It's what we do with it that counts.
- **Remembering doesn't work.** The person who counts on his or her memory has a fool for a filing system. Studies have shown we forget 50 percent of what we hear in four hours.
- **Make it work for you, not against you.** With your CRM system, two things count most: It's fun and it works.
- **You have to give a piece of your mind to get peace of mind.** You can utilize the insight and vision of your whole network to help you "see around corners."
- **Make connections the old-fashioned way.** You don't have to know everything. Seek out people who know the things you don't.
- **You can improve on human nature.** With practice, using your CRM system becomes more than a discipline; it's a way of life.

How good are your network-building skills? I developed the following self-test several years ago. See how you stack up. Answer these questions and rate yourself on a 1–5 scale, 1 being not true and 5 being very true:

1. I have a large network of people I can call upon when I need help, information, or a resource. (Score ___)

2. When I meet someone new, I record and file information about that person within 24 hours, and I reach out to connect with him or her on social media. (Score ___)

3. I add someone new to my CRM system at least every week. (Score ___)

4. I follow up with new contacts right away—sending an email, making a phone call, forwarding a link, or writing a note. (Score ___)

5. I keep track of special things that matter to my contacts like their family, hobbies, and achievements. (Score ___)

6. I can easily find out when I was last in contact with someone. (Score ___)

7. When I email or mail something out—a resume, sales letter, change of address—I can count on having correct name spellings, titles, and addresses for everyone in my network. (Score ___)

8. I know about and acknowledge special dates like birthdays, anniversaries, and graduations. (Score ___)

9. When I want to give a business gift, I can count on my CRM system to provide me with an excellent idea of what the person might appreciate. (Score ___)

10. I make it easy for others to add me to their networks by providing my email and social media information, handing out my business card, notifying them of address changes, and informing them about my career progress. (Score ___)

11. When friends ask me for the name of a good resource, I have no trouble providing one. (Score ___)

12. When the moment comes, I can really "wow" a customer, prospect, or potential employer with special information or an idea that shows I care. (Score ___)

Total the points above and score yourself:

0–24   You're in rough shape. It's time to make a change.

25–36   You're doing some things right. Now let's get to work.

37–44   You're off to a great start. Build on what you've done so far.

45–55 You've got superstar potential. All you need is the polish.

56–60 You're already there. Keep up the great effort!

MACKAY'S MORAL

The more you exercise your networking muscles, the stronger they get—and the easier networking becomes.

Get to know the gatekeeper

Whether you're looking to make a sale, land a job, or receive a charitable contribution, getting through the fence to the top dog is a lot easier if you know the gatekeeper.

Gatekeepers can include security personnel at the entrance, receptionists, special assistants, executive assistants, or whoever might screen you from reaching the decision-maker.

When you're trying to gain access to a decision-maker, always be courteous to these people because they hold the key to your success. These individuals may be the allies you need to get the desired outcome from Mr./Ms. Big. Correct technique and good manners can transform interactions with corporate gatekeepers from frustrating to fruitful.

Gatekeepers are real people like you and me. Unfortunately, it's all too common to get off to a poor start with gatekeepers because they often aren't treated respectfully. Too many people concentrate on how to get past the gatekeeper to the decision-maker. The gatekeeper, however, has radar that goes up quickly, especially when salespeople are involved. Remember, you're not entitled to see someone or be seen.

Gatekeepers are not inherently uncooperative. They screen calls and inquiries to limit unnecessary interruptions and distractions for the boss. Your first contact needs you to somehow assure the person that you deserve an appointment or voicemail or even an email address, if you haven't found that on the company website.

Your message better be good or you'll be treated like everyone else. You won't get through. You have about 10 seconds to build some rapport and spark his or her interest. Take time to prepare your message that will set you apart. Do your homework. Find out about the company and the players involved. Look for any connection or commonality.

Don't ever settle for voicemail because your phone calls will seldom be returned. The same is true for emails. Always talk with a human being.

Whether I'm selling envelopes or promoting a charitable cause, I never place a call to a prospect without first finding out the name of his or her assistant and how to correctly pronounce it. A mispronounced name can kill the conversation before it starts. It's easy enough to discover. You simply ask the receptionist. Then when my call goes through, the stage is set for a nice one-on-one, because I'm immediately able to address the gatekeeper by name.

I've had even better results by not even trying to talk directly with Mr./ Ms. head honcho. I tell the assistant, "I would like to work directly with you regarding" an appointment, charitable pledge, study, interview, or whatever it happens to be.

When I'm talking with the assistant, I'm talking with the person I "want" to talk to. If the Big Kahuna has enough faith in that person to appoint him or her to that position, that's good enough for me. By taking this approach, all I'm asking is that the assistant use his or her judgment to decide whether I'm making a reasonable request. If I am, I'm assuming that the person is going to give me the best effort to see to it that what I'm asking for gets done.

> *When I'm talking with the assistant, I'm talking with the person I "want" to talk to. If the Big Kahuna has enough faith in that person to appoint him or her to that position, that's good enough for me.*

Over the years, I have had a lot better success working with people in this fashion than trying to run over or around them. Having gatekeepers in your network and having a relationship with them matters. I look at it like a checking account. You can't withdraw more than you put in. You have to give in order to receive.

It's much easier to talk with people the second time you meet them. You don't have that much more to talk about than you did in your previous encounter, yet somehow everything is just more at ease. When gatekeepers get to know you, they will trust you and want to help you. Friends do anything for friends. It's human nature.

Treat the gatekeepers with dignity. Respect their power. And by all means, acknowledge their help. Not with lavish gifts. That's gauche. Just little niceties. A creative handwritten note. A humorous card or e-card. A plant or flowers. A book. A separate visit where you stop by to see them, and not the boss.

Little things don't mean a lot. They mean *everything*.

MACKAY'S MORAL

A lot more people would be in heaven if they knew St. Peter, the most well-known gatekeeper.

MAKE FRIENDSHIPS WORK AT WORK

I've always felt that the real title to every book I've written is *Prepare to Win*. But I have a fondness for catchier titles, so for my networking book, I went with *Dig Your Well Before You're Thirsty*. Bottom line: Networking is all about preparing to win.

In my networking book, I wrote a chapter about people who should be in your network: doctors, travel agents, bankers, insurance agents, auto mechanics, ticket brokers, recruiters, community and religious leaders, real estate brokers, and on and on.

These are all great and musts to have—especially for me—but one of the areas I later realized that I neglected to cover is connections to cultivate inside the workplace, which are crucial to succeeding in anyone's career. After all, there's a reason we call them *connections*. You have to connect.

That's exactly what I did when I started my career many moons ago at Quality Park Envelope Company. My gut instinct told me that if I could figure out who I could befriend and impress with my business qualities, I would be able to move up in the organization. Sure enough, within a couple months, I moved from the plant to the sales department.

All it took was for me to do the best I could do, make sure the assistant plant manager knew it, and latch on to a guardian angel—someone who was equally eager to escape the plant and who took me with him when he wrangled his way into sales.

I was beginning to learn the finer points of internal networking. Networking is not a numbers game. The idea is not to see how many people you can meet; the idea is to compile a list of people you can count on.

I was beginning to learn the finer points of internal networking. Networking is not a numbers game. The idea is not to see how many people you can meet; the idea is to compile a list of people you can count on.

This was my first exposure to what I later learned was called the *sausage theory*. When one link moves, the other links follow. I've seen this play out many times over the years. When people get a different job in an organization or jump to a key job at another company, they often bring a lot of their coworkers with them.

Here are some of the coworkers to get to know who can help you move up:

- **A best friend (or two or three).** Find a few people you can count on for support and assistance. You'll be more productive knowing you've got them to talk to about work. Don't make it a one-sided relationship, of course—be available to listen and help out your friends as necessary.

- **A Human Resources rep.** Get to know at least one person in your HR department so you have someone to go to with questions and concerns. You'll be more comfortable discussing issues if you don't walk in only when you have a problem.

- **A mentor.** Seek out a senior worker in your organization to go to for career advice. Let the person know you respect his or her reputation and would value any tips he or she can share. With luck, you'll gain a sponsor who can help you move upward in your organization. I owe much of my success to my mentors.

- **A rival or challenger.** You're often in competition for top assignments. Instead of treating it like a battle, get to know the people with the same goals and ambitions you have. You may find common ground that will help you both succeed. Competition makes you better.

- **Gatekeepers.** The best way to open doors is to know gatekeepers. Get to know the people who have access to executives and senior managers, and make sure they know you. This can be very important for getting through to people who can approve your ideas and help you get ahead.

Bottom line, your career can be linked with the careers of others. As your friends and mentors move up, so can you, especially if you have been a key contributor to their promotion or success.

It doesn't matter how far down the food chain you are when you start out; networking can pay off big time. It isn't where you start. It's where you finish that counts.

Just remember, there are no dead-end jobs. If you build a network, you will have a bridge to wherever you want to go.

MACKAY'S MORAL

Working your way up is much easier if you're networking your way up.

15

PEOPLE SKILLS

Ten Commandments for the Office

It's just business as usual, day in and day out. The fast lane gets faster. Competition for business and jobs gets meaner. The world gets smaller every day. You've dealt with a hundred coworkers, customers, vendors, and the irritating kid who works at the lunch counter. It's time to go home and unwind.

The traffic jam gives you an opportunity to replay some of the day's encounters. Regrettably, you wish you would have handled a few things quite differently. How can you make tomorrow better?

My mother always told me, "You don't have to like everybody, but you do need to learn to get along."

Over the years, I've developed a list, a "Ten Commandments for the Office," which makes my commute home a little less guilt-ridden. Better yet, it's improved my commute *to* the office. If I follow my own advice, I won't have to spend my time apologizing for what I should have done in the first place. Try it out.

1. **Be respectful.** This includes respect for other people's property, ideas, and time. Frankly, this commandment should about cover everything. If you are respectful of others, you can usually work out most issues—even if it's agreeing to disagree. An added bonus is that when you treat others with respect, they are more inclined to return the favor.

2. **Follow through.** If you promise to do something, do it. No ifs, buts, or maybes. No excuses, no whining. You are only as good as your word. There will always be a place in this world for the person who says, "I'll take care of it." And then does it.

3. **Think before you speak.** Don't say whatever is on your mind, unless you want your mindless thoughts to come back to haunt you. Those ghosts can rise up years later, just when that promotion looks so promising. And while we're on the topic, remember that *how* you say something is as important as *what* you say.

4. **Help out.** So what if it's not in your job description. If you have an opportunity to be useful, jump at it. Even if the rewards are not in the form of a paycheck, your coworkers will remember who helped them when they needed it. Taking on a little extra work—or a lot— shows that you are a team player, an employee worth watching.

5. **Learn something new every day.** It could be a new skill. Maybe the latest developments in your industry. Or just the name of a person you see daily at the copy machine. You have millions of brain cells just waiting to work for you!

6. **Pay attention.** If you go directly to your cubicle and barricade yourself all day, you're missing important developments in your workplace. Not the gossipy events, of course, but the really good stuff—new procedures, new ideas, and so on. This commandment also covers those occasions when the value of your input depends on your familiarity with the situation at hand. In short, always keep your antennae up!

7. **Ignore pettiness.** Rise above it, or you will be dragged down with it. There will always be someone who will make a mountain out of a molehill. It better not be you.

8. **Be patient.** Not to be confused with tolerating incompetence, this commandment covers a multitude of situations. Someone misunderstood you. A job is taking longer than you planned. You are missing every traffic light. What will you gain by losing your cool? I'm not a patient guy by nature, so I've really had to work at this one. If I can do it, you can too!

9. **A good attitude is up to you.** It takes a lot for the world to come to an end, so don't act like it's happening every day. Be encouraging, be cheerful. Refuse to be brought down by minor—or major—setbacks. Bad attitudes are contagious. The good news is that positive attitudes are catching, too.

10. **Do your best.** Like commandment #1, this should also cover just about everything. No one can ask you to do more.

It's important to decide early on how you will conduct yourself. Then, when a crisis erupts or challenge arises, you won't have to think twice about the right thing to do. I've always said that perfect practice makes perfect. These rules are no exception. And just for the record, these commandments work outside the office too.

MACKAY'S MORAL

Some rules are made not to be broken.

BAD MANNERS
ARE BAD FOR BUSINESS

If your mother was anything like my mother, good manners was her middle name. Please and thank you were just the beginning, followed by respect, tact, patience, consideration, and all the other forms of etiquette so important in a civilized world.

Today, I consider myself incredibly fortunate that she and my dad took such pains to impart such values to my sister and me.

Good manners are never out of style or out of date, although lately, I'm seeing less and less of them. My theory is that as business in general becomes more impersonal, people become less concerned with the long-term ramifications of their actions.

In other words, you can now do business by phone, Internet, email, or fax and be essentially anonymous. You've probably been put on hold, paced through a phone menu, pressed every button, transferred to several incorrect departments, and nobody but the machine knows or even cares. There's little pressure to be polite, just businesslike and efficient. Sadly, it soon becomes the rule rather than the exception. Sooner or later, you have no other choice than to put up with it.

As customers do business farther away from home, the likelihood that your next door neighbor is also your banker or grocer or school principal lessens. We lose some of the sense of community that helps us behave civilly even when we are disappointed.

Customer loyalty is at an all-time low. Consumers are shopping wherever and whenever it's convenient, in part because the same products are available at many outlets, but also because the stores aren't enticing them to come back. They can zip over to the net any time. Could it be we're not getting the kind of treatment we want?

My favorite example is the telemarketer who calls at a time most likely to interrupt your dinner, hawking a product that precious few people are likely to buy over the phone. How many of you have actually bought insurance/phone service/mortgages/credit cards or similar offerings from an unknown faceless solicitor who doesn't have the decency to ask if you're busy? Is this what business has become?

Well, business may have changed, but people haven't. They still have feelings, and they'd like a little consideration. The best part is that it's sooooo easy to do. (And free!)

I'd like to start a campaign to return good manners to business. I'd like the folks on the other side of the cash register or order book to see me as more than just another account. I don't necessarily want to get personal— I just want to be a person. I'd like to leave the transaction feeling like a valued customer who is worth their best behavior.

Exhibiting good manners does not make a person appear to be weak or wimpy. Rather, it demonstrates that person's maturity and ability to appropriately respond to business situations. Who would you rather have working for you—the sales rep whom customers look forward to dealing with or the bulldozer who'll stop at nothing to get the order?

Bad manners are bad business.

Wouldn't it be great if all your meetings and appointments started on time because nobody was late? Punctuality is just good manners.

The voice on the phone identifies herself before you have to ask? Wow! What a concept!

Somebody actually reloaded the copier paper when he used up the supply? This is starting to sound too good to be true.

A little consideration goes a long way. And it's really all so basic. Everyone could benefit from reading Emily Post's classic best-seller, *Etiquette in Society, in Business, in Politics, and at Home.* Some aspects of our society may have changed in the century since she penned her book, but the core principles of proper etiquette and professional behavior are timeless.

As Eleanor Roosevelt said, "What we need in the world is manners.... I think that if, instead of preaching brotherly love, we preached good manners, we might get a little further. It sounds less righteous and more practical."

More simply put, good manners are like a roadmap for society. They help us navigate through tough situations. We don't have to backtrack because we haven't taken wrong turns. We will reach our destination without the road rage.

MACKAY'S MORAL

Good manners are free, but they are also priceless.

MAINTAIN A CIVIL TONGUE

Rudeness rules the headlines these days—seems we can't escape it no matter where we go. Crudeness is the norm rather than the exception. Can we even call ourselves a civilized society anymore?

From the hallowed halls of Congress to the usually civilized tennis world to television talk shows to music awards: what are these people thinking? That no one will notice? That they are exempt from the rules? That their behavior won't have a profound effect on their futures?

I would refer all these offenders to a few hours of Disney movies, where the Golden Rule prevails without fail and conversation is G-rated and uplifting. Bambi's little friend Thumper could teach them all a lesson: "If you can't say somethin' nice, don't say nothin' at all."

This is not just kid stuff. Knowing that few of us would take Thumper's advice literally, I'll rephrase: If you can't say something nicely, don't say anything at all.

There is always a dignified way to get your point across, and you won't end up having to apologize or explain your actions. Believe it or not, people actually listen to reasoned arguments. They don't give much credence to hotheads.

We all know how damaging and hurtful an outburst can be in our personal lives, and often we assume our family and friends will forgive our bad behavior and overlook our lapses.

But in a business setting, where those we deal with don't necessarily have to deal with us again, rudeness or disrespectful behavior is never a good option. A lapse in judgment can easily translate to a collapse in business. Word travels fast—and your reputation is at stake. Your future is at stake.

Walk away, count to 10, bite your tongue, whatever works for you. Practice self-control at every opportunity. You may not have much control over a situation, but you can control how you respond to it.

A Carnegie Foundation study once found that only 15 percent of a businessperson's success could be attributed to job knowledge and technical skills, which were considered to be an essential element but overall, a small contribution. A whopping 85 percent of one's success could be determined by the "ability to deal with people" and "attitude."

The lesson for anyone wanting to get ahead and still get a point across is that self-control and consideration are critical ingredients that supersede even a superior product or top knowledge. The "scorekeepers" in business are not so very different from the line judges and umpires in tennis: you will lose points if you lose control.

As my friend motivational guru Zig Ziglar said, "You are free to choose, but the choices you make today will determine what you will have, be, and do in the tomorrow of your life."

"No one characteristic will help one to advance, whether in business or society, as politeness," said B.C. Forbes, founder of *Forbes* magazine. "Competition is so keen today, there is so much standardized merchandise, there are so many places where one's wants can be satisfied, that the success or failure of a business can depend on the ability to please customers or clients. Courtesy—another name for politeness—costs nothing, but can gain much both for an individual and for an organization." It is interesting to note that Forbes made those comments more than 50 years ago. Clearly, some things never change.

As Mark Twain observed: "Indecency, vulgarity, obscenity—these are strictly confined to man; he invented them. Among the higher animals there is no trace of them. They hide nothing; they are not ashamed. Man, with his soiled mind, covers himself. He will not even enter a drawing room with his breast and back naked, so alive are he and his mates to indecent suggestion ... Man is the Animal That Blushes. He is the only one that does it—or has occasion to."

Dear readers, what do you say we try to reverse this trend?

It is perfectly acceptable—even occasionally necessary—to disagree with those around you. But you needn't be disagreeable. It's okay to make waves; it isn't necessary to drown the other person. But lose your cool, lose your temper, lose control, and you'll find you are the one who's all wet.

MACKAY'S MORAL

Giving someone a piece of your mind rarely gives you peace of mind.

2, 4, 6, 8—WHO DO YOU APPRECIATE?

A university professor began reflecting on the people who had a positive impact on his life. In particular he remembered a schoolteacher who had gone out of her way to instill in him a love of poetry. He hadn't seen or spoken to her in many years, but he located her address and sent her a letter of thanks. A short time later, he received this reply:

"My dear Willie, I cannot tell you how much your note meant to me. I am in my eighties, living alone in a small room, cooking my own meals, lonely, and, like the last leaf of autumn, lingering behind. You will be interested to know that I taught school for 50 years and yours is the first note of appreciation I ever received. It came on a blue-cold morning, and it cheered me as nothing has in many years."

The teacher's note brought the professor to tears—and then he began searching for others who'd shaped his life, just to say thanks.

If only more people held onto gratitude the way they hold a grudge!

None of us got to where we are alone. Whether the assistance we received was obvious or subtle, acknowledging someone's help is a big part of understanding the importance of saying thank you.

It's more than just good manners. Saying thank you—and meaning it—is never a bad idea. It appeals to a basic human need to be appreciated. It sets the stage for the next pleasant encounter. And it helps keep in perspective the importance of receiving and giving help.

It's more than just good manners. Saying thank you —and meaning it—is never a bad idea. It appeals to a basic human need to be appreciated.

Retailing giant Sam Walton wrote 10 rules for success, and the Walmart founder didn't mince words when it came to being thankful. The fifth of Walton's rules is "Appreciate everything your associates do for the business."

I wish I could convince every business owner and manager to adopt that attitude. If you have hired well and provided the necessary tools that allow your staff to perform their jobs, and they have achieved accordingly, the next logical step is acknowledgment of their efforts.

The cost of praising someone is nil—but a recent study has found that the payoff can be huge. Employees want to be seen as competent, hardworking members of the team. Good managers want satisfied, motivated, and productive staff members. What better motivator than thanking employees for their contributions to the company's success?

A *Personnel Today* survey of 350 human resources professionals found that the greatest factor in workplace productivity is a positive environment in which employees feel appreciated. According to the survey, two-thirds of the respondents said they felt a lot more productive when they received recognition for their work, while the remainder said they felt a little more productive.

Just *feeling* productive can be motivating in itself. When workers don't feel productive, frustration sets in, according to 84 percent of the survey respondents. Here's a startling result: 20 percent said they felt angry or depressed when they weren't able to work as hard as they could.

How to best praise effectively? Try these ideas:

Be sincere. Give praise only where it is due.

Give public praise. The goal is to encourage employees to keep up the good work, while simultaneously encouraging others to put out greater effort. Praising in public raises general morale. Doing this in a department-wide email or the company's newsletter helps, but doing it in meetings or at in-person events is even better.

Be specific in your praise. Identify exactly what the employee worked on and what he or she accomplished. Don't just say, "Well done, Maggie." If the employee feels the praise isn't genuine, it could have a negative effect.

Provide some lasting recognition. Consider a letter in the employee's file or a simple celebration for the department that overcame a tough challenge. Appreciation is not a one-shot event. It needs to be ongoing.

A smart manager will establish a culture of gratitude. Expand the appreciative attitude to suppliers, vendors, delivery people, and, of course, customers.

All links along the chain are essential to your success. It's so easy to ignore the person who delivers office supplies, the tech who unfroze your computer, or the customer who referred you to a great new account. Big mistake. They all deserve acknowledgment, especially if you want to preserve the relationship.

And while you're at it, don't forget your favorite teacher.

MACKAY'S MORAL

An attitude of gratitude should have wide latitude.

HARVEY'S SHORT COURSE IN CLASS

You have probably heard the term, "He (or she) is a class act." Of course, it's always a compliment. But exactly what does that mean?

Class is easy to recognize but much harder to define. Similarly, the absence of class is easy to detect—and a serious flaw for anyone who aspires to be successful.

First of all, class is not an "act." It's a deep-seated way of life for those who possess it. Having class involves good manners, politeness, pride without showboating, empathy, humility, and an abundance of self-control. The actions of class-act people speak louder than their words. You can see it in their body language and the way they carry themselves. Class always shows without being announced.

People can tell whether you have class by the way you interact with others. If you have class, you don't need much of anything else to be a winner. If you don't have it, no matter what you do, it won't make up the difference. Money, notoriety, or success by themselves won't give you class. Class comes from within, not from external sources.

As an explanation, I've created an acronym of what it means to be a class act:

C is for calm, courteous, and in control. People who have class carry themselves in a certain way. They stay calm under pressure and don't lose their tempers. They are respectful and use good manners. They don't use crude language or criticize or complain in public. They don't interrupt others.

L is for living by high standards. Class acts set goals in both their careers and personal lives. They are not afraid to step out of their comfort zones and push themselves beyond their limits to see how successful they can become.

A is for above it all. Class acts take the high road and refuse to stoop to the level of their adversaries. They don't have to apologize for their unfortunate words because they know better than to give in to the heat of the moment.

S is for self-respect, and respect for others as well. They don't gossip or say mean and petty things about others. They take every opportunity to make others feel good about themselves and appreciated.

S is for self-confidence without being arrogant. Class acts understand their abilities and are not afraid to use them. You can develop confidence, just like any muscle or character trait, if you are willing to work hard. Class acts also increase the confidence of others.

A is for accountability. Class acts take responsibility for their actions and results, whether it's a success or failure.

C is for compassion. Classy people understand that helping someone up will never pull you down. Compassion is a vital part of class acts. Compassion feels and whispers, "I'll help." Class acts really care.

T is for trust. Truthfulness and integrity are the basis for trust. Classy people are trustworthy and understand the importance of maintaining confidentiality. To me the most important five-letter word in business is T-R-U-S-T.

In his book *The Success Principles*, my friend Jack Canfield lists "Be a Class Act" as Principle #55. What I found most intriguing are some of the reasons he lists as why being a class act helps you succeed.

He writes: "People want to do business with you or become involved in your sphere of influence. They perceive you as successful and someone who can expand their possibilities. They trust you to act with responsibility, integrity and aplomb. Class acts tend to attract people who are at the top of their game."

That's true in the game of life or sports. Class athletes have an edge over their opponents. Why? Their poise allows them to concentrate better. They exhibit better confidence to play to their potential. An added plus: classy athletes usually have the crowd behind them.

So take a close look at your network of friends, coworkers, customers, and so on. Are they class acts? Whether you realize it or not, they are a reflection of you. The good news is that you can change.

Make a decision to re-create yourself as a class act and see what kind of people you start attracting. Do fewer things, but do them better. Change your behavior for the better. Raise the quality of your attitude. When you have a higher level of personal standards, you get better treatment from everyone around you.

MACKAY'S MORAL

A class act can say a lot without uttering a word.

WHO'S BUTTERING YOUR BREAD?

Former U.S. Senator Bill Bradley told this story on himself years ago. He was in Philadelphia and went into a restaurant and ordered dinner. The busboy came up to him and put a roll and pat of butter down before him. Bradley looked at the busboy and said: "I'd like another pat of butter."

"One pat of butter to a customer, sir," replied the busboy.

Bradley looked at him and said: "Don't you know who I am?"

The busboy said: "No, who?"

He said: "My name is Bill Bradley. I graduated #1 in my class at Princeton University ... Associated Press First String All-American in basketball ... drafted in the first round in the NBA ... Rhodes Scholar ... elected U.S. Senator!"

The busboy replied, "Those are very impressive credentials, Mr. Bradley, but don't you know who I am?"

"No, who?"

"I'm the man in charge of the butter."

There will always be someone in charge of the butter, the plates, and everything else. We need to get along with everyone. We can't put ourselves ahead of others. Many people are important and can keep us from getting what we want. It doesn't matter if it's a waiter, parking lot attendant, mail person, UPS driver, ticket seller, or whoever; everyone is important.

There will always be someone in charge of the butter, the plates, and everything else. We need to get along with everyone. We can't put ourselves ahead of others.

When you are good to others, you are best to yourself. I make it my business to get to know the managers and servers of the top restaurants in town, just as I do the bell captains and so on. Similarly, I let them get to know me. It doesn't take a $100 tip for someone to remember you. But I will guarantee you, the minute you are rude, demanding, arrogant, or otherwise dismissive, they will remember you—for all the wrong reasons. Don't even think about asking for a second pat of butter then. From my perspective, there are way too many people who are so arrogant, they have chapped lips from kissing the mirror too much.

Terry Paulson, author of *They Shoot Managers, Don't They?*, witnessed an angry executive take apart a baggage handler who was working as fast as he could. After the executive left, Paulson sympathized with the poor fellow, but he replied, "Don't worry, I've already gotten even."

"What do you mean?" Paulson asked.

With a sly smile, the baggage handler replied, "He's going to Chicago, but his bags are going to Japan."

A prime people skills tutorial is the election season. Have you ever watched a truly seasoned politician work a crowd? Yeah, sure, they know where the money might come from, and they might give those folks a little special attention at the $1,000-a-plate dinners. But why would a candidate for the highest office in the land spend a few hours in Podunkville, USA, in a hot factory, answering the same questions he's been asked a million times, shaking every hand until his own is swollen to twice its size? Because that astute candidate knows that every vote counts and he might only have one chance to meet and greet these humble but all-important voters. The photo ops are not at the black-tie dinners. They're among the "real" people whose work keeps this country running.

Perhaps one of the finest testimonials to looking out for those who are taking care of you is the story of Greg Booker, the attendant at the parking lot where the Minnesota Twins players and luxury suite holders park. Booker was a cheerful fellow, always polite, always helpful. He died during the baseball season a few years back, and the players, on their way to the airport for a road trip, made a special stop at his wake to pay their respects. Important, famous, well-paid players, making sure they said goodbye to the fellow who said hello to them every day at the ballpark. He was as much a part of the organization as the guys on the highlight films. As a final tribute, the Twins named the street into the stadium after Booker. That's how it should be.

MACKAY'S MORAL

Life is a dance. If you're smart, you learn the steps.

THE BEST SHIP TO SAIL—FRIENDSHIP

"Friendship is the hardest thing in the world to explain. It's not something you learn in school. But if you haven't learned the meaning of friendship, you really haven't learned anything." I've heard this quote many times, including from my good friend, the late Muhammad Ali.

I have friends whom I've known since I was a little boy, friends from college, friends who started out as business contacts, golfing friends, friends who share my passion for community service, and friends I met last week. And they all have one thing in common: We like each other for what we are, not what we want each other to be.

Greek philosopher Socrates was asked, "What is the most beneficial thing a person can acquire?"

He answered, "A friend who gives sincere advice."

I am fortunate to have friends who aren't afraid to ruffle my feathers when it comes to advice. If I need to adjust my attitude, alter my course, back off, or move forward, I have friends who will tell me. And because I value their friendship, I listen. And I will return the favor, if necessary. And we will remain friends because friendship is like a bank account: You cannot continue to draw on it without making deposits.

I am fortunate to have friends who aren't afraid to ruffle my feathers when it comes to advice. If I need to adjust my attitude, alter my course, back off, or move forward, I have friends who will tell me. And because I value their friendship, I listen.

Friendship must have been a hot topic among the Greek philosophers. A century later, Aristotle viewed friendship among the highest virtues. It was an essential element in a full, virtuous, and worthwhile life. He identified three kinds of friendship:

Friendship of pleasure. Two people are wonderfully happy in each other's company.

Friendship of utility. Two people assist one another in everyday aspects of life.

Friendship of virtue. Two people mutually admire one another and will be on best behavior in order not to jeopardize their relationship.

We need all three kinds of friends. Chances are we have some in each category, as well as friends who meet all the criteria.

Great literature, movies, and music lyrics are full of references to friendship. The Beatles got by "with a little help from my friends." James Taylor reminded us that when you need a helping hand, "you've got a friend." Bette Midler gave us a long list of reasons why "You've got to have friends." One of the most successful and longest-running television shows of all time was *Friends*, which will probably continue to run in syndication when the stars are old and gray.

And contrary to popular belief, dogs may not be man's best friends! However, they are extraordinarily loyal and trustworthy—and one reason a dog has so many friends is that he wags his tail instead of his tongue.

We have wonderful opportunities to make friends wherever we go. I jump at those opportunities! I love meeting new people because I get a different view of the world. I may not agree with everything I hear, but what a way to expand your mind.

One day a father of a very wealthy family took his son on a trip to the country with the purpose of showing his son how poor people live. They stayed with a very poor family.

When they returned, the father asked the son what he thought of their trip.

"It was great, Dad."

"Did you see how poor people live?" the father asked.

"Oh yeah," said the son.

"So, tell me, what did you learn from the trip?" asked the father.

The son answered: "I saw that we have one dog and they had four. We have a pool that reaches to the middle of our garden and they have a creek that has no end. We have imported lanterns in our garden and they have the stars at night. Our patio reaches to the front yard and they have the whole horizon. We have a small piece of land to live on and they have fields that go beyond our sight. We have servants who serve us, but they serve others. We buy our food, but they grow theirs. We have walls around our property to protect us; they have friends to protect them."

The boy's father was speechless.

Then his son added, "Thanks, Dad, for showing me how poor we are."

Isn't perspective a wonderful thing? Appreciate every single thing you have, especially your friends!

MACKAY'S MORAL

The best vitamin for making friends is B-1.

16

PERSISTENCE

NEVER TOO LATE TO SUCCEED

A poor boy named Harlan with only a sixth-grade education wouldn't have made anyone's list of the most likely to succeed. His first major success came at the age of 39, when he was able to come up with the financing to open a small-town gas station and restaurant.

He did pretty well, but with the onset of World War II, Harlan's once-solid customer base left the small town to enlist in the military or take factory jobs in the city. He managed to hold on until a new interstate highway eliminated his drive-by trade. Then, after nearly 30 years in business, Harlan was forced to sell his dream to pay off his debts.

Almost broke and approaching age 70, Harlan could have walked away from his dreams. Instead, he hit the road, offering to share his pressure-cooking techniques with other restaurant owners if they'd agree to become his franchises. He sold only five in the first two years, but he stuck it out.

Four years later the self-proclaimed Colonel Sanders had sold more than 600 Kentucky Fried Chicken franchises. And by the time Harlan Sanders died at age 90 in 1980, KFC was a worldwide brand. Today, KFC is the world's second-largest restaurant chain (measured by sales) after McDonald's, with 18,875 outlets in 118 countries and territories.

Persistence is one of the traits I look for in hiring any new employee, especially a sales rep. There is no substitute.

I remember when I was first starting out as an envelope salesman and asking an experienced colleague I respected how many calls he would make on a prospect before giving up. He said, "It depends on which one of us dies first."

When giving up is not an option, you have to find ways to maintain your motivation. Give yourself a pep talk, and then roll up your sleeves and look for the next reasonable steps you need to take. Do you need more education? Do you need more staff? Do you need to tweak your idea to make it more attractive to potential clients? Do you need to channel your efforts in a completely different direction?

Bob Nelson, author of *1,001 Ways to Take Initiative at Work*, says it's best to focus on what you *can* accomplish rather than on what you can't. This will help you stay positive. Use your energy to work toward a goal, rather than against an obstacle, he suggests.

If you identify a roadblock to your goal, develop a plan to address whatever is in your way. Be patient; remember Colonel Sanders's example. Success may be elusive at first, but give it time.

Some of Nelson's other pointers include finding ways to make it easy, even desirable, for your colleagues to say yes to your requests. When you give coworkers options, they should be able to choose how they can best help you.

Be assertive, but not aggressive. Always be polite, but don't give up on your direction in order to be liked. If you believe in what you are doing, you need to be able to stand firm when nay-sayers try to shoot down your plans.

Be assertive, but not aggressive. Always be polite, but don't give up on your direction in order to be liked. If you believe in what you are doing, you need to be able to stand firm when nay-sayers try to shoot down your plans.

A prime example of shooting down plans actually came when the early space explorers were trying to shoot rockets up into the great unknown. One of America's space pioneers was a physicist named Robert Goddard. His story is one of unwavering persistence in the face of "learned" skepticism.

Professor Goddard helped launch the Space Age by experimenting with a 10-foot rocket in a New England cabbage field. His belief in rocketry as a viable technology for flight was met with great cynicism.

Even the *New York Times* dismissed his plans in a 1920 editorial. The *Times* soundly panned Goddard's thesis: "Professor Goddard clearly lacks the knowledge ladled out daily in high schools."

Yet Goddard persevered until he proved his firm belief, that rocket engines can create thrust in a vacuum. Two of his 214 patented inventions—a multi-stage rocket and a liquid-fuel rocket (both patented in 1914)—were important milestones toward spaceflight.

The theory was proved 40 years later by other space pioneers who did indeed reach extreme altitudes. Years after his death, at the dawn of the Space Age, he came to be recognized as the founding father of modern rocketry.

Unless you are Robert Goddard, persistence is not rocket science. If you are willing to stick with it, you can take your ideas to the moon!

MACKAY'S MORAL

When you feel like giving up, remember why you held on for so long in the first place.

TRYING TIMES ARE NO TIME TO QUIT TRYING

When the going gets tough, it's time to make a trip to the zoo for inspiration. That's where you'll find my ingredients for success: a hide like a hippopotamus, the courage of a lion, the memory of an elephant, the perseverance of a beaver, the endurance of an Alaskan sled dog, the speed of a greyhound, the agility of a monkey, and the stubbornness of a mule.

One of those traits, perseverance, stands out during down times, when we are so often tempted to give up. Among life's greatest pleasures in life is doing what people say you can't. When things seem bleakest, you have to carry on to succeed.

Marshall Field, the famed Chicago department store merchant, once offered a list of 12 reminders to those who would have happiness and success in life. Number two on the list was perseverance.

In building a firm foundation for success, *Forbes Scrapbook of Thoughts on the Business of Life* listed 20 steps, including perseverance.

Businessman H. Ross Perot said: "A lesson I've learned from the lives of great inventors ... the most successful people in the world aren't the brightest. They are the ones who persevere."

And finally, oil magnate John D. Rockefeller added: "I do not think there is any other quality so essential to success of any kind as the quality of perseverance. It overcomes almost everything, even nature."

I'll never forget watching *The David Susskind Show* years ago. He had three guests on who were self-made millionaires. These men, in their mid-thirties, had averaged being in a dozen different businesses before they hit it big.

The line between failure and success is so fine that we scarcely know when we pass it; so fine that we are often on the line and do not know it. How many people have thrown up their hands at a time when a little more effort, a little more patience, would have achieved success?

In business, prospects may seem darkest when really they are about to turn. A little more perseverance, a little more effort, and what seemed a hopeless failure may turn into a glorious success. There is no failure except in no longer trying.

History abounds with tales of perseverance. Theodor Geisel died in 1991 at the age of 87. Before he died, he wrote 47 books that sold more than 100 million copies in 18 languages. What most people don't know about Dr. Seuss is that he didn't write his first book until he was 33 and it was rejected by 28 publishers before Vanguard Press picked it up.

Then there was a little girl from Tennessee who was born to face poverty, obesity, a broken home, and physical abuse. Today, Oprah Winfrey is one of the most admired celebrities in the world.

Similarly, there are many tales of experts who were convinced that the ideas, plans, and projects of others could never be achieved. However, accomplishment came to those who said, "I can make it happen."

- The Italian sculptor Agostino d'Antonio worked diligently on a large piece of marble. Unable to produce his desired masterpiece, he lamented, "I can do nothing with it." Other sculptors also worked this difficult piece of marble, but to no avail. Michelangelo discovered the stone and visualized the possibilities in it. His perseverance resulted in one of the world's masterpieces—his statue of David.

- Even the great Thomas Edison discouraged his friend, Henry Ford, from pursuing his fledgling idea of a motorcar. Convinced of the worthlessness of the idea, Edison invited Ford to come and work for him. Ford remained committed and tirelessly pursued his dream. Although his first attempt resulted in a vehicle without reverse gear, Henry Ford knew he could make it happen. And, of course, he did.

- "Forget it," the experts advised Madame Curie. They agreed radium was a scientifically impossible idea. However, Madame Curie insisted, "I can make it happen."

- Finally, as you read these accounts under the magnificent light of your environment, consider the plight of Benjamin Franklin. He was admonished to stop his foolish experiments with lightning. What an absurdity and waste of time! Why, nothing could outdo the fabulous oil lamp! Thank goodness Franklin knew he could make it happen.

You too can make it happen!

MACKAY'S MORAL

Never give up: The mighty oak was once a little nut that held its ground.

17

QUALITY/VALUES

GOOD ENOUGH NEVER IS

There's a good reason why Debbi Fields of cookie fame is so successful, and she summed it up in an aphorism I'll never forget: "Good enough never is."

Debbi told me how she coined that phrase after she visited one of her first stores. She walked in unannounced and saw a large crowd of customers in line. The problem was she noticed the most recent batch of cookies was overcooked, and she didn't want those cookies sold. When she confronted the manager he said, "They are good enough." Debbi responded with her now famous line, "Good enough never is." And she threw the entire batch in the trash and made the staff start over. She went through the line explaining what had happened. After apologizing to everyone, she said their orders would be free, if they came back and gave them another chance to show they were the best cookies in the world.

I can attest to how good they are because Debbi made a batch for my wife and me when we visited her at her Aspen home. What a cookie, and what a lesson!

I also learned another valuable lesson from Debbi. She started cooking at an early age because her mother's cooking was just "good enough," and Debbi wanted better. Initially her mother was not in favor of Debbi starting her cookie business because she thought it would fail.

That made Debbi realize that there are two sides of life. There is the negative side that points out the risks and wants to rain on your parade. Then there is the positive side that cheers you on and roots for your success. It's up to you to determine the best path.

Fortunately, Debbi Fields chose the positive side, as the company now has 400 franchised and licensed locations throughout the United States and in 33 other countries since she opened her first store in 1977.

Giving 100 percent in everything you do is so important. According to statistics compiled by the Communications Division of Insight, Syncrude Canada Ltd., if 99.9 percent were good enough, then:

- 107 incorrect medical procedures will be performed by the end of the day today.
- Two million documents will be lost by the IRS this year.
- 22,000 transactions will be deducted from the wrong bank accounts in the next 60 minutes.

- 1,314 phone calls will be misplaced by telecommunication services every minute.
- 268,500 defective tires will be shipped this year.
- 14,208 defective PCs will be shipped this year.
- 103,260 income tax returns will be processed incorrectly this year.
- 5,517,200 cases of soft drinks produced in the next 12 months will be flatter than a bad tire.
- 3,065 copies of tomorrow's *Wall Street Journal* will be missing one of the three sections.
- 18,322 pieces of mail will be mishandled in the next hour.
- 291 pacemaker operations will be performed incorrectly this year.
- 880,000 credit cards in circulation will turn out to have incorrect cardholder information on their magnetic strips.
- $9,690 will be spent today, tomorrow, next Thursday, and every day in the future on defective, often unsafe sporting equipment.
- 55 malfunctioning automatic teller machines will be installed in the next 12 months.
- 20,000 incorrect drug prescriptions will be written in the next 12 months.
- 114,500 mismatched pairs of shoes will be shipped this year.
- 315 entries in *Webster's Third New International Dictionary of the English Language* will turn out to be misspelled.
- Two plane landings daily at O'Hare International Airport in Chicago will be unsafe.
- 12 babies will be given to the wrong parents each day.

Given statistics like those, does a pan of overbaked cookies seem like such a big deal? It is, if your standards are as high as they should be. And never stop trying to exceed those standards.

Take it from Orison Swett Marden, founder of *SUCCESS* magazine, "The quality of your work will have a great deal to do with the quality of your life."

Here's a work/life example that illustrates his point.

In ancient Rome, when the scaffolding was removed from a completed Roman arch, the law read that the Roman engineer who built the arch had to stand beneath it. The point was that if the arch came crashing down, he would experience the responsibility first hand. As a result, the Roman engineer knew that the quality of his work was crucial and would have a direct personal impact on his life.

MACKAY'S MORAL

There is no substitute for quality.

DO IT RIGHT THE *FIRST* TIME

I've often extolled the virtues of learning from your mistakes. Don't be afraid to make them, I've advised, but be sure not to make the same mistake two or three times.

At the same time, however, I'm a huge proponent of trying to do things right the first time. Mistakes are fine, if they're on your own time. Otherwise, you will be staring down financial and customer relations problems that could have been avoided with a little care.

Let me share my neighbor's experience. These folks decided it was time to replace an aging kitchen floor. Theirs is an older house, the kind we refer to as "solid." They chose the new floor and arranged for installation. The contractor arrived on time, set to work, and at the end of the day, invited the homeowners to inspect his masterpiece.

The floor looked great, but why did he shave off an inch from the bottom of the door into the kitchen?

"Oh, that. I was going to raise the threshold, but then decided to re-do the floor underneath. Don't worry. I can add some wood to the bottom of that door and it will look just fine."

No, my neighbor said, you must put another door on there. The original door was not pieced together, and this is not acceptable.

Several months, several dozen phone calls and several thousand dollars later, a new custom-made door sports the welcome sign. The contractor paid more for the replacement door than the original floor job was worth.

What's worse than his losing money on this job, though, is that he will never work in this neighborhood again. He could probably have retired off the contracts he would have picked up around there.

It would have been so simple to take the time to do it right the first time.

Stanley Marcus's father, the founder of Neiman-Marcus, was constantly seeking ways to improve his store's merchandise. He wanted to offer his customers only perfect products, because after all, his reputation was at stake. Shortly after the first store opened in 1907, he established an inspection department, a concept unheard of in the retail business at the time. Every single piece of clothing was tried on a model form and inspected for flaws in the cut of the garment, the fabric, or any other defects on close inspection.

Quality control to the extreme, you think? Maybe so, but as a customer, I would be grateful to Mr. Marcus and loyal to his store. He took the time to do it right the first time.

Most companies would be fairly content with a 95 percent customer satisfaction rating. But during World War II, parachute packers had to do better. Their record was unacceptable: only 19 out of 20 parachutes opened. The manager decided to let the packers test their work by jumping from a plane. You guessed it—quality quickly rose to 100 percent.

Doing it right involves a commitment of not only a little more time but often a little more money—at the outset, anyway. Sometimes doing things that make the bean-counters cringe turns out to be the golden bricks that are the foundation of a company's reputation.

Doing it right involves a commitment of not only a little more time but often a little more money—at the outset, anyway. Sometimes doing things that make the bean-counters cringe turns out to be the golden bricks that are the foundation of a company's reputation.

For example, Maytag, with the motto of "ten years' trouble-free operation," has built its entire advertising campaign around the lonely repairman. Maytag appliances are not the cheapest models available, but customers swear by them because they value the dependability and quality. Maytag remains a leader in the field because they do it right the first time.

A quality operation is not an accident. It is a commitment from the top that extends to the newest hires. Only when every level demonstrates a superior commitment to doing a job, making a product, or performing a service does the concept of doing it right the first time really work.

At MackayMitchell Envelope Company, our goal is to be in business forever. Doing jobs right the first time is the first and probably most important step. You don't get a second chance to make a first impression.

MACKAY'S MORAL

If you don't have time to do it right the first time, when are you going to find time to do it over?

VALUES DETERMINE WHO WE ARE

In Antoine de Saint-Exupery's famous novel, *The Little Prince*, a fox becomes the best friend of the young royal on a fictitious planet. When the fox must depart from the prince forever, he offers to tell him the world's most wonderful secret if the prince meets certain conditions. The little prince agrees, does what is expected, and then asks to be told the greatest secret.

"Only that which is invisible is essential," the fox replies.

The most valuable things in life cannot be seen with the naked eye: love, friendship, hope, integrity, trust, compassion, and values.

You can't see values, touch them, taste them, or smell them. Yet they are critical, intangible essentials that bring continuity and meaning to life. And they are every bit as important for organizations as they are for individuals.

"It's not hard to make decisions, once you know what your values are," said Roy E. Disney. Roy Disney was the partner and co-founder, along with his younger brother Walt Disney, of Walt Disney Productions, since renamed The Walt Disney Company. The Walt Disney Company is the epitome of a values-driven organization. While it may be overshadowed by its retail prowess, its primary product is happiness. Their "Disney courtesy" concept is based on four key values: safety, courtesy, show, and efficiency. Every one of their performance standards is based on these encompassing beliefs. Customer service is a lifestyle for all Disney employees. Employees are expected to think, walk, talk, and breathe safety, courtesy, show, and efficiency. This lifestyle creates happiness for their guests.

Defining your values is not just an academic exercise. "Clarifying your values is the essential first step toward a richer, fuller, more productive life," said Carl Rogers, an American psychologist and a founder of the humanistic approach (or client-centered approach) to psychology. Rogers is widely considered to be one of the founding fathers of psychotherapy research and was widely honored for his pioneering research.

If you want to clarify your own values, ask yourself these questions:

- What do I believe in?
- In what guiding principles can I become constructively obsessed?
- What governs my life?
- What do I stand for?

- What puts meaning in my life?
- What qualities are important for my life to be complete?

Hey—I never said this was easy! This is not a quick-and-dirty exercise. Values are not a spur-of-the-moment action. They are non-negotiable principles that guide your everyday life. Your personal convictions, not those of others, determine how you live. You cannot separate personal value from personally held values.

Nor can you separate corporate value from corporate values. Customers and competitors should be able to see your values in action every day. Honesty, fairness, respect, and trustworthiness are among values that should be front and center with every transaction.

> *Customers and competitors should be able to see your values in action every day. Honesty, fairness, respect, and trustworthiness are among values that should be front and center with every transaction.*

The often-quoted Chinese philosopher Confucius, who lived in the fifth century B.C., wrote: "The rule of life is to be found within yourself. Ask yourself constantly, 'What is the right thing to do?' Beware of doing that which you are likely, sooner or later, to repent of having done."

When you are in a position of having to repent, do it quickly and sincerely. That is another value that is essential to a good life: being able to admit mistakes and correcting them.

I will never forget when my good friend Lou Holtz was coaching Notre Dame in the 1989 Fiesta Bowl against West Virginia. His players learned a valuable lesson about their coach's values that day, which resulted in a national championship.

Notre Dame was penalized on two consecutive plays for "taunting" the opposition. Despite knowing that his actions would bring another penalty, Holtz ran out on the field and asked the referee which of his players were doing the taunting, since this was before referees identified players by numbers. Then Holtz—with a national TV audience watching—grabbed the player and told him what was expected of him.

Holtz has always believed strongly in his players, but he demands that they follow his three simple values:

1. Do what is right. Be on time, polite, honest, remain free from drugs, and if you have any questions, get out your *Bible*.

2. Do everything to the best of your ability in the time allotted. Mediocrity is unacceptable when you are capable of doing better.

3. Show people you care.

MACKAY'S MORAL

Decide what you will stand for or you won't have a leg to stand on.

18

ROADBLOCKS

IF YOU DON'T HAVE A PLAN B, YOU DON'T HAVE A PLAN

You might have heard about the Chinese proverb that says, "When planning for a year, plant corn. When planning for a decade, plant trees. When planning for life, train and educate people." And part of that training should be developing a backup plan.

You may have made the best-laid plans, but what if something unexpected happens? I can't emphasize enough how important backup plans are. You should always have a plan B and possibly plans C and D. The bigger the deal or event, the more detailed your backup plan should be.

I can't emphasize enough how important backup plans are. You should always have a plan B and possibly plans C and D. The bigger the deal or event, the more detailed your backup plan should be.

As I was building my envelope manufacturing company, whenever we had a big event I would always ask everyone on my team, "What can go wrong?" And just as important, "What is our backup plan?"

Planning is time-consuming and, let's face it, many people don't like to do it. But when you think about it, in business you don't put all your eggs in one basket. That would be regarded as rash or unprofessional. That's why you need a plan and, equally important, a backup plan.

I'm a big believer in being prepared. How many special events, meetings, weddings, or businesses have been ruined because people didn't have backup plans? We live in an imperfect world. Regardless of whether we plan for something to go wrong, something inevitably will.

Maybe it's an out-of-town speaker who can't make it to your event due to bad weather, traffic, or plane or car trouble. Or your audiovisuals go down, or there are transportation issues. There are a myriad of things that can go haywire.

I recently attended a charity event in a rural area. Ten minutes into the party, the lights went out. All the electricity was off. Bye-bye catering. That also meant the plumbing was inoperational, because it ran on an electric pump. This was an evening event, so sunlight was not an option. Guests stumbled in the dark to their cars, leaving all the silent auction items still artfully arranged on the tables. The night was a total bust. The rescheduled event six weeks later—at an area hotel—drew fewer than half the original guest list. And raised half the anticipated funds.

People don't plan to fail; they fail to plan. Did anyone give any thought to an emergency generator?

When I'm asked about important skills for leaders, it's hard to beat a hungry fighter, but there are a lot of other traits that I look for, like planning skills.

Even if what you're planning seems like a sure thing, it's always good to consider the worst-case scenario. For example, in the early 1950s, Hewlett-Packard Company founders Bill Hewlett and Dave Packard needed an additional manufacturing plant to keep up with the company's growth. However, they approached the venture with caution. They chose a general design that, in the event of a company failure or hard times, could easily double as a supermarket space they could lease.

Planning, and backup planning, save precious time because you are prepared to act if any unforeseen circumstances arise. Rather than switching into panic mode, you can react with confidence.

When I am preparing to give a speech, I have some specific requirements, including a second microphone, spare batteries, and a technician in the room. I carry a ruler and tape so I can enlarge the lip on the lectern so my papers don't scatter all over the floor. I tape over the door latches so the noise doesn't distract the audience if someone comes in late. When you have worked hard to deliver a quality product, it hardly makes sense to ignore the details. Plan ahead to prevent disasters.

Do you back up your computer files? Have you ever been working on your computer for an hour or two on an important document, when suddenly a power surge wipes out your masterpiece? You'll quickly learn to back up frequently.

Your career is no place to wing it. You need a career plan, and you need to review that plan on a regular basis. From getting an education to developing skills to finding the first job, knowing what path you want to take requires forethought. Assessing your career progress is part of your plan. If you decide to quit your job, you'd better have a backup plan. Or you can plan to be right back where you started.

MACKAY'S MORAL

A plan isn't a plan until you have a backup plan.

STOP PROCRASTINATING BEFORE IT STOPS YOU

Procrastination is a thief. It robs you of the one commodity that you just can't buy back: time. It throws off schedules. It replaces accomplishment with inaction. It turns dreams into nightmares.

When faced with a task that we just don't want to do, many of us simply put it off until tomorrow. That's why tomorrow is often the busiest day of the week. And "one of these days" becomes none of these days. As Mark Twain once said, "Why put off until tomorrow that which you can put off until the day after tomorrow?"

Putting off an unpleasant task until tomorrow simply allows more time for your imagination to make a mountain out of a possible molehill … more time for anxiety to sap your self-confidence.

Most of us can relate to occasional bouts of procrastination—the phone call you have been dreading to place, the project that you just can't get excited about, the meeting that you should have scheduled two weeks ago. But why can't we just get in gear?

Thomas A. Harris, author of *I'm OK, You're OK*, said there are three things that give people the "wantivation" to change: They must hurt sufficiently, they must experience despair or boredom, or they must suddenly discover they can change. He explained, "Until one of these three is realized, any excuse not to change will suffice."

Dr. Gail Saltz, author of *Becoming Real: Defeating the Stories We Tell Ourselves That Hold Us Back*, says that 20 percent of Americans are considered "chronic procrastinators." But it's not about laziness, it's about fear, she says. Among the reasons:

- **Fear of failure.** Are you so paralyzed by the fear of failure that you'd rather just not try at all?
- **Fear of success.** Do you think that if you succeed at something then the bar will be set so high that you will never reach it again? Or are you afraid that you don't deserve success?
- **A need to be defiant.** Is life generally a battle for control? Are you taking a passive-aggressive approach to control by procrastinating?
- **A thrill-seeker procrastinator.** Are you trying to avoid the boredom of daily tasks? Does boredom terrify you? Do you need to create a crisis to keep things interesting?

Understanding procrastination will help you break the paralyzing habit of putting off what you need to do. Then you can begin to make the changes that will help you tackle your work with more determination.

Start prioritizing so you won't get overwhelmed. Create to-do lists and figure out what's important. As the old saying goes, "Well begun is half done." Knowing what you need to do is not enough. You need to plan to track your progress.

Then do just one step. Gather some preliminary information, call one person, or figure out what tools you need. Once you've completed that task, give yourself permission to do something else. In many cases, once you've begun you'll be more inclined to keep on working. Even if you don't, you'll be one step closer to success when you come back to the task later.

I find it helpful to set a deadline, even when the project isn't time-sensitive. That way, there's nothing hanging over my head that is cluttering up the rest of my workload. I also write down my to-do list so that I can focus on one item at a time.

Procrastination is a problem at all levels. Charles M. Schwab, who founded Bethlehem Steel Company in 1904, was a master of his schedule. He made it a practice of investing five minutes each day analyzing the problems he should tackle the next day. He would write down those tasks in the order of priority.

When he arrived at his office the next morning, he would start with the top issue on his list and move on in order. "This is the most practical lesson I've ever learned," he claimed, and shared this example to prove his point: "I had put off a phone call for nine months, so I decided to list it as my number one task on my next day's agenda. That call netted a $2 million order."

I'm not sure what that would translate to in today's economy, but I'd be happy with a $2 million order any day! Make the call!

MACKAY'S MORAL

Overcoming procrastination helps your to-do list become your all-done list.

DON'T LET FEAR OF SUCCESS HOLD YOU BACK

Legend has it that one day a man was walking in the desert when he met Fear and Plague. They said they were on the way to a city to kill 10,000 people. The man asked Plague if he was going to do all the work.

Plague smiled and said, "No, I'll take care of only a few hundred. I'll let my friend Fear do the rest."

Can you actually die from fear? Most likely not. What fear kills is your spirit, your ambition, your confidence.

Several years ago I penned my "The Second Ten Commandments." (See the "Final Thoughts" section.) Commandment II stated: **Thou shall not be fearful, for most of the things we fear never come to pass.** Every crisis we face is multiplied when we act out of fear. Fear is a self-fulfilling emotion. When you fear something, you empower it. If you refuse to concede to fear, there is nothing to fear.

Success usually depends on overcoming your fears: fear of taking a risk, fear of asserting yourself, fear of exposing your deepest self to other people, and ultimately, fear of failure. But for some people, the real fear is—believe it or not—success itself.

Success usually depends on overcoming your fears: fear of taking a risk, fear of asserting yourself, fear of exposing your deepest self to other people, and ultimately, fear of failure. But for some people, the real fear is—believe it or not—success itself.

Fear of failure can be crippling, but fear of success can paralyze your efforts just as severely. Avoiding success may seem irrational, but success brings change, and change is often threatening.

We fear success because success can bring expectations of continued success. Achieving a major goal is hard work. What happens if people expect you to keep doing it indefinitely? Can you continue to produce?

Another concern is that coworkers may look to you for advice or assistance once you've proved you can succeed. You may lose control over your time or your privacy. Or you might offer advice that doesn't work as well as hoped. Then your achievements might become suspect.

And you certainly don't want to make enemies of the people you work with. Some people delight in taking down successful people. Envious or hostile peers can make life miserable. Can you bring them on board on another project so they can also celebrate some success?

The prospect of actually reaching a goal can be terrifying: What comes next? How will people react? What if your goal turns out to be meaningless? These worries can lead to procrastination and self-sabotage. To overcome them, and achieve the success you were meant to enjoy, follow this advice:

- **Face your fears.** Explore the emotions you have about success. Analyze what you're really afraid of, and it will usually lose its impact.

- **Focus on the process.** The end result may be important, but as with any journey, the individual steps can be more meaningful than the destination. Concentrate on what you're learning, the people you meet, and the experiences you collect as you move closer to your goal.

- **Analyze past successes.** Look at projects or achievements from your past. What obstacles did you face? How did success make you feel? What changed as a result? This will help you sort through and clarify your fears and your ability to overcome them.

- **Anticipate the changes.** Ask yourself, "What will happen when I succeed?" By confronting fears, you take away their power, and you'll be able to identify strategies for moving beyond them.

- **Select worthwhile goals.** Pursue goals that address your needs, not anyone else's. Take the time to think through what success will really mean before committing yourself. You'll only be excited about success if it's what you truly want.

- **Think about the rewards.** Don't let concerns about the future distract you from the positive benefits of reaching your goals. Visualize the upside: the final product, a satisfied customer, a check, or some other tangible results.

- **Create new behaviors.** After you've looked through the issues, start devising strategies for moving forward. How can you reinforce your self-confidence? What excuses do you need to eliminate? How can you sustain your motivation?

- **Be realistic.** Remember that success won't solve all your problems, but the feeling of accomplishment can make everyday irritations easier to tolerate, even if you can't erase them.

Benjamin Franklin had some timeless advice for those who are afraid of success and failure: "The man who does things makes mistakes, but he never makes the biggest mistake of all—doing nothing."

MACKAY'S MORAL

If you want to be successful, you must first succeed in conquering your fear.

19

SALES AND MARKETING

LAW OF LARGE NUMBERS
PAYS LARGE DIVIDENDS

If you can't be number one, the best position you can shoot for is number two.

It doesn't matter if it's politics or business, number two is the strongest position to be in, because when number one has trouble or messes up in some way, number two is there to take over.

Many people have the attitude that if they can't be number one, who cares if you're number two or number 10. You still aren't the winner.

Vince Lombardi once said, "There is no room for second place. There's only one place, and that's first place."

That may be true for athletics, but it's certainly not true for business. You have to think long term and what can happen in the future. In sales, if you don't get the order, shoot for runner-up.

Consider Jacob Bernoulli's Law of Large Numbers, which states that if an experiment is repeated a certain number of times, the relative frequency of an occurrence tends to be a fixed number. An entire industry, insurance, is built on the principle of the Law of Large Numbers. There are 329 million living Americans. The insurance people can tell you within one-fourth of 1 percent just how many of us are going to die within the next 12 months—and how—and where—and in what age bracket, sex, color, and creed. That's pretty amazing. The only thing they can't tell us is *which ones*!

Being an envelope guy, one of my favorite examples of the Law of Large Numbers is direct mail. How many pieces of advertising do you receive each day? Companies keep sending mailings because they know a certain percentage of us will buy.

Telemarketing works on the same principle. For all the calls a telemarketer makes, a certain percentage will respond positively.

The lottery is another industry that fits the Law of Large Numbers. Lottery America Calculated Results Tables show, among other things, the calculated results in one column and the actual results in another column for each of the different types of number combinations. Once you see the comparison, you understand why lotteries are classic examples of the Law of Large Numbers.

Some people find it surprising that there are more than 16 million others on the planet who share their birthdate. At a typical football game with attendance of 50,000 people, most fans are likely to share their birthday with about 135 others. The notable exception will be those born on February 29. There will only be about 34 fans born on that day.

Avis, the gigantic car rental company, had a slogan that focused on the importance of being second, "We're number two and we try harder." They were primed for Hertz to stub its toe, big time. Over the years, Avis shortened its slogan to "We try harder," and it is one of the 10 most recognizable slogans in business today. It stands as a model of quality and service and a spirit that keeps customers returning.

If you are in sales, apply the Law of Large Numbers to your prospect list. Position yourself as number two to every prospect on your list and keep adding to that list. I can promise you that if your list is long enough, there are going to be number ones who retire, die, are terminated, or lose their territories for a hundred reasons and succumb to the Law of Large Numbers. What I can't tell you is *which ones*.

If you are in sales, apply the Law of Large Numbers to your prospect list. Position yourself as number two to every prospect on your list and keep adding to that list.

But fortunately, as in the insurance business, "which one" doesn't matter. All that matters is that you have the perseverance and patience to position yourself as number two to enough different people, and the Law of Large Numbers will do for you what it has done for the insurance industry: You will be an extremely successful and wealthy salesperson.

That's why I say if you're standing second in line, in enough lines, sooner or later you're going to move up to number one. And the amazing thing is that few people ever use this strategy.

MACKAY'S MORAL

Let the Law of Large Numbers work for you, and your numbers will get large.

WHAT MAKES A GOOD SALES REP?

I've been a salesman all my life, and I've been hiring sales reps for nearly as long. So I think I know a thing to two about sales. Recently a friend asked me to identify the traits of a sales superstar. Here's my recipe:

Hungry fighter. If I had to name only three traits that make a great sales representative, they would be (1) hungry fighter, (2) hungry fighter, and (3) hungry fighter. That's how much I think of this trait. Every good salesperson I've ever encountered is driven. They have a strong work ethic and a high energy level. They work harder and longer than their peers. When the economy is poor, they are still out there pounding the pavement or making calls.

Tell the truth. I've always believed that telling the truth is the best policy. In business, especially today, it's a must. A few years back, the Forum Corporation of Boston, Massachusetts, studied 341 salespeople from 11 different companies in five different industries. Their purpose was to determine what separated the top producers from the average producers. When the study was finished, the results were startling. It was not skill, knowledge, or charisma that divided the pack. The difference came down to one trait: honesty. When customers trust salespeople, they buy from them!

Positive attitude. Your attitude, not your aptitude, will determine your altitude. Ninety percent of success is mental. You can alter your life by altering your mind. In tough economies, it may not be your fault for being down, but it is certainly your fault for not getting up. You have to be a believer to be an achiever.

Know your product. Strong sales reps know their products backward and forward. They also know their competitors' products and are prepared to point out the differences.

Be prepared. I still remember my old Boy Scout motto: "Be prepared." Well, it's true. It takes a lot of unspectacular preparation to produce spectacular results.

Reputation. You can't buy a good reputation ... you must earn it. If you don't have a positive reputation, it will be difficult to be successful in whatever you do.

Likeability. I have never known anyone to buy from someone he doesn't like. Are you genuine? Pleasant? Easy to talk with?

Good first impression. You never get a second chance to make a good first impression. Are you neat and well groomed? Underdressed or overdressed?

Set goals.... measurable, identifiable, obtainable, specific, and in writing. Winners set goals; losers make excuses. Remember the Italian proverb: "You never climb higher than the ladder you select." Goals give you more than a reason to get up in the morning; they are an incentive to keep you going all day. Most important, goals need to be realistic: beyond your grasp today but within your reach in the foreseeable future.

Service mentality. I've often said the sale begins when the customer says yes. Good salespeople make sure the job gets done on time—and done right. There's one thing no business has enough of: customers. Take care of the customers you've got, and they'll take care of you. You must have a fanatical attention to detail!

Great listener. You can't learn anything with your mouth open. For many people, good listening means, "I talk, *you* listen." Listening is a two-way process. Yes, you need to be heard. You also need to hear the other person's ideas, questions, and objections. If you talk *at* people instead of *with* them, they're not buying in—they're caving in. Believe it or not, being a good listener is more important in sales then being a good talker.

Sense of humor. It is impossible to overrate the importance of a sense of humor. When there are inevitable setbacks along the way, try some humor and laugh about them.

Thirst for self-improvement. You don't go to school once for a lifetime. You are in school all your life. Good salespeople are constantly working to become better. They take courses, read books, listen to audio recordings and podcasts, and inhale everything they can to improve. We live in the information age, so it's easy to take every opportunity to learn and grow at any hour of the day. Remember, the largest room in the world is the room for improvement.

MACKAY'S MORAL

A salesperson tells, a good salesperson explains, and a great salesperson demonstrates.

PUTTING THE SWAY IN PERSUASION

A man opened a fish market and displayed a sign that said, "Fresh Fish for Sale Here."

His first customer showed up, looked at the sign and said, "Why does it say 'fresh'? You wouldn't sell them if they weren't fresh, would you?" So the shopkeeper, not wanting to upset his customers, painted over the word "fresh."

Then another customer arrived. "Why does your sign say 'here'? This is where you are selling them, right?" So the shopkeeper got out his paint again and wiped out "here."

A third customer glanced at the sign and asked: "Why does it say 'for sale'? You're in business to sell fish, right? You aren't giving them away." The sign was painted again, and all it said was "Fish."

The shopkeeper figured he might finally sell some fish. But a fourth customer had a question, too. "Why do you even need to say 'fish'? You can smell them a block away." Certain that his customer was on to something, he took his sign down.

Soon there were no customers at all. The shopkeeper went out of business.

He had failed Marketing 101: If you want to sell your product, no matter what it is, you have to persuade people to buy it. The trouble with the shopkeeper was that everyone else persuaded him to do business their way.

Bringing others around to your way of thinking is an art. Persuasion is much more than putting a positive spin on things. In fact, sometimes the reverse psychology approach is more powerful. (Think teenagers!) Perhaps you need to demonstrate a negative result to sway opinions. Sometimes, actions speak louder than words. To bring others around to your way of thinking, or to some specific action, you must be able to articulate your position so that others can see the advantage of following your plan: What's in it for them?

Anyone who is involved in negotiations knows the importance of persuasion. But there is a distinct difference. Negotiating means we both get some of what we want. You are satisfied with your deal, and I'm satisfied with what I got. That's the desired result.

But persuasion means you get what I want, and you thank me for giving it to you. That's a better result for both of us, because I'm not asking you to give anything up, just to get a different, and more advantageous, result.

But persuasion means you get what I want, and you thank me for giving it to you. That's a better result for both of us, because I'm not asking you to give anything up, just to get a different, and more advantageous, result.

Benjamin Franklin was a master persuader. His methods required patience and endurance. He assumed people are won over slowly, often indirectly. Here are five of his bargaining strategies:

- Be clear, in your own mind, exactly what you are seeking.
- Do your homework, so that you are fully prepared to discuss every aspect and respond to every question and comment.
- Be persistent. Don't expect to "win" the first time. Your first job is just to start the other person thinking.
- Make friends with the person with whom you are negotiating. Put your proposal in terms of his or her needs, advantages, and benefits.
- Keep your sense of humor.

I would add one more bit of advice: Be honest and aboveboard. As Aristotle said, "Character may almost be called the most effective means of communication." Getting caught in a lie will persuade others, all right: To do the polar opposite of what you're asking.

Great political orators in history—Abraham Lincoln, Thomas Jefferson, and Ronald Reagan—brought about positive societal changes with their persuasive powers. They were successful ultimately because they were passionate about their beliefs and presented their cases in such a manner that no one could misunderstand their messages.

At an international conference, I witnessed a business training exercise that illustrates how persuasion can produce the desired result. The leader drew an imaginary line on the floor, and put one person on each side. Then she told each to convince the other to cross the line to come over to his side. Interestingly, players from the United States almost never convinced one another, but their Japanese counterparts simply said, "If you'll cross the line, so will I." They traded places—and both won!

MACKAY'S MORAL

To get others to see things your way, you must look through their eyes.

Sales—up close and personal

In the Broadway musical *My Fair Lady*, Professor Higgins has driven his prodigy Eliza Doolittle to exhaustion teaching her how to speak proper English. The professor shows little acknowledgment of her hard work, even when her pronunciation improves markedly.

Later in the play, Eliza is again frustrated when her would-be sweetheart Freddie talks about his affection for her in romantic phrases—but keeps his clumsy distance and doesn't kiss her.

"Words! Words!" Eliza explodes. "I am so sick of words! I get words all day through. First from him, now from you! Is that all you blighters can do?"

Then she admonishes him: "Don't talk of stars burning above; if you're in love, show me! Tell me no dreams filled with desire. If you're on fire, show me!"

There is a profound lesson here for salespeople as well as lovers. Or, for that matter, for anyone trying to persuade someone to a point of view. An old proverb says: Tell me, and I will forget. Show me, and I may remember. But involve me, and I'll understand.

Everyone in sales is familiar with the four Ps—product, price, place, and promotion. I think there should be a fifth P—personal, as in make it personal.

Everyone in sales is familiar with the four Ps—product, price, place, and promotion. I think there should be a fifth P—personal, as in make it personal.

There are any number of ways to personalize your product and approach. I'm not just talking about making things personal by customization. Plenty of products out there can have a name or monogram stenciled on, from jewelry to towels to furniture. Hundreds of thousands of U.S. businesses offer some level of personalization for their products. And this trend is certainly not slowing due to our ego-centric marketplace.

But to really hit close to home, I'm talking about making things personal by helping people understand how they will be affected. Showing people what a product or service will mean to them. Taking the pitch right to their level, so that it seems the product is made for them and no one else. Because in reality, it is.

A personalized approach is even more important today with so much of our communication on a very impersonal level. People order online and do their banking at ATMs with no social interaction. Infomercials clog the airwaves, followed by automated phone ordering. Even grocery and home improvement stores have self-checkout lanes, making it possible to shop with a hundred other people and not speak to anyone. Online stores and brick-and-mortar stores now deliver to your door, so you don't even have to see the other shoppers. We've lost a lot of that human touch.

Ever notice how the most effective commercials on television have a spokesperson who could be your next-door neighbor? Someone you could trust, someone who would be completely straight with you.

A prime example right now is the health care debate. Doctors and patients are telling their stories, sharing very personal experiences. Both sides of the debate know that those representatives will be more effective than the politicians who are absent from the ads, even though they will be making the decisions.

Politicians in campaign mode operate quite differently. They shake hands and make appearances in the tiniest of towns, just to reach voters. A surrogate wouldn't have the same effect.

Similarly, when you have an opportunity for face time with a customer, make it really memorable. Seemingly mundane products are necessary to most businesses, but your approach needn't be boring.

Our company sells envelopes by the millions, but I still get excited when I can help customers improve their business, present a sharper image, or streamline procedures. Who knew an envelope could do all that? What I am selling isn't the envelope; it's what the envelope will do for them.

During World War II, the U.S. government began offering soldiers a life insurance policy with a $10,000 benefit if they were killed in combat. In one unit, a young lieutenant delivered a polished presentation on the details of the plan. No one signed up. Then an older sergeant quietly asked the lieutenant if he could talk to the troops.

"Men," he said, "if you get this life insurance and you get killed, the government is going to send your family $10,000. If you don't get this insurance and you get killed, the government isn't going to send your family anything. So who do you think they're going to send up to the front lines—the ones who'll cost $10,000 when they're killed, or the ones who won't cost anything?"

All the soldiers immediately signed up.

MACKAY'S MORAL

If you want to really grab your audience, use a personal touch.

KNOWING SOMETHING ABOUT YOUR CUSTOMER IS JUST AS IMPORTANT AS KNOWING YOUR PRODUCT

I remember when legendary NFL quarterback Peyton Manning switched teams from the Indianapolis Colts to the Denver Broncos. I was listening to a national sports radio program and the two talk show hosts were discussing the enormous impact Manning was having in his new football home, Denver. They mentioned that Manning had already learned the entire playbook, but even more interesting was the fact that he learned the names of the entire press group and knew as much as he could about them and their families. One show host opined how "brilliant" that was of Manning, and what is most impressive is that he took the time to read and find out as much information as he could.

Perhaps he did this because he knew the value of scouting reports, which colleges and major sports leagues use to assess their competition and draft choices.

I don't know whether Peyton Manning is familiar with the Mackay 66-Question Customer Profile, which I wrote about in my book, *Swim with the Sharks Without Being Eaten Alive.* However, Manning certainly knows the power that it yields when used properly to build relationships.

I have been preaching about the power of the Mackay 66 for my entire career. It's a tool to help you humanize your selling strategy. To be successful in life—and especially in sales—you must have a deep-down burning desire to help people. Studies show that you can't talk business all the time. Your customers are people first!

I developed this 66-question customer profile when I was 21 years old. (The Mackay 66 is available for free on my website—www.harveymackay.com.) At MackayMitchell Envelope Company we require all of our salespeople to fill it out about each of their customers.

You wouldn't believe how much we know about our customers. The IRS wouldn't believe how much we know about our customers.

And I'm not talking about their taste in envelopes either. We want to know, based on routine conversation and observation, what our customers are like as human beings. What do they feel strongly about? What are they most proud of having achieved? Are there any status symbols in their offices? In other words, we want to know the person behind the desk.

And remember ... this is not just for our customers. It's also for our suppliers. We want the best paper suppliers in the country. We want the best ink suppliers.

Use the Mackay 66 for employees and competitors—anyone whom you can benefit from knowing more about. Each time you encounter those persons, you learn a little bit more about them and keep building your list. You will probably never fill out all 66 items, but 30 are better than 20, and 15 are better than 10, things like education (high school and college), family (married, kids, and names), anniversary, hobbies and interests, favorite sports teams, vacation habits, previous employment, professional and trade associations, clubs, and so on.

Question number 66—Does your competitor have more and better answers to the above questions than you have?

The Mackay 66 is a concept, philosophy, and tool. You still must perform. But perform and build a good relationship and you not only get the order, you get all the reorders.

The Mackay 66 is a concept, philosophy, and tool. You still must perform. But perform and build a good relationship and you not only get the order, you get all the reorders.

You simply cannot know enough about your customers, employees, suppliers, and competitors.

Here's a story that dates back about 100 years that illustrates the importance of noticing the little things and knowing your audience:

Sir Arthur Conan Doyle, the creator of Sherlock Holmes, was quite impressed with the observational powers of a cab driver who picked him up at the train station after a vacation in the south of France. As he stepped into the cab and put his suitcase on the seat next to him, the driver surprised him by asking him, "Where would you like to go, Mr. Doyle?"

Doyle was surprised that he knew his name, and asked whether they had ever met before.

The driver said no, which prompted Doyle to ask how he knew who he was.

The driver replied, "This morning's paper had a story about you being on vacation in Marseilles. This is the taxi stand where people who return from Marseilles always come to. Your skin color tells me that you have been on vacation. The ink spot on your right index finger suggests to me that you are a writer. Your clothing is very English, and not French. Adding up all those pieces of information, I deduce that you are Sir Arthur Conan Doyle.

"That, and your name is on your suitcase."

MACKAY'S MORAL

People don't care how much you know about them ... once they realize how much you care about them.

Use the Mackay Sales Scalpel to sharpen selling techniques

Everyone is in sales. Why? Because from the time we wake up until our heads hit the pillow at night, we are continually communicating, negotiating, persuading, influencing, and selling ideas.

Do you want to nail the sale? The tool I use is called the Mackay Sales Scalpel. It's my sure-fire way to sharpen and pinpoint every sales situation.

As I see it, expert selling demands five essentials:

- Fire—the drive to strive.
- Formulate—the art of planning.
- Fascinate—the gift of sizzle.
- Follow-through—the discipline to control.
- Finalize—opening the door to maximum opportunity.

Let's start with *Fire*. You have to have fire. You have to love the fight. You have to know how to ignite it and to keep it lit.

When you love what you do, you will never have to work another day in your life. In fact, the subtitle to one of my books reads: "Do what you love. Love what you do. Deliver more than you promise." That's the spirit of the salesperson's creed.

When times are tough, it may not be your fault for being down. But it is always your fault for not getting up. You have to be a believer to be an achiever. Only a fired-up, high-energy workplace ignites tomorrow's ideas. The job of sales management? It's to keep the fire roaring.

But no amount of fire will take you anywhere without a plan. People don't plan to fail; they fail to plan. That brings us to ingredient #2 of the Mackay Sales Scalpel: *Formulate*. You need to formulate a plan.

Central to your plan: Figure out how you'll demonstrate the product.

Dawn, the dishwashing liquid giant, came up with a brilliant product demonstration. Remember the catastrophic Gulf of Mexico oil spill of 2010? Dawn went to work sprucing up oil-caked wild ducks and made them spanking clean using their product. What could be more convincing? Great salespeople are always on the lookout for potent proof of product effectiveness. Dawn seized an unforgettable moment.

Statistics are at the heart of formulating your plan, starting with where you get the bulk of your business. Can you identify the top 20 percent of your customers? Most salespeople are familiar with the 80/20 rule:

80 percent of your business comes from 20 percent of your customers. Well, this trend is headed strongly for 90/10. That gives you a great idea of how to prioritize your time.

The third essential of the Mackay Sales Scalpel is *Fascinate*. Advertising pioneer David Ogilvy said no one ever sold anyone anything by boring them to death. There's not a lot of difference between showmanship and salesmanship. Mostly, you have to be likable, pleasant, and listen well. In our cold and unfriendly world, it can be fascinating to meet up with a genuine, honest, and attentive person. I have never known anyone to buy from someone he or she doesn't like.

Want to fascinate people? Start by smiling and listening. Oh yes, there's one other thing to keep in mind, but you probably know that already: The sweetest sound in the English language is the sound of your name on someone else's lips.

That brings us to the fourth element of the Mackay Sales Scalpel: *Follow-through*.

Why is follow-through so important? Selling is easy, but only if you work hard at it. You have to do the details—relentlessly.

Few things drive repeat sales more than expert customer service. No customer service, and pretty soon, no business.

In customer service, nothing counts like honoring commitments and meeting deadlines. In sales, you have to nail the exact practices before-hand with manufacturing, IT, distribution, finance, and other pertinent departments.

The key is to latch on to your customers and hold them fast. Don't just meet their needs. Anticipate them. Don't wait for them to tell you there's a problem. Go out and ask them if there is a problem.

Now we come to *Finalize*—the fifth and final edge of the Mackay Sales Scalpel. It's all about closing.

The close is only the very last stage of the process. You'll never close effectively without mastering the whole process of negotiating first. Find ways for both sides to legitimately win. At any close, the super salesperson is already thinking about the service needed to support the deal or the referrals that a satisfied customer is bound to deliver.

MACKAY'S MORAL

The sale begins when the customer says yes.

SALES IS EVERYONE'S BUSINESS

Everyone is in sales. To me, job titles don't matter. Everyone has to be thinking about sales. It's the only way any company can stay in business.

There are no jobs if you don't bring the business through the front door. That's why I have a sign on my office door: "If you know where you can get us some business, come on in."

At our company, a sales mindset is a requirement. From the factory floor to the reception desk to the boardroom, figuring out what the customer wants and finding a way to deliver it must be at the forefront of every job. Whether you are selling a product, services, or a corporate image, you are in sales.

A while back I received an email from a fellow who used to be in sales but switched to information technology as a help desk technician. Even though he was now on the side of delivering service rather than sales, he understands the personalized approach with customers, be it computer operators, network administrators, or engineers.

He wrote:

"When it comes to identifying and resolving technical issues, it's important to remember the human side of technology. I only have the phone to work with, but quite often those little or long pauses while waiting for a procedure to cycle through or a test result to return can be used to build rapport, ease tension, or otherwise get to know the other person(s) on the line.

"The important thing to keep in mind here in taking advantage of these opportunities is that these people talk to the people who ultimately buy the company's services. If the service they receive at any point along the line is poor, or if the vendors' techs are impersonal or worse—abrasive or condescending—the salesperson talking with the decision-maker is going to have a rough time of it when it comes to renewing the contract."

So you can see how having a sales mindset—no matter what role in the company—can have an impact on sales.

From the moment we get up in the morning to the time we go to bed, we are negotiating, communicating, persuading, and influencing. If we aren't selling products or services, we are selling ideas.

From the moment we get up in the morning to the time we go to bed, we are negotiating, communicating, persuading, and influencing. If we aren't selling products or services, we are selling ideas.

If you want to be successful in sales, remember the 4 Ws and the H.

- **Who?** Know your customers. Get into the mind of your buyer—what does he or she really want? What does he or she really need? Sometimes those two options are not the same, so be prepared to guide people to the best solution for their situation.

- **What?** Target a clear outcome. Before approaching a customer, be certain of what you want to achieve. In some cases you may not be seeking an immediate sale, but more information about what the customer wants. Walk in with a clear plan—and backup options—so you aren't wasting their time or yours.

- **Why?** Listen to people. Successful selling isn't about talking to customers, but listening to their needs so you can find out how your product or service can help. Asking questions is critical... and pay attention to the other person's problems before offering your solution.

- **When?** Get to the point quickly. Once you determine that you have what the customer needs, resist the urge to launch into a lengthy lecture about what you have to offer. Pick one or two of the customer's most important needs and briefly demonstrate how you can help. Customers buy on their schedule, not yours. Contact them frequently (without getting annoying) so they learn to think of you when they have a problem you can help them solve.

- **How?** Solve customers' problems. Address their needs, large and small, and show how you can help them. And here's some advice that some might consider heresy: If you can't help them, refer them to someone who can. There will be times your product or service isn't the best fit, and your customers will appreciate your willingness to put their needs first.

Don't forget to measure your results. Keep track of successes and failures. Analyze what helped you succeed and where you may have slipped up. Identify some best practices that have led to success, and incorporate them into every customer interaction. Keeping score of your record can help you stay motivated and productive during dry spells, and reinvigorate you when you're doing well.

MACKAY'S MORAL

Selling isn't rocket science—it's people science.

20

SELF-
IMPROVEMENT

WHO DO YOU WANT TO BE WHEN YOU GROW UP?

I've always been fascinated by the Japanese carp, otherwise known as the koi. It's a fish with seemingly unlimited growth potential. If you put the koi in a small fish bowl, it will only grow to be two or three inches long. In a larger tank or a small pond, it will reach six to ten inches. A bigger pond, and it gets to be a foot and a half. But if the koi is placed in a large lake, where it can really stretch out, it can grow up to three feet long. The size of the fish is proportional to the size of its home.

Well, it works that way with people too. We grow according to the size of our world. Not physically, of course, but mentally. You too can be a mental giant!

They say you learn something new every day. I would take that statement one step further and say that you *need* to learn something new every day.

Waiting for someone to teach you a lesson (translation: the hard way) is a poor way to get an education. You have to make the effort to learn and grow so that you are worth more to your employer, coworkers, friends, and family. Your potential is unlimited.

The beautiful part is that you can grow as much as you want. Your mind has plenty of room to hold information. In fact, I recently read that we typically use only 10 percent of our brains. Would you be satisfied to get that little service out of any other part of your body?

My guess is that most folks fall into some comfortable habits and are content with the status quo. When anything has been done the same way over a long period of time, sometimes it's a good sign it's been done the wrong way. Now don't go changing things just for the sake of change. Try something new because the result could be better.

Is it up to your supervisor to prepare you for a promotion? Maybe a little, but the real responsibility belongs much closer to home. You have to let your boss know that you're always ready for a new challenge and will do whatever it takes to prepare. You want to be qualified before the next job opens up, not disappointed after. You want to be interesting at the office and after hours. Your coworkers and friends can only hear the same stories so many times.

I'm a big proponent of lifelong learning. You don't go to school once for a lifetime; you are in school all of your life. That's why they call graduation "commencement"—it's just the beginning.

I'm a big proponent of lifelong learning. You don't go to school once for a lifetime; you are in school all of your life.

There are growth opportunities everywhere for both work and leisure. Take a class. Get a library card—and use it. Learn to play a musical instrument. Study a foreign language. Visit an art museum. Sign up with a Toastmasters group. Drive home a different way. Taste a new food. Surf the net on a topic you've wanted to know more about. Coach a team. Read a different section of the newspapers or websites where you normally get your information. Volunteer for a job that nobody else wants. Cut your apple in half horizontally instead of vertically and look for the star in the middle.

Grow. Stretch. Transform yourself. A simple bar of iron is worth about $5. Made into horseshoes, the value rises to about $50. Transform it into needles, and now you're talking $500. But if you take that bar of iron and make it into springs for a Swiss watch, it could be worth a half million bucks. You started with the same raw material; the value grew as the material was formed and developed. It's the same with people.

My friend Zig Ziglar challenged his audiences: "Go as far as you can see and when you get there, you will always be able to see farther." Christopher Columbus took his advice and didn't even know it!

We live in the information age, the space age, the new millennium. Technology has given us access to facts and figures and people and places at the touch of a button. We have every opportunity to learn and grow at any hour of the day. Today is the right time to start expanding your mind.

MACKAY'S MORAL

The biggest room in the world is the room for improvement.

NEVER LEAVE WELL ENOUGH ALONE

A baseball manager made an announcement to his team at the hotel on the morning of the game that there would be two buses leaving for the ballpark. "The 2 p.m. bus will be for those players who need extra work, and the *empty* bus will be leaving at 5 p.m."

We all need extra work if we want to improve.

Everyone is fascinated with big plays—a "Hail Mary" pass in football, a grand slam in baseball, a hat trick in hockey. However, quite often it's the smaller plays, like a base hit, negotiating a new labor contract, or finding a way to improve a manufacturing process, that consistently achieve success. This kind of improvement isn't as dramatic, but it's the kind that everyone can work on.

Continuous improvement is one of the four basic concepts of Total Quality Management. (The others are a focus on processes, measurement, and empowerment of people.)

Quality is about creating a corporate culture that strives for continuous improvement—about operating the organization in a more efficient way.

There's no magic to it. It happens incrementally. There's no formula for instant improvement. Human beings are not like a package of mashed potatoes. You can't add water and achieve a reformed human being.

Marshall Field, the famed Chicago department store merchant, offered his employees 12 reminders to bring happiness and success in life—both in their personal lives and at work. Guess what was on the list: Improve your talents.

Maybe you can depend on your company for further training. Perhaps you're better at self-directed learning. Whichever path you follow, the main message is to keep contributing. If you don't get the raises or promotions you feel you deserve, it's no excuse for slacking off on contributions to your work.

In fact, a setback like that may be just the push you need to show what you have to offer.

After years of service, a veteran employee met with his manager for his annual review. "I appreciate the good work you've done, but I can't promote you," she said. "You've probably reached a point in your career where you'll likely only receive cost-of-living raises until you retire."

After the employee picked himself up off the floor, he decided not to give up but to continue to do a good job and focus on a few of his promising ideas. For example, he had an idea for simplifying the company's order process. He sold the idea to management and saved the company a ton of money.

The experience energized him, but the icing on the cake came when his manager called him into her office and said, "Remember what I said about not being able to give you a raise? I was wrong." She then handed him a paycheck reflecting a nice increase.

None of this would have happened if the employee had chosen to drown in self-pity rather than try to improve.

Abraham Lincoln is another who went through some self-doubt but pulled himself up by continuous improvement. His early career was without much distinction, but from his teenage years onward, Lincoln was keen to advance, pursuing a rigorous program of reading, study, and self-improvement. We all know what President Lincoln achieved. His law partner, William Herndon, later said that Lincoln's ambition was "a little engine that knew no rest."

The American Society for Quality Control has published a booklet called "The Hare and the Tortoise Revisited: The Businessman's Guide to Continuous Quality Improvement."

One story in it tells about a Japanese quality expert who stresses the need for patience and discipline. He likens the quality process to farming bamboo. Once the bamboo seed is planted, the farmer waters it every day. He does that for four years before the tree even breaks ground. But when it finally does, it grows 60 feet in the next 90 days.

It's that kind of commitment to the long view that marks the companies that have been most successful in achieving outstanding quality.

MACKAY'S MORAL

Good, better, best; never rest till good be better, and better, best.

STRENGTHEN YOUR MEMORY

"Do you know what today is?" a wife asked her husband one morning.

"Of course I know what today is," grumped the husband. "I can't believe you would think I would forget such an important day." And with that the husband rushed to his car to conceal his panic and embarrassment. Had he forgotten their wedding anniversary again?

That evening the husband returned home bearing a dozen roses and a beautiful dress from his wife's favorite boutique. "This should win me some points," he thought to himself.

His wife could barely contain her excitement. "My goodness!" she exclaimed. "A dress AND flowers. What a wonderful surprise. But tell the truth, do you know what day this is?"

"Of course," said the husband confidently.

His wife said, "Today is Arbor Day!"

Will he forget Arbor Day ever again? Probably not. But he will have a tough act to top for his anniversary!

Most people who claim they have a poor memory actually have an untrained memory. Twenty percent remember by hearing, so say things out loud. Forty percent remember by seeing, and the other 40 percent by doing, so write things down to prove to yourself that you know it.

But this isn't anything new. Confucius said 2,500 years ago: "What I hear, I forget. What I see, I remember. What I do, I understand."

Pale ink is better than the most retentive memory. In other words, write it down. Brain clutter and interruptions can detour the best intentions to remember.

Pale ink is better than the most retentive memory. In other words, write it down. Brain clutter and interruptions can detour the best intentions to remember.

Ever had a great idea that you forgot almost right away? Most of us have, and it can happen more frequently as we grow older. It's often said you can't teach an old dog new tricks, but just about any healthy person can improve his or her memory.

Take, for example, Scott Hagwood, who follows a regimen to improve his memory similar to those athletes use to train their bodies. Hagwood suffered from thyroid cancer, and one of the side-effects of his radiation treatments was memory loss. Hagwood, who most would consider an average college student, entered a contest called the U.S.A. Memoriad—a sort of memory Olympics. Contestants memorize poetry, decks of cards, lists of numbers, words, and so on. Hagwood won.

You can improve your memory and keep it strong at any age by following a few basic tips:

- **Get plenty of rest.** Lack of sleep can diminish your brain's ability to solve problems, think creatively, and form memories. A good night's sleep is essential.

- **Exercise.** Physical activity increases the flow of oxygen to your brain and keeps you healthy in other ways. You become more alert and relaxed, thereby improving your memory. Relaxation techniques can be helpful to improving memory.

- **Socialize.** Stay in touch with friends. Good relationships are important to emotional health and mental processes because they provide stimulation and laughter. Volunteer, join a club, or get a pet.

- **Reduce stress.** You may not be able to eliminate all unpleasant situations and activities from your life, but do your best to manage your reaction to them.

- **Eat the right food.** A nutritious diet can help you stay in shape mentally as well as physically. Research shows that foods with Omega-3 fatty acids may lower your risk of Alzheimer's disease, and fruits and vegetables supply antioxidants that are good for your brain.

- **Organize your thoughts.** Learning new material or retaining facts works best when you group related information until you have mastered it, and then move on to other concepts.

- **Spend extra time for really difficult material.** Learning the names of a couple new coworkers is a breeze—but when you need to identify every member of your new department, allow yourself a little more leeway. Study lists so the names themselves become familiar.

- **Keep your brain active.** Spend more time reading and doing crosswords or Sudoku puzzles than watching TV. A good mental workout will keep your mind in shape to process and remember important information.

- **Minimize distractions.** Pay attention. Distractions can make you quickly forget even simple items. The ability to concentrate and focus can't be understated. If you're easily distracted, pick a quiet place where you won't be interrupted.

MACKAY'S MORAL

Exercise your brain so your memory doesn't get flabby.

EXPERIENCE IS THE NAME
PEOPLE GIVE TO THEIR MISTAKES

I received an interesting letter from one of my cronies:

"I have to share with you my favorite story about my six-year-old grandson, Matthew. When he was starting first grade, we were discussing the reason he got in trouble at school.

"He replied, 'I was disrespectful to my teacher.'

"I asked if it was wrong and he said, 'Yes, I shouldn't have done it.'

"I said that we all make mistakes, and it's okay to make mistakes if we learn from the mistakes. People who learn from their mistakes are smart, and those that don't are stupid.

"Matthew thought for a while and then said, 'I've got to make a lot of mistakes, so I can get really smart.'"

That's pretty observant for a first-grader. He's already willing to make mistakes to learn from them.

Of course, an equally important point is that you can't make the same mistake three times … or you're out. Like Yogi Berra said when explaining a poor season, "We made too many wrong mistakes."

Managers shouldn't hesitate to talk openly with their employees and to reward a job well done. But what about dealing with the mistakes people make? The person who made a mistake isn't the only one who can learn from that experience.

Here are some tips to help turn mistakes into lessons from which everyone can learn:

Ask whether anyone else can learn from a mistake an employee made. The mistake no one hears about can be repeated by others if not addressed. Before a pattern develops, assess the cause.

Dale Carnegie, the great American writer and speaker, referenced mistakes in two of his 10 ways to be a leader: "Talk about your own mistakes before criticizing the other person," and "Call attention to people's mistakes indirectly."

Attack the problem, not the person or people involved. There is no gain in embarrassing an employee by broadcasting an individual's foibles. The lesson is what's important, whether it's how to avoid the same mistake or what changes might occur because of it. Further, you run the risk of creating a hostile work environment if employees fear for their jobs if they make an unintentional error.

Let people know that risk taking means making mistakes. This is fundamental thinking for successful companies. And it allows managers to more easily bring attention to a mistake for the purpose of improvement and progress.

Thomas Watson, the founder and first president of IBM, was quoted in *Reader's Digest* as saying: "Double your rate of failure.... Failure is a teacher—a harsh one, perhaps, but the best.... That's what I have to do when an idea backfires or a sales program fails. You've got to put failure to work for you ... you can be discouraged by failure or you can learn from it. So go ahead and make mistakes. Make all you can. Because that's where you will find success. On the far side of failure."

I've always said if you want to triple your success ratio, you have to triple your failure rate!

Start the process using yourself as an example. Start your regular meetings by talking about a mistake you've made in the past couple of weeks and what you learned from it. Sometimes I go back even further—these young tigers don't have to learn everything the hard way! When the boss can 'fess up to a blunder or two, and still be the boss, employees learn not to fear failure. They learn from it and move on.

Finally, remember that some amazing discoveries were made by mistake. Christopher Columbus opened up a whole new world based on a mistaken navigation plan. Marie Curie had a bad idea that turned out to be radium. Vulcanized rubber (think tires) was an accidental discovery at Goodyear. So maybe what's important is not just learning from your mistakes—it's capitalizing on them too.

MACKAY'S MORAL

There are really no mistakes in life ... there are only lessons.

21

SUCCESS

The Seven Cs of Success

Success is a journey, not a destination, or so it's been said. You may take a few detours, hit some roadblocks, and arrive at a different place than you'd planned. I'm still on my journey, and I'm offering you my map for smooth sailing, traveling the Seven Cs of success.

Clarity

Eighty percent of success comes from being clear about who you are, what you believe in, and what you want. But you must remain committed to what you want and make sure those around you understand what you're hoping to accomplish.

A young mathematician during wartime was commissioned as captain of a submarine. Eager to impress his crew and to stress how important it was to strictly observe all safety procedures, the young captain called them all together for a meeting. His instructions went like this:

"I have developed a simple method that you would all do well to learn. Every day, count the number of times the submarine has dived since you boarded. Add to this the number of times it has surfaced. If the sum you arrive at is not an even number—don't open the hatches."

Competence

You can't climb to the next rung on the ladder until you are excellent at what you do now. Practice makes perfect ... not true. Perfect practice makes perfect.

Just remember two things: (1) the person who knows "how" will always have a job, and (2) the person who knows "why" will always be the boss.

Constraints

Eighty percent of all obstacles to success come from within. Find out what is constraining in you or your company and deal with it.

The Gallup Organization conducted a survey on why quality is difficult to achieve. The greatest percentage listed financial constraints. Often our lives and careers are shaped by the kind of surroundings we place ourselves in and the challenges we give ourselves.

Consider, for example, the farmer who won a blue ribbon at the county fair. His prize entry? A huge radish the exact shape and size of a quart milk bottle. Asked how he got the radish to look just like a quart milk bottle, the farmer replied: "It was easy, I got the seed growing and then put it into the milk bottle. It had nowhere else to go."

CONCENTRATION

The ability to focus on one thing single-mindedly and see it through until it's done is critical to success.

Great athletes are notorious for their concentration and focus. Golf great Ben Hogan stood over a crucial putt. Suddenly a loud train whistle blared in the distance. After he had sunk the putt, someone asked Hogan if the train whistle had bothered him.

"What whistle?" Hogan replied.

And let's not forget Yogi Berra, who said, "You can't think and hit the ball at the same time."

CREATIVITY

Be open to ideas from many sources. Surround yourself with creative people. Creativity needs to be exercised like a muscle: If you don't use it you'll lose it.

Statistics indicate that between the ages 5 and 17, there is an extreme drop in the creative level in both male and female students. In fact, as you grow older, your creativity level decreases proportionally. The good news here is that this trend is reversible, if you keep challenging yourself. Ask Grandma Moses, who didn't start painting until age 80 and went on to produce more than 1,500 works of art.

COURAGE

Most in demand and least in supply, courage is the willingness to do the things you know are right.

At times we can all be like the lion in *The Wizard of Oz*, running a little low on courage. Courage, contrary to popular belief, is not the absence of fear. Courage is the heart to act in spite of fear. Deep down, the cowardly lion had it. You do, too. Don't be afraid to use it.

CONTINUOUS LEARNING

Set aside some time every day, every week, and every month to improve yourself. Read trade publications or books, or listen to podcasts during your commute to and from work to keep you miles ahead of the competition. Go back to school and take additional classes or join groups or organizations, take lessons … whatever it may be, just never stop learning.

MACKAY'S MORAL

Learn to navigate the seven Cs if you want smooth sailing to success.

SUCCESS IS THE DIFFERENCE BETWEEN WORKING HARD AND HARDLY WORKING

Long ago the people of a very successful civilization thought they had all the answers to success. The king called the wisest people in the kingdom together and said, "I want you to put down all the reasons why we are successful. Place them in writing so future generations will be able to read it and duplicate our success."

They worked for approximately two years and came back with the answer, and it consisted of nine volumes.

The ruler looked at it and said, "This is impressive, but it's too large." He then challenged them to simplify their findings. They worked another year and narrowed it down to one book. The king said, "This is better, but it is still too lengthy. Refine it."

They worked another year, and finally reported back with their results, now contained on one page. The king said, "You have done a great job, but it is still too long. Please reduce our formula for success to the lowest common denominator."

They worked another year and pared it down to one paragraph. The king said, "That's an improvement, but it is still far too complicated. Keep working until everyone understands why we are so successful."

Six months later they came back with their formula confined to one sentence. The king looked at it and said it was perfect. If all future generations understood this, they would be in a position to conquer anything.

The sentence read, "There ain't no free lunch."

No one can take anything for granted. You must continue to work at everything you do to get better, to grow, and to maximize your skills and potential. Do not, however, confuse growth with making your work more complicated.

No one can take anything for granted. You must continue to work at everything you do to get better, to grow, and to maximize your skills and potential.

Stanley Marcus was a giant in retailing, having built the famous Neiman-Marcus chain. He was a good friend whom I admired and respected greatly. He has always had a remarkable ability to inspire growth in his employees.

One of his favorite stories follows:

"I once visited the bridge of a naval vessel where the brass gleamed like gold. I asked the captain how often they had to shine the brass.

"'Every day,' he told me. 'The minute you stop polishing it, it starts to tarnish.'

"This incident," said Marcus, "can be correlated to people. None of us is made of gold; we're all made of brass, but we can look like gold if we work hard at polishing ourselves as the sailor polishes the brass on his ship. We can be better than we are if we will make the effort.

"That may sound trite," said Marcus, "but it must have made an impression on many people, because almost every week some member of our staff comes up to me and says, 'I'm sure polishing my brass today.'"

I would submit that any employee who is willing to work to improve his or her skills is worth his or her weight in gold. The best merchandise in the world wouldn't sell at Neiman-Marcus were it not for the people who work there. The fastest ship in the Navy is in dry dock without a hard-working crew. The most sophisticated computers in the world can only do so much without human programming. It's the effort expended that makes a company successful.

I've heard it said that there are four main bones in every organization:

- **The wish-bones.** Wishing someone else would do something.
- **The jaw-bones.** Doing all the talking but very little else.
- **The knuckle-bones.** Those who knock everything.
- **The back-bones.** Those who carry the brunt of the load and do most of the work.

Thomas Edison was definitely in the back-bone category. The story goes that one evening the famous inventor came home from a long day at work, and his wife said to him, "You've worked long enough without a rest. You must go on a vacation."

"But where on earth would I go?" asked Edison.

"Just decide where you would rather be than anywhere else on earth," suggested his wife.

"Very well," said Edison, "I'll go tomorrow."

The next morning he was back at work in his laboratory.

MACKAY'S MORAL

There are many formulas for success, but none of them work unless you do.

MAKE LIKE A PENCIL
AND GET THE LEAD OUT

A young boy asked his mother what he should do in order to be a success when he grew up. The mother thought for a moment, and then told her son to bring her a pencil. Puzzled, the boy found a pencil and gave it to her.

"If you want to do good," she said, "you have to be just like this pencil."

"What does that mean?" her son asked.

"First," she said, "you'll be able to do a lot of things, but not on your own. You have to allow yourself to be held in someone's hand.

"Second, you'll have to go through a painful sharpening from time to time, but you'll need it to become a better pencil.

"Third, you'll be able to correct any mistakes you might make.

"Fourth, no matter what you look like on the outside, the most important part will always be what's inside.

"And fifth," the mother finished, "you have to press hard in order to make a mark."

Great advice. His mother touched on five important topics: teamwork, being able to accept criticism, correcting mistakes, self-confidence, and working hard. Let's take them one at a time.

Teamwork. As I like to say, even Batman had Robin. You can't do it all alone. My definition of teamwork is a collection of diverse individuals who respect each other and are committed to each other's successes. Teamwork sometimes requires people to play roles that aren't as glamorous as they'd like.

For example, I once asked a symphony conductor which instrument is the most difficult to play. Without missing a beat, the conductor replied: "Second fiddle. I can get plenty of first violinists. But finding someone who can play second fiddle with enthusiasm is a real problem. When we have no second violin, we have no harmony." And you just can't be successful without harmony or teamwork.

Criticism. Giving and taking criticism is no easy task, but it is necessary if you want to become better. If you ignore the problem and hope it goes away, you are not going to improve. Every office I've ever worked in or done business with has been made better because of suggestions or criticisms of the people who spend their working hours there. No one ever choked to death swallowing his or her own pride! Admit you aren't perfect. Remember that the goal of honest criticism is to make you better than you were before.

Mistakes. Everyone makes mistakes. What's important is that you learn from them. President Ronald Reagan said: "What should happen when you make a mistake is this: You take your knocks, you learn your lessons, and then you move on."

The greatest mistake a person can make is to be afraid to make one. In fact, you often need to increase your failures to become more successful. Mistakes don't make you a failure. How you respond to a mistake determines just how smart you really are.

It's important to remember that the person who made a mistake isn't the only one who can learn from that experience. Talk about mistakes, so they are not repeated by others.

Self-confidence. When I'm interviewing potential employees, one of the traits that I look for is confidence. Confidence doesn't come naturally to most people. Even the most successful people have struggled with it in their careers. The good news is that you can develop confidence, just like any muscle or character trait, if you're willing to work at it. My advice: track your success, practice being assertive, accept that failure is not the end of the world, step out of your comfort zone, set goals, keep improving your skills, and above all else, don't compare yourself to others.

Work hard. Success comes before work only in the dictionary. Many people look for a magic formula to turn things around, but there is no magic formula. Sure, natural talent can make a big difference. But show me a natural .300 hitter in the major leagues, and I'll show you someone who bangs the ball until his hands bleed trying to keep that hitting stroke honed. Ask any surgeon about how much sleep she got for the 8 to 10 years it took her to get through medical school, internship, and residency. It takes iron determination and lots of hard, hard work.

MACKAY'S MORAL

If you want to make your mark, sharpen your skills.

SAM WALTON'S RULES FOR SUCCESS

Sam Walton, the legendary founder of Walmart, had 10 rules for running a successful business. They are simple and straightforward, but guess what? I would bet the farm that a great many businesses don't follow them—and they'd be better off if they did.

Read these (my comments follow) and see how they might fit into your business plan. Take note that even in a tough economy, Walmart is prospering.

1. **Commit to your business. Believe in it more than anyone does.** Passion is at the top of the list of the skills you need to excel. When you have passion, you speak with conviction, act with authority, and present with zeal. If you don't have an intense, burning desire for what you are doing, there's no way you'll be able to work the long, hard hours it takes to become successful.

2. **Share profits with your employees. If you treat them as partners, they will treat you as a partner, and together you will perform beyond your wildest dreams.** Employees are the life-blood of any good company. Many companies seem to have fancy incentive programs for the big wheels, but smart companies have bonuses and profit-sharing all the way down the line.

3. **Motivate your partners. Money and ownership are not enough. Set high goals, encourage competition, and then keep score.** Competition makes you better and stronger. You should not only welcome stiff competition, but you should actively seek it. You'll never realize your full potential unless you're challenged. Similarly, if you don't set goals to determine where you're going, how will you know when you get there? You must stay focused on your goals above all else. Truly dedicated individuals won't let anything interfere with attaining their goals.

4. **Communicate everything you possibly can to your employees. The more they know, the more they will understand.** Information is power, but it must be used to empower your workforce. You will be amazed how a few snippets of information can transform a business into a powerhouse.

5. **Appreciate everything your associates do for the business.** In addition to point #2, find ways to let your employees know that you

value their contributions. Invite your customers to share their stories of great service and post them for all to see. Catch people doing a good job and let them know you notice. It keeps everyone motivated and does wonders for retention. Remember that your successes result from a group effort.

6. **Celebrate your successes. Find some humor in your failures. Don't take yourself so seriously.** Maintain a positive tone, even when things don't go as planned. Although a failure may not be funny at the time, there's always a lesson to be learned. Often, the lesson learned is humility.

7. **Listen to everyone in your company, and figure out ways to get them talking.** Many people think that communication means getting others to do what you want them to do. For them, good listening means, "I talk, *you* listen." These people have forgotten the basic truth about being a good listener: *Listening is a two-way process.* Yes, you need to be heard. You also need to hear the other person's ideas, questions, and objections. If you talk *at* people instead of *with* them, they're not buying in—they're caving in.

8. **Exceed your customers' expectations.** There's one thing no business has enough of: customers. Take care of the customers you have and they'll take care of you by coming back—and bringing their friends. On the flip side, disappoint customers, and they'll disappoint you— and then disappear.

9. **Control your expenses better than your competition does.** Walmart tries to help its customers follow this rule. If you aren't already watching pennies, start now.

10. **Swim upstream. If everyone else is doing it one way, there is a good chance you can find your niche by going in the opposite direction.** Following the crowd leaves you with very little room to maneuver.

MACKAY'S MORAL

If a business can survive and thrive in tough times, they must be playing by some smart rules.

BECOME "THE MOST LIKELY TO SUCCEED"

Were you voted "most likely to succeed" back in high school?

That moniker had mixed implications. A recent survey reported in the *Wall Street Journal* showed that about one-third of the respondents described the award as a "burden," creating pressure to live up to expectations. I suppose that could create some uncomfortable moments at the high school reunion.

But about 40 percent who received that designation found themselves more motivated to live up to the title. They are probably the folks you call "the boss."

And then there are the rest of us. We didn't necessarily have more brains, more talent, more money, or more opportunities. But we knew what we wanted and we had the desire to get there.

Success comes in many forms and means different things to different people. In the working world, it is often defined as landing the perfect job, achieving a targeted income level, occupying a corner office, or owning a business.

However you measure it, success is sweet. And it doesn't happen overnight.

Bumps in the road—and there will be plenty of bumps—can derail a successful career and lead down a path of negativity. Discouragement, disappointments, even occasional failures, are not the end of the road. Reroute your thinking. Zero in on your achievements. Take a success inventory. Focus on these five categories:

1. **Education.** List the classes you have completed, the degrees you have earned, professional certifications, and specialized training.

2. **Professional positions.** Include every major job you've ever had, and identify the responsibilities and authority you held. Don't forget those entry-level positions that probably taught you lessons you will never forget.

3. **Projects.** Start with the job-related projects that have been successful because of your contributions. Then move on to volunteer projects that worked with your involvement. You should also make note of community events, church activities, and hobbies that you are proud of.

4. **Accomplishments.** This category is for career achievements such as awards, promotions, significant praise from supervisors, letters of commendation, or recognition that represents your importance to your organization, community, family, or self.

5. **Potential.** What are you prepared to do with all that successful experience? Is throwing in the towel an option anymore?

Now make your list work for you. You did it before, and you can certainly do it again. Instead of being overwhelmed by failure, be inspired by success.

Rethink your strategy if necessary. Surround yourself with positive people who can provide the encouragement that will help you realize what is possible.

Re-evaluate your goals. Are they realistic, achievable, specific, and measurable? All those components are necessary if you want to measure your success. How else will you know you have succeeded?

Focus on improvement, not perfection. You can always do more, achieve more, get more. Track your progress so you can see how much closer you have come to reaching your goals and ultimate success.

Be proactive. Create your own opportunities by working on what you can control instead of what's beyond your reach. Before you know it, more will be within your reach.

Create your own opportunities by working on what you can control instead of what's beyond your reach. Before you know it, more will be within your reach.

Don't be afraid to fail. Put your ideas out there and give them a chance to succeed. Learn from your mistakes. The annals of business history are full of stories of how splendid successes resulted from colossal failures. Make history repeat itself!

A man walking down a narrow, twisting road spotted a guru sitting on the grass in meditation. He approached the guru and asked, "Excuse me, master, is this the road to success?"

The old man nodded silently and pointed in the direction the traveler was headed. The traveler thanked the guru and went on his way.

An hour later, the traveler returned, bleeding, exhausted, and angry.

"Why did you tell me that was the road to success?" he asked the guru. "I walked that way, and right away I fell into a ditch so deep it took me almost an hour to climb out. Why did you tell me to go that way? Was that some kind of joke?"

The guru stared at him. After a long pause, he started to speak. "That *is* the road to success. It lies just beyond the ditch."

MACKAY'S MORAL

It's never too late to be "Most likely to succeed."

FOR LONG-TERM SUCCESS, GIVE UP THESE DETRIMENTAL TRAITS

Success isn't always about dominating the landscape. Sometimes, to be successful, you have to be prepared to give up some counterproductive behaviors that are holding you back—and you may not even realize you're guilty.

Old habits are hard to break. And if you don't even realize that you are practicing some of these behaviors, you may not see a problem. But if others perceive you as a difficult coworker, it's time to take another look at what you are doing.

Be brutally honest with yourself or ask a trusted associate; see whether any of these traits describe you. If the answer is yes, an attitude adjustment may be in order:

- **The need to be right.** Concentrate on getting results, not on proving your own intelligence and accuracy. Be open about your mistakes. Don't worry about who gets the credit for victory. Help others succeed, and you'll share in the glory.

- **Speaking first.** You don't have to dominate every meeting and conversation. Ask for others' ideas and opinions. Give them the opportunity to share their thoughts, and they'll become more comfortable communicating with you.

- **Making every decision.** Ask others what they would do, and be willing to accept that there may be more than one way to accomplish a task. Don't insist that everyone do things your way.

- **Control.** You can't stay on top of every task and decision. Identify what you really need to handle, and delegate responsibility for tasks that others can do just as well. Accept that some things are beyond your control so you can concentrate on the influence you have.

- **Inflexibility.** If you find yourself balking at new ideas, or resisting change with "but we've always done it this way," it's time for an attitude adjustment. Different situations demand different solutions. And it's better to be part of the solution than part of the problem.

- **Disloyalty.** Bad-mouthing your company, coworkers, products, or services never improves any situation. Disagreement is not disloyalty. It's natural to have differences of opinion. But it is not professional to disparage another in an attempt to make yourself look better. Criticism must be constructive, not destructive.

- **Dishonesty.** Just tell the truth. Honor confidential conversations. If you prefer not to answer a question, say so, but don't lie or evade questions. Trust is the most important word in business, in my opinion.

- **Tunnel vision.** Projects that require cooperation among departments should not provoke competition, but teamwork. But if each department sees its contribution as the most important, rather than focusing on the big picture, the big picture will be way out of focus.

- **No sense of humor.** It's important to take your work seriously, but that doesn't mean you can't have fun at work. In fact, I'm a big fan of enjoying your job and making work enjoyable for those around you. As long as the language is appropriate, that is, not offensive, demeaning, or vulgar, a dose of humor can bring people together and make situations more comfortable.

- **Poor listening skills.** There is a difference between hearing and listening. Pay attention to what's being said, and ask questions if you are unclear about the message. Avoid interrupting, evading eye contact, rushing the speaker, and letting your attention wander. You can win more friends with your ears than with your mouth.

- **Disorganization.** A messy workspace does not demonstrate how busy you are. Clutter gets in the way of clear thinking. If you can't find what you need the moment you need it, you need to get organized.

- **Lack of accountability.** Blaming mistakes or poor results on others, refusing to take responsibility for obvious errors, making excuses instead of finding solutions—it can't always be someone else's fault.

- **Poor time management.** First things first. Setting priorities and meeting deadlines is fundamental to the success of an organization.

If one of the key players operates on a different schedule, the whole project suffers. Wasting time is wasting money.

- **Impulsiveness.** Learn to think before you speak or act. You can't un-say words, and apologies often ring hollow. Count to 10, count to 100, count to whatever it takes to prevent rash and regrettable actions.

- **Vulgarity.** Watch your language. Even as more and more four-letter words creep into everyday use, they have no place in a respectable business.

MACKAY'S MORAL

Clean up your act, or be prepared to clean out your desk.

22

TEAMWORK

Look for these traits
in successful team players

It was a cold winter. The hedgehogs, realizing the situation, decided to bunch together to keep warm. However, the quills from each hedgehog pierced their next-door neighbors, so they decided to move apart. But then they started to freeze and die alone, so they made the decision to cuddle back together and live with the little piercings caused by the close connection with their companions in order to receive the heat that came from the group. This allowed them to survive.

And that, my friends, is the perfect definition of teamwork.

No team is composed entirely of perfect people. Whether you're a superstar or a benchwarmer, you are an important member of the team.

Individuals working together as a group make a team successful. The success of any team—be it in sports or in business—is dependent on every person working toward a common goal. The role of every team member, no matter how seemingly insignificant, is valuable to the team's overall success. Success doesn't come from what you do occasionally; it comes from what you do consistently.

Andrew Carnegie, business magnate and philanthropist who led the expansion of the American steel industry in the late 19th century and often identified as one of the richest people ever, said: "Teamwork is the ability to work together toward a common vision, the ability to direct individual accomplishments toward organizational objectives. It is the fuel that allows common people to attain uncommon results."

Do you think he knew about hedgehogs?

Helen Keller said, "Alone, we can do so little; together we can do so much."

That's hedgehog talk if I've ever heard it!

I always get a kick out of when someone refers to someone else as a self-made man or woman. Let me tell you, there is no such thing. No one reaches his or her goals without the help of many others.

As Steve Jobs, the founder of Apple, said, "Great things in business are never done by one person. They are done by a team of people."

Michael Jordan said, "There is no 'i' in 'team' but there is in 'win'."

Whether you're forming a fully self-directed work team or leading a group that just needs to collaborate effectively, you must recruit the right people. Keep your eyes open for these abilities and traits:

- **Willingness to contribute.** Is the person ready to put the team's goals first? This doesn't mean ignoring personal needs, but it does mean that team members must put their primary energy into contributing to the team so they can share in its success.

- **Acceptance of roles.** People on a team have specific jobs, tasks, and roles. Although they should be willing to stretch themselves, they won't be effective or helpful if they insist on going outside the boundaries of what the team needs from them.

- **Eagerness to assist.** On a team, no one can back off and say, "That's not my job." Look for people with a track record of pitching in to help wherever they're needed as situations call for it.

- **Identification with the group.** Effective team members take pride from their association with the group. Find out what other teams, task forces, and committees a potential team member has worked on. How does he or she describe the experience?

- **Responsible attitude.** Everyone's eager to share credit. Is your team made up of people willing to accept responsibility for failure? Look for people who can be honest about their mistakes and willing to learn from experience.

Perhaps the best example of teamwork I've ever heard is one I share with my audiences whenever I give a speech. It's about mules, not hedgehogs, but the message is every bit as effective.

A salesman is driving on a two-lane country road in a rainstorm and gets stuck in a ditch. He asks a farmer for help. The farmer hitches up Elmo, his blind mule, to the salesman's car and hollers out, "Pull, Sam, pull!" Nothing happens. He then yells, "Pull, Bessie, pull." Still nothing. "Pull, Jackson, pull." Still nothing. Finally he hollers, "Pull, Elmo, pull." And Elmo rips the car right out of the ditch.

The driver is confused and says, "I don't understand. Why did you have to call out all those different names?"

"Look, if he didn't think he had any help, he wouldn't even try!"

MACKAY'S MORAL

For a winning team, recruit hedgehogs, not attention hogs.

WHEN WE FIND EACH OTHER, A MIRACLE BEGINS

Excitement gripped the world when two men became the first to climb Mt. Everest, the world's tallest peak. It was in May 1953 and the intrepid explorers were Edmund Hillary, a New Zealand beekeeper, and Tenzing Norgay, his Sherpa guide from Nepal. They reached the summit of the 29,000-foot peak together, and soon their names would be known around the world.

During their descent, Hillary slipped and started to fall. But Norgay immediately dug in his ice axe and braced the rope that held them together. Except for this quick action, Hillary most certainly would have fallen to his death.

At the bottom of the mountain, the news media was waiting and they soon learned of Hillary's near accident, and Norgay's lifesaving maneuver.

"Tell us all about it," the reporters shouted, focusing on the modest Sherpa guide.

Norgay looked at them with great calm. In a quiet voice, he replied simply: "Mountain climbers always help each other."

It's hard to think of a better description of teamwork and professionalism than this description of how the earth's highest mountain was scaled without any loss of life or injury.

That's why in sports the team with the most superstars usually doesn't win championships. The Boston Celtics won 13 NBA championships and never had the leading scorer in the league. They accomplished it with phenomenal teamwork.

The Chicago Bulls with Michael Jordan couldn't win as a team while Michael was racking up stratospheric stats. Then one day … shazam! … the coach and strategy changed and Michael started giving up the ball more and including his teammates. The rest is history … six NBA titles.

Remember when Lee Iacocca took over at Chrysler? He said, "People in engineering and manufacturing almost have to be sleeping together. These guys weren't even flirting." A few zillion minivans later, Chrysler clearly had mastered the teamwork concept.

When you have a team member who thinks he is indispensable, you should have him stick his finger in a bowl of water and notice the hole it leaves when he pulls his finger out.

No one is more important than the team. The key is how to build the team and make it more successful.

No one is more important than the team. The key is how to build the team and make it more successful.

I've had the unusual opportunity to travel around the world and speak weekly to a Fortune 1000 size company or association. In doing my homework on a speech client and talking to several people who would be in the audience, I always pick up a few tricks.

Bill Hoel, an executive with the hugely successful International Paper, based in Memphis, gave me one of the best examples I've ever heard of fostering teamwork.

At every Lead Team Meeting all the members must take a turn before the meeting and tell something about themselves. It can't be business. For example, someone might talk about a new granddaughter or that she just ran her first marathon.

Bill knows that in order to foster teamwork, you must first get to know each other better.

This reminds me of a teamwork tactic I've been using at MackayMitchell Envelope Company for 40-plus years. Before every sales meeting, all of our sales reps must tell a joke or a story.

This loosens everyone up and helps them to feel more a part of the team. It also makes for better presentations and a comfortable atmosphere.

Rick Pitino, in his bestselling book, *Success Is a Choice*, tells a great teamwork story about when he took over as coach of a down-in-the-dumps University of Kentucky basketball team. Kentucky has a rich basketball tradition, and they weren't used to losing.

During the first day of practice, Pitino sat all the players down and asked them how close they were with their teammates. They all said, "Oh, we're real close, coach." Then Pitino proceeded to ask each player about his teammates. Do you know what their fathers and mothers do? How about brothers and sisters? And not one person knew one thing.

MACKAY'S MORAL

You can't clap with only one hand.

WHEN "GO, TEAM, GO" BECOMES "STOP, TEAM, STOP"

When was the last time you were at a conference or seminar that didn't include at least one session on teambuilding? Did it include the old introduce-yourself-to-the-people-next-to-you-and-come-up-with-a-plan-to-save-the-imaginary-company? Or an elaborately staged cheerleading event? These are a couple exercises most companies have used to emphasize the fundamental importance of promoting teamwork within their corporate structure.

And while some of the activities designed to promote cooperation are downright hokey, the concept of being able to work with others is critical to the success of every business I know.

What's even more important is the ability to work with different groups of people—different teams for different projects.

Nothing kills teamwork faster than a bad attitude. Let me share some of the most common teamwork killers that I hear. It doesn't seem to matter what kind of business you're in, these themes are universal:

Nothing kills teamwork faster than a bad attitude.

I can't work with _____. It's time to put personality issues aside and stay professional. Sure, there are people you really don't care to be around, but don't let them bring out the worst in you.

It's my way or the highway. Someone has to be in charge, but never confuse leadership with knowing it all. Your way may lead to the highway sooner than you'd like if you keep up this attitude.

Why do I always get stuck babysitting the new people? I'd take that as a compliment! Someone in charge thinks you're a good mentor and has recognized your talent at bringing along the recent hires. The suits don't usually let underachievers interfere with the care and feeding of their rising stars.

I'm too busy. The old saying about asking a busy person if you want something done is true. If you truly can't devote adequate time to a project because of your other demands, speak to your supervisor about priorities. You've probably been assigned to the new project because you're a good fit, not because you're being punished. (If the latter is the case, dust off your resume, update your LinkedIn profile, and start looking for a new team pronto.)

This is a dumb project. Do you really know all the details of this project and how your work will fit in the big picture? A clearly defined goal should be the starting point of any project. If it's not, you don't have the information you need to accomplish your mission. If you do have that information, but can't see where you fit in, see the above note about dusting off your resume and updating your LinkedIn profile.

Are we just doing this to make the boss look good? Well, maybe you are, but your boss is probably holding your next promotion or next raise in his or her hands. That should be some incentive! Besides, the boss's boss knows that the boss didn't do the job all alone; don't blow your chance to shine.

Whose bright idea was this? Does it really matter? If it's a good idea, be thankful that you have the opportunity to develop it. If it's a bad idea, that fact will show up soon enough. Don't make the mistake of dismissing any idea solely because of the source. I'm a firm believer that everybody's got a few good ideas floating around in the gray matter.

Can't someone else do this? Sure they can, and maybe even better than you. Are you that eager to give them the opportunity? Give it your best shot and show that not only are you a team player, you're the "go-to" guy or gal.

I'll do it/You do it. Either way, the team concept is missing. Some projects can succeed with just one person on the job, but two heads are better than one. Don't shun help just to make things "easier." It usually backfires.

What happens if we fail? Who said you were going to fail? Starting out with a negative attitude is your first and worst mistake. From my experience, most people don't plan to fail, they fail to plan. Better you should plan to succeed and keep your goal clearly in the center of your plans.

There is an idiom in Japanese, "to eat from the same pot." In any business, everyone eats from the same pot regardless of the job title: president, factory worker, switchboard operator, legal counsel, payroll clerk. If the pot disappears, everyone goes hungry. But when the pot is full, the fruits of labor are shared by all.

MACKAY'S MORAL

If you want to "eat from the same pot," add to the stew.

NONE OF US IS AS GOOD AS ALL OF US

Teamwork might seem like a complicated subject, but to some creatures it comes naturally as a way to survive and to expend the least amount of energy.

According to a BBC News Online story, scientists taped heart monitors to great white pelicans. These birds had been trained to fly behind a light aircraft and a boat, and a team was able to observe them during their flight. Pelicans, it is known, fly in "squadron" formation, or in a "V," and they flap in time with their leader. Scientists, now able to observe and gather data from the heart monitors, found that the birds' heartbeats were lower when they flew in formation than when they flew solo. This was because they were able to benefit from each other's air streams. They were also able to glide more.

Working together, the birds were able to accomplish their migratory goals by expending less energy and being able to fly farther than when they are alone. It seems that there is a lesson here, and it's not for the birds. Animals of all types evolve certain behaviors because it helps them to migrate, feed, or survive more easily. The entire group benefits because less energy is required to perform the great task at hand.

In human terms, even the most seasoned pilots need a control tower and ground crew.

Lester C. Thurow, economist and dean of the Sloan School of Management, said:

"There is nothing antithetical in American history, culture, or traditions to teamwork. Teams were important in America's history—wagon trains conquered the West, men working together on the assembly line in American industry conquered the world, a successful national strategy and a lot of teamwork put an American on the moon first (and thus far, last).

"But American mythology extols only the individual—the Lone Ranger or Rambo. In America, halls of fame exist for almost every conceivable activity, but nowhere do Americans raise monuments in praise of teamwork."

Why is that? I can think of no single feat that was accomplished without a little help. From the greatest minds in the world to the most successful corporations, no one can honestly claim they did it all alone. It's often said it takes "a village to raise a child." I believe that village is also necessary to contribute to any level of success in adulthood as well. This world is simply too big a place to go it alone.

A story in the *Harvard Business Review* illustrates the importance of teamwork at every level. While many Westerners might think that consensus is characteristic of Japanese culture, institutionalized conflict is an integral part of Japanese management:

"At Honda, any employee, however junior, can call for a 'waigaya' session. The rules are that people lay their cards on the table and speak directly about problems.

"Nothing is out of bounds, from supervisory deficiencies on the factory floor to perceived lack of support for a design team.

"'Waigaya' legitimizes tension so that learning can take place."

That example emphasizes the importance of every member of the team and how a real team should function. Each member should be able to contribute strengths and ideas; otherwise the concept of team is meaningless.

Once upon a time there was an enterprising businessman who had a fantastic idea. He figured out a way to build the perfect automobile. He hired a team of young engineers and told them to buy one of every car model in the world and dismantle them.

He instructed them to pick out the best part from every car and to place it in a special room. Soon the room was filled with parts judged by the group to be the best engineered in the world—the best carburetor, the best set of brakes, the best steering wheel, the best transmission, and so on. It was an impressive collection—more than 5,000 parts in all. Then he had all the parts assembled into one automobile—the pick of the world so to speak.

There was only one problem. It didn't work! The automobile refused to function. The parts would not work together.

It's the same with people. A team of people or things with a common objective and harmony can be superior to a group of individual "all stars" any day.

MACKAY'S MORAL

TEAM: Together Everyone Accomplishes More.

23

TIME MANAGEMENT

HOW TO KEEP TIME ON YOUR SIDE

I had a project I had been trying to write for several days, but too many things kept getting in the way. One interruption after another. All of them important. All of them necessary. But few of them urgent. No one would leave me alone!

Remember the lessons our parents and teachers taught us—interrupting is rude. Somehow, that all changes in the workplace. But should it? Try to remember (if you can) the last time you got through a project from start to finish without being pulled in another direction.

My friend Alan Freitas of Priority Management in Boston says productivity's number-one enemy is interruptions. He's offered a few suggestions for dealing with them. I've added several of my own. Now my hope for you is that you can get through this uninterrupted.

- **Hang out a "Do Not Disturb" sign, and insist that others honor it.** Set aside a period of time each day—even if it's only 10 minutes—when you are unavailable for anything less than a four-alarm fire. That goes for office visitors, telephone calls, email, and carrier pigeons. Trust me, people will think your sign does not apply to them. If that doesn't work, try coming in to work early or staying late.

- **Just say no.** It's up to you to decide whether the task at hand is more important than the subject of the interruption (see the "four-alarm fire" reference above). Schedule time later in the day or week for the interrupter and address that issue—uninterrupted.

- **It's not about how many balls you can keep in the air at one time.** Superman fights one crime at a time, and finishes the job. Multi-tasking only works when a task is accomplished. We all have more than one project on our desks. The question is: how many of them will actually get done, on time, and satisfactorily?

- **Provide a regular meeting time during which key people can "bundle" interruptions into a single meeting.** This practice helps people plan ahead and anticipate many of the pesky details. Naturally, some issues will need to be revisited, but when the expectation is that you come prepared, no one wants to look foolish.

- **Be a great listener.** Do not interrupt while someone else is talking. Good communication is essential for understanding the issues at hand. This may well prevent unnecessary interruptions later. ("What was that you said earlier?" … and so on.)

- **Limit distractions, especially if you have a short attention span.** Do not decorate your office with "executive toys" or any other temptations that cause you to lose focus.

- **Take a break when you feel yourself zoning out.** Walk around. Get a drink of water. Clear your head for a few minutes. Set a limit on how long you'll be away from your desk, or you will become your own worst interruption.

- **Can it wait?** Encourage coworkers to consider whether an interruption is really warranted right at the moment. Amazingly, many of those disruptions can be put in email or voicemail to be acted on later, or saved for the scheduled meetings.

- **Be respectful of your coworkers' time.** If you expect them to honor your "Do Not Disturb" sessions, you must reciprocate.

Getting your staff on board may take some time and gentle reminders, but the results will be worth it. Even if everyone doesn't buy into the new program, you will still have far fewer distractions.

Now, let me tell you what I consider to be legitimate interruptions: *customers.* I am never, ever too busy or too absorbed in what I am doing to help a customer. If your business is customer-driven, you shouldn't be too busy either. Otherwise, you may never be busy again.

L.L. Bean and McDonald's, two superstars in the customer service arena, share some rules that have become guidelines for many successful companies. One of the cardinal rules reads: "A customer is not an interruption of our work; they are the purpose of it."

That's been the rule at MackayMitchell Envelope Company ever since we started looking for business more than 40 years ago. In fact, I have a sign in my office that reads, "Our meeting will not be interrupted ... unless a customer calls."

MACKAY'S MORAL

You must have a sense of what your time is worth for others to value it.

TAKE THE TIME
TO MANAGE YOUR TIME

Have you ever wondered where all your time goes?

You're not alone. People have been talking about time for centuries. Consider this excerpt from *The Book of Fate*, written by Voltaire in the 17th century:

"Of all the things in the world, which is the longest and shortest, the quickest and the slowest, the most divisible and the most extensive, the most disregarded and the most regretted, without which nothing can happen, which devours everything that is little, and gives life everything that is great?

"The answer is time. Nothing is longer, since it is the measure of eternity. Nothing is shorter, since it is lacking in all our plans. Nothing is slower for him who waits. Nothing is quicker for him who enjoys. It extends to the infinitely little. All men disregard it. All men regret the loss of it. Nothing happens without it. It makes forgotten everything unworthy of posterity, and it immortalizes the great things."

I have a saying that I've often used: "Killing time isn't murder; it's suicide." We all start out in life with one thing in common; we all have the same amount of time each day, each week, each month, and each year. Now it's just a matter of what we do with it.

I have a saying that I've often used: "Killing time isn't murder; it's suicide." We all start out in life with one thing in common; we all have the same amount of time each day, each week, each month, and each year. Now it's just a matter of what we do with it.

I've seen estimates that the average person spends seven years in the bathroom, six years eating, four years cleaning house, five years waiting in line, two years trying to return phone calls to people who aren't there, three years preparing meals, one year searching for misplaced items, and six months sitting at red traffic lights.

That's nearly 30 years and doesn't include a lot of what you might need or want to do. Prioritizing your time should be a top priority.

Getting more done doesn't always mean doing more things. Sometimes it's about doing less. Don't try to schedule every minute of every day. When you make and prioritize your to-do list, leave yourself some flexibility to handle interruptions and unplanned tasks that are bound to come up during the day. You should block out segments of your day for important tasks, but be sure to reserve enough time so that you don't have to rush through things. Taking your time can sometimes be the best use of your time.

Do you need to manage your time better at work? Who doesn't? One of the first things you have to take control of is your time. It always seems like there's not enough time to accomplish everything when you're working hard, but Bob Nelson in *1,001 Ways to Take Initiative at Work* says there are some steps you can take to rescue your time. Here is some of his advice:

- When you get to the end of your day, make a to-do list for tomorrow. Put whatever's most important to accomplish at the top of your list. That way, when you walk in, you'll know just what you need to do and where to start.

- Make a commitment to arrive at work a half hour early every day. Then you can get started on whatever's most important and work without interruption for that period of time.

- Don't jump down on your list to lower-priority tasks until you have made sufficient progress on your higher-priority tasks.

- Use a calendar and plan. It will organize you, and you won't have to spend time asking what you're supposed to be doing. You'll already know.

- Go through your in-box at least once a day and prioritize it.

- Say goodbye to unimportant meetings. If you don't need to be there, don't go. It will waste your time, and your list won't get any smaller.

- Focus on what only you can do. Then, when possible, delegate to others.

- Take a couple of hours every week to sit down and look at your big picture goals. Are you making progress? Set or reset goals appropriately.

- Learn to say no. Be polite, but firm. Otherwise, you won't have the focus or energy to attain your goals.

Benjamin Franklin famously said, "If we take care of the minutes, the years will take care of themselves." A minute doesn't seem like much, but the cumulative value of those minutes determines the quality of a lifetime. Don't waste another second!

MACKAY'S MORAL

If you want to have the time of your life, make the most of your minutes.

MAKE THE CALL
TO IMPROVE PHONE SKILLS

The world is getting smaller every day. Thanks to advances in technology, we can connect to points around the globe in seconds through our computer, phone, or other devices. Businesses can easily reach people and places that were inaccessible just a few years ago.

This is why I say the phone is one of the most awesome tools available. We've all had years and years of experience using a phone, so why are so many people bad at using it?

Here are some of the techniques that I use.

First, when your call is answered, always ask whether this is a good time to talk. This simple step can add years to your life—and your career.

Get the assistant's name if he or she answers the phone. I can get a lot of work done just working through assistants. And use their names. They are very important in getting your message across.

Obviously, you want to answer the phone on the second or third ring. Speak slowly and project so people can understand. When I switch to a speaker phone, I want to make sure the connection is still acceptable. Try not to interrupt. Don't get distracted when you are on the phone. Focus on the caller. Listen to what he or she has to say. Turn your phone ringer off on important calls when talking on your office line. Be sensitive to the tone of your voice. Don't eat or chew gum or type audibly on a keyboard.

When someone calls you on the telephone, you should always greet him pleasantly and tell them how happy you are to hear from him. That has to be evident in your voice. I ask our employees at MackayMitchell Envelope Company to answer the telephone with a smile because you can hear it in a voice. You want every customer to feel like she is your most important customer and virtually the only customer you have.

Try to start every phone conversation with good news, even when you have bad news to report. And also have a good close. Have an agenda of what you want to accomplish. Every crucial phone call should have clarity of focus and clarity of purpose. Think through what you want to say and discuss before you even make a call. That's how you build a network.

Start early in your career to keep track of the 100 to 300 most important people in your network. Find out their birthdays and call them every year on their special days. If you work in sales, make sure to call your customers on their birthdays. You won't believe how much business you will write up.

I was one of the first people to get a car phone, and now it is hands-free. Driving without communicating is every salesperson's biggest time-waster. I'll do anything to make the time more productive, so I even stopped making cold calls. I call ahead to make sure the buyer is in.

I never leave my name for a return phone call without a designated time I can be reached. Don't risk playing telephone tag. I don't care to squander my time any more than the other person cares to squander his or hers.

And this is especially crucial: If my assistant or gatekeeper answers the call, I make sure he or she says, "Mr. Mackay is expecting your call." This makes the caller feel special.

Can't get a call-back? Leave a message no one can ignore. I picked up this tip from my Florida realtor. Start with your name, day, date, and time, and then a pledge: "Leave your name and number, and I guarantee I will call you back within 24 hours. If I fail to do so, I will make a $100 contribution to your favorite charity—as long as the charity is not you."

Keep to a schedule whenever possible. Minimize interruptions by returning phone calls at a specific time of day. For me it's usually the end of the day. Of course, you will need to take some calls, but those that aren't urgent, you can return when you have time to best deal with them.

I'll let you make the call: How important are your phone skills to your career?

MACKAY'S MORAL

Don't let your phone skills be a hang-up.

24

TRUST

WHO PACKED YOUR PARACHUTE TODAY?

Charles Plumb was a fighter pilot in Vietnam. He flew 75 combat missions before his plane was destroyed by a surface-to-air missile. He survived by ejecting and parachuting behind enemy lines.

He was captured and spent six long years in a North Vietnamese prison. The most remarkable lesson he learned, though, may have been one he learned after he returned home.

Plumb was sitting in a restaurant one day when a man from a nearby table approached him and said, "You're Plumb! You flew jet fighters in Vietnam from the aircraft carrier Kitty Hawk. You were shot down!"

Plumb was stunned. "How in the world did you know that?"

"I packed your parachute," the man replied. "I guess it worked!"

"It sure did," Plumb responded. "If my chute hadn't worked, I wouldn't be here today."

That night Plumb couldn't sleep, thinking about the man who had likely saved his life. He wondered what the man might have looked like in his Navy uniform. He thought about how many times he might have ignored the sailor, because he, Plumb, was after all, a fighter pilot, and the other man, just a sailor.

Then Plumb's thoughts turned to the many hours the sailor had spent at a long wooden table in the bowels of the ship, carefully folding the silks of each parachute, holding in his hands the fates of pilots he didn't know.

Now, when Plumb lectures, he asks his audience, "Who is packing *your* parachute?"

Everyone has someone (or several someones) who provides what he or she needs to make it through the day, whether they realize it or not.

Plumb also points out that he needed many kinds of parachutes the day his plane was shot down over enemy territory: his physical parachute, his mental parachute, his emotional parachute, and his spiritual parachute. He needed all those supports to get through his long ordeal.

The parachute-packers of the world keep the rest of us from free-falling to certain failure. So I'll pose the question to you: Who is packing your parachute?

And you might want to consider a few more questions too. Who made that parachute? Was the fabric substantial, the stitches strong and even? Who taught you how to use that parachute? Was it a seasoned veteran who made sure that your first time wouldn't be your last time? There are very few second chances where parachutes are involved.

The military presents a perfect example of watching out for each other and working together. Extensive training, both physical and mental, ensures that all the members of a unit understand their roles and can perform under pressure. In life and death situations, it can be no other way.

In business, the pressures are less dramatic, but nonetheless important. So it's equally important to realize who is making your success possible.

Do you know who is watching out for you, at the next desk or at the daycare or on the freeway? More importantly, have you taken a minute to recognize the folks who go out of their way to make sure you make it? Whether or not you know their names, their conscientious attention to their work affects everyone they touch.

MACKAY'S MORAL

No matter what level you are at in your organization, learn how to pack parachutes.

WHOM DO YOU TRUST?

According to a recent study, Americans have fewer people to confide in today than they have had in the past two decades.

In fact, the study, conducted by Duke University and the University of Arizona, found the number of Americans who say they have no one with whom to discuss important matters has more than doubled.

"The evidence shows that Americans have fewer confidants and those ties are also more family-based than they used to be," said Lynn Smith-Lovin, professor of sociology at Duke University. "This change indicates something that's not good for our society. Ties with a close network of people create a safety net. These ties also lead to civic engagement and local political action."

The study was published in the *American Sociological Review*. The survey found:

- The mean number of people with whom Americans say they can discuss important matters dropped nearly one-third—from 2.94 people in 1985 to 2.08 people in 2004.

- The percentage of people who depend only on family members to discuss important matters increased from about 57 percent to 80 percent.

Many of the individuals I read about and admired while growing up—Dale Carnegie, Thomas Edison, and Henry Ford—always formed groups of five or six people to meet regularly to problem-solve, brainstorm, and motivate each other.

That's why shortly after I founded Mackay Envelope Company years ago, I set up an alliance with five other envelope manufacturers from around the country. We were all in the same business and yet not competing with each other because of our geographic locations.

We were similar in size, number of employees, and sales mix. Therefore, we could compare apples to apples … meaningful data. We just wanted to learn from each other.

We met at least once a year for 10 years and would communicate quarterly to exchange financial data, marketing ideas, creative selling examples, manufacturing cost systems, bonus plans, and salaries.

I received and implemented many great ideas.

I've always been a strong believer in having a "kitchen cabinet" of advisers for most of the areas in which I've been involved—business transactions, banking, public speaking, writing books, health care, and so on. You have to surround yourself with people in whom you can confide and brainstorm. And it must work both ways. You have to help them, as well.

I've always been a strong believer in having a "kitchen cabinet" of advisers for most of the areas in which I've been involved—business transactions, banking, public speaking, writing books, health care, and so on. You have to surround yourself with people in whom you can confide and brainstorm. And it must work both ways. You have to help them, as well.

As the years go by and the projects change, my trusted group of advisers changes, too.

New ideas and insights are always welcome, but I never forget the people who have been instrumental to my past successes.

This approach isn't so very different from how many companies operate, with a board of directors. Corporations large and small compete for the best and brightest minds to help the "inside" people—the president and other officers—make major decisions. A good board isn't necessarily made up of people who are in the same business. It has members with a variety of skills, experience, and interests to bring a broad view to the issues at hand.

That model may seem out of reach for small business owners, but it doesn't have to be elaborate to be successful. If you don't know where to begin, look first at your local business association, the Chamber of Commerce, Rotary, or a trade organization. Find the leaders in those groups and take them to lunch to pick their brains. Whom do they rely on for advice or to bounce around ideas?

You may not be in the same business, but you are all in business. Chances are, you have more in common than you think. Often the solutions for one business can be adapted to fit another. Then the rest is up to you. You can decide whether the advice will work for you, or perhaps you need to find a different solution.

As Malcolm Forbes said, "Listening to advice often accomplishes far more than heeding it."

Either way, it's a win-win. You have gained a confidant who isn't your direct competitor, and you have expanded your network.

Don't forget to return the favor when you are asked for help. And don't be offended if your confidant doesn't follow your advice; that's his or her prerogative. What is important in the end is the relationships that you build. As I always say, dig your well before you're thirsty.

MACKAY'S MORAL

Don't be afraid to ask for help unless you're afraid of succeeding.

25

VISION/
VISUALIZATION

VISUALIZATION HELPS YOU LIVE YOUR DREAMS

Our brain is divided into two halves: the right half of our brain learns facts and figures and the left half houses our creativity. We work hard to develop the right half of our brain in school, but sometimes the left half gets ignored.

One of the best ways to use your imagination is to visualize or fantasize. Long ago I came to realize that projecting myself in a successful situation is the most powerful means of attaining personal goals.

That's what a place-kicker does when he comes on the field to kick a winning field goal. Three seconds left in the game … 80,000 screaming fans … 30 million people watching on TV, and the game is in the balance. As the kicker begins his moves, he makes the final adjustments necessary to achieve the mental picture he's formed in his mind so many times—a picture of himself kicking the winning field goal.

The ability to project is a common trait among all great athletes. They have future vision. They see things a split second before they happen.

Jack Nicklaus, considered by many the greatest golfer of all time and a PGA Tour Hall-of-Famer, was asked about his tremendous success, especially in making crucial tournament-winning putts. He thought about it for a bit and said, "I never missed a putt in my mind."

Nicklaus is not considered to be the best at hitting his woods, long or short irons, or even chipping and putting. But everyone considers him the greatest thinking golfer of all time. There was no equal at the mental part of the game, which makes up 50 percent of golf.

Thomas Watson Sr. was 40 when he took over as general manager of a little firm that manufactured meat slicers, time clocks, and simple tabulators. He had a vision for a machine that could process and store information long before the computer was a commercial reality. To match his lofty vision, Watson renamed his company International Business Machines Corporation. Toward the end of his life, Watson was asked at what point he envisioned IBM becoming so successful. His reply was simply, "At the beginning."

Fred Smith's vision of an overnight, nationwide, air express delivery service was first unveiled in the early 1970s in a term paper for an economics class at Yale University. Unfortunately, his professor didn't share Smith's excitement and gave him a "C." Smith, however, took the idea and created an exceptional company known as Federal Express.

Success is no surprise to visionary people. They know what they want, determine a plan to achieve it, and expect positive results.

Success is no surprise to visionary people. They know what they want, determine a plan to achieve it, and expect positive results.

Billy Graham prayed, "God, let me do something, anything for you." Henry Royce was unwilling to accept anything but automobile perfection. Orville and Wilbur Wright were inspired at a children's birthday party when they saw a toy with a wound-up rubber band take to the air. Marie Curie held high her commitment to scientific excellence in spite of doubters and made important contributions until the day she died. Mohandas K. Gandhi and Martin Luther King Jr. held a dream of a better life for all people. Lee Iacocca preached, "I have one, and only one, ambition for Chrysler; to be the best. What else is there?"

These people were able to visualize, above and beyond the majority, a condition that was just right. They taught us that a vision begins with imagination, coupled with a belief that dreams can one day be realized.

A man by the name of Viktor Frankl owes his long life to his ability to project himself. He passed away at the age of 92. He was a renowned Viennese psychiatrist before the Nazis threw him into a concentration camp. I heard him speak a number of years ago, and he held the audience spellbound.

He said, "There's one reason why I'm here today. What kept me alive in a situation where others had given up hope and died was the dream that someday I'd be here telling you how I survived the concentration camps. I've never been here before. I've never seen any of you before. I've never given this speech before. But in my dreams I've stood before you in this room and said these words a thousand times."

MACKAY'S MORAL

People begin to become successful the minute they decide to be.

YOUR VISION SHAPES YOUR REALITY

A railroad crew was making repairs to a section of track when a train rolled up on a parallel track. Several men in suits disembarked from one of the passenger cars and began inspecting the work that was being done. A tall man in a blue suit looked over at the crew and nodded. He began to smile and walk toward them.

"Ted, is that you?" he asked of the crew's chief.

"Yes, it is," the chief replied as he shook hands with the visitor. "It's good to see you, Dale!"

The two men chatted briefly, inquiring about each other's health and families. Before they parted, they shook hands again and promised to keep in touch. When the man in the suit walked away, a member of the crew asked the chief, "Was that Dale Willis, the head of the railroad?"

"Yes, it was," the chief replied.

"It seems like you two are old friends," the man said.

"We are," the chief replied. "We started out together on this job on the same day 20 years ago."

"So how is it that you're here laying track with us?" someone asked.

"Well," the chief replied, "I had a vision of working for the railroad, while Dale had a vision of running the railroad."

And if Ted is content working for the railroad, his vision was realized. Dale's vision, on the other hand, set him on a path that he could accomplish only through a step-by-step plan to move ahead. This story from *Bits & Pieces* perfectly illustrates the importance of vision.

A study done by *Fortune* magazine examined 120 entrepreneurs over a three-year period. They were asked, "What do you need most to be a success?"

The study, headed by Robert Baum, an assistant professor of entrepreneurship at the University of Maryland's Robert H. Smith School of Business, pointed to the need to have vision in order to reach goals. Baum said that 60 percent of people he talks to have wanted to start their own businesses, but that most of what he hears is "I wanna, I wanna." The people who actually succeeded were the ones who had a vision and knew clearly where they wanted to go.

The American Marketing Association did a study several years back and asked 500 CEOs: What do you have to do to survive the next five years? Eighty-one percent said creativity and vision. But of the 500 CEOs, 81 percent of them said that their company is not doing a good job at it.

I suspect that part of the problem is that many companies don't know how to formulate a realistic vision. They confuse it with goals and objectives, which should come out of the corporate vision. Vision doesn't do the planning, and it doesn't anticipate the obstacles. It gives a real idea of what is possible, if only they want it bad enough.

Base your vision on principle. An effective vision isn't about processes or products, but principles—guidelines for action and behavior. Explore the values that guide the organization. Rely on principles that are timeless and easy to grasp, even if they're sometimes difficult to live up to.

A vision that inspires people to action doesn't come out of a single afternoon brainstorming session. Every member of your team needs to spend time asking questions about the organization, your industry, customers, competitors, trends—everything that affects the success of your vision. You have to build a foundation of learning before you can go forward.

Don't base your vision on where you are today, but on where you want to be in 5 years, or 10, or 25. Think about the direction you want to take and the obstacles you will have to overcome in order to succeed.

Don't base your vision on where you are today, but on where you want to be in 5 years, or 10, or 25. Think about the direction you want to take and the obstacles you will have to overcome in order to succeed.

When I speak to corporate America, I tell the story of Helen Keller, who was left blind and deaf at age 19 months from a childhood illness. Yet she became a brilliant author and lecturer who graduated cum laude from Radcliffe College. She was making a speech on a college campus, and during the question and answer session a mean-spirited questioner asked her the following: "Tell me Miss Keller, is losing your eyesight the worst thing in the world that can happen to anyone?"

"No," she said. "It's losing your vision." You see, eyesight is what we see in front of us. Vision is all the way down the road.

MACKAY'S MORAL

Vision without action is a daydream. Action without vision is a nightmare.

26

WATCH YOUR LANGUAGE

WE LEARN MORE BY LISTENING THAN BY TALKING

We spend 45 percent of our waking time listening, yet we forget 50 percent of what we hear.

Listening is a critical skill in everyone's life. Remember the old game of "telephone," where the first person in line whispers a message to the next person, and it gets passed down the line? This usually results in a completely different message or statement. Many of us played that game as children, sometimes with hilarious results. In real life, if you're not a good, careful listener, the results can be less than amusing—even damaging or life changing.

Hearing is one of the body's five senses, but listening is an art. Being a good listener can make or break a career. Your success could hinge on whether you have mastered the skill of listening.

Believe it or not, there's an International Listening Association website which offers some interesting facts:

- Eighty-five percent of our learning is derived from listening.
- Listeners are distracted, forgetful, and preoccupied 75 percent of the time.
- Most people only remember about 20 percent of what they hear over time. But I would advise here that trying to commit the important things to memory should be accompanied by some efficient note-taking.
- People listen at about 125 to 250 words per minute, but think at about 1,000 to 3,000 words per minute.
- There have been at least 35 business studies indicating listening is a top skill needed for success. Frankly, I think the experts can agree that another study will not produce any different results. Now it's time for teaching effective listening skills to those who don't already possess them.

Television and radio have enhanced the importance of listening. Instead of having the facts before you in print, as with newspapers and magazines, you need to be able to process what you are hearing. The same is true if using audio and video learning over the Internet instead of reading on it. In the business world, reports and memos take the place of the print media, while the spoken messages in meetings test your listening skills. It's no wonder that for people with poor listening skills, meetings are perceived as punishment rather than an opportunity for good give and take.

Bill Marriott, chairman and CEO of Marriott International, the world's largest hotel chain, described "the biggest lesson I have learned though the years."

"It is to listen to your people. I find that if you have senior managers who really gather their people around them, get their ideas, and listen to their input, you make a lot better decisions."

Marriott said he learned this lesson from a visit with President Dwight Eisenhower when Marriott was a young ensign in the Navy. He had been in the Navy for six months, and the President was a visitor at Marriott's home at Christmastime. It was extremely cold outside, but his father had put up targets outside for shooting and asked the President whether he wanted to go outside and shoot or stay inside by the fire.

"He just turned to me," said Marriott, "and said, 'What do you think, Ensign?'"

Marriott said he told the President it was too cold outside for shooting and to stay by the fire, which they did.

To this day, Marriott says, that lesson (asking someone else's opinion) has stayed with him and has been a big asset in his business.

Remember, most people won't listen to what you're saying unless they already feel that you have listened to them. People who feel like they're being listened to will feel accepted and appreciated rather than isolated and rejected. When we feel we are being listened to, it makes us feel like we are being taken seriously and that what we say really matters.

Remember, most people won't listen to what you're saying unless they already feel that you have listened to them. People who feel like they're being listened to will feel accepted and appreciated rather than isolated and rejected.

So if you want to be listened to, avoid these anti-listening gaffes:

- Interrupting
- Avoiding eye contact
- Rushing the speaker

- Letting your attention wander
- Rushing ahead and finishing the speaker's thoughts
- Not responding when appropriate
- Use of negating phrases such as "yes, but …"
- Trying to top the speaker's story
- Forgetting what the speaker has already told you

MACKAY'S MORAL

You can win more friends with your ears than with your mouth.

WASH YOUR MOUTH CLEAN OF THESE CAREER-KILLING PHRASES

How many of you remember your mom or dad washing your mouth out with soap when you said a bad word or got caught lying? I don't know whether it's still a common practice, but many people of my generation remember the awful taste this left in their mouths and dutifully passed this teaching opportunity to their children.

My dad always told me, "Think before you speak." Easier said than done. However, over the years you learn NOT to use certain words that you know will invite a negative reaction or worse.

Words matter. They can uplift or they can knock down. They can unite or divide. They can paint a masterpiece idea or rust an ironclad agreement. Use your words wisely.

You can be bright and cheerful on the inside, but your words and behavior can sabotage your best efforts. I have compiled a list of phrases that you should banish from your workplace vocabulary.

"It's impossible." Any variation of "I can't do that" will generally mark you as someone who doesn't want to work hard or take on a new challenge. Unless you're being asked to violate the laws of physics (or your state), make an honest effort to do what's asked of you.

"That's not my job." Teamwork is essential to any organization's success. Don't hide behind your job description to get out of assignments you don't want. Too many people take their job descriptions so literally, often ignoring the "and other duties as necessary." If you're too busy, or the task is outside your field of expertise, say so. If not, do your best to accommodate requests and follow instructions whether they're officially part of your job or not.

"I'll try." Too often this can be seen as an alibi. You'll make some effort, but you're not really committed to success. Replace "try" with "will" to motivate yourself—and to inspire other people's confidence in you. Learn from the wisdom of Yoda, the *Star Wars* Jedi master: "Do or do not. There is no try." They don't pay off on effort; they pay off on results.

"It's not fair." You don't want to get a reputation as a whiner. Complaining about every injustice or slight at work will alienate the people you want to get along with. Focus on doing your job to the best of your ability, whatever happens.

"Who comes up with this stuff?" Yes, we've all thought it. And there are times when it is a completely legitimate question. But I will guarantee you, the minute that sentiment is uttered aloud the boss who proposed the idea will appear around a corner and wonder who is unwilling to give it a go.

"That's bizarre/stupid/unreasonable." Don't be offensive and demean a coworker. This shows you are not a team player. Ask for details to see whether you have misunderstood what is being proposed. If you don't like the idea, explain why politely. It always helps to have a workable solution in your back pocket too.

"You should have ..." Avoid anything that sounds like you're searching for blame or scapegoats instead of solutions. Try to join forces instead. Ask what happened so you can figure out what to do next. And keep in mind, many great ideas have sprung up from mistakes on the first go-round. (We prefer to call that "research.")

"That's the way we've always done it." When anything's been done the same way over a long period of time, sometimes it's a good sign it's being done the wrong way. So what am I saying? Think big, think bold, think creative, think stretch, think quantum leaps. Always think becoming a differentiator, think vision, think speed, think customize, think focus, think flexible. Sometimes it's risky not to take a risk.

"This may be a dumb question, but ..." Don't diminish your point before you've even made it. What is really dumb is to proceed when you don't understand what you are supposed to do or what outcome you are seeking.

I have always thought that some of the best communication advice ever offered came from Thumper, the young bunny in the Disney movie *Bambi*: "If you can't say somethin' nice, don't say nothin' at all." It's so much easier to have said nothing than to have to try to walk back a thoughtless statement.

As President Calvin Coolidge said, "I have never been hurt by anything I didn't say."

MACKAY'S MORAL

Sticks and stones can break your bones, but words can come back to haunt you.

SPREAD THE WORD: DON'T GOSSIP

One day in ancient Greece an acquaintance met the great philosopher Socrates and said, "Socrates, do you know what I just heard about your friend?"

"Hold on a minute," Socrates replied. "Before telling me anything I'd like you to pass a little test. It's called the Triple Filter Test."

"Triple Filter?"

"That's right," Socrates continued. "Before you talk to me about my friend, it might be a good idea to take a moment and filter what you're going to say. The first filter is Truth. Have you made absolutely sure that what you are about to tell me is true?"

"No," the man said, "actually I just heard about it and…."

"All right," said Socrates. "So you don't really know if it's true or not. Now let's try the second filter, the filter of Goodness. Is what you are about to tell me about my friend something good?"

"No, on the contrary…."

"So," Socrates continued, "you want to tell me something bad about him, but you're not certain it's true. You may still pass the test though, because there's one filter left: the filter of Usefulness. Is what you want to tell me about my friend going to be useful to me?"

"No, not really."

"Well," concluded Socrates, "if what you want to tell me is neither true nor good nor even useful, why tell it to me at all?"

There would be no or little gossip if everyone followed Socrates' Triple Filter Test. But that is not the case. Gossip runs rampant.

It's no wonder legendary American humorist Erma Bombeck said: "Some say our national pastime is baseball. Not me. It's gossip."

Someone has calculated that, if a rumor was started at midday, and was repeated within two seconds by everyone who heard it to two other people, who repeated it and kept the cycle going, by about 6:30 p.m. the same day, everyone on earth would have heard it.

Of course, the Internet has brought gossiping up to warp speed. A rumor posted online can make it around the world in milliseconds. And although the post may seem anonymous and, therefore, "safe," the damage is potentially irreparable. Snopes, the urban legends reference site, can't debunk everything, after all.

Office gossip in particular is a major concern for a number of reasons. The Triple Filter Test could prevent plenty of misunderstandings and hard feelings in the workplace, where teamwork and cooperation are often central to productivity. How does someone work with another who insists on passing along information that may not be true, good, or useful?

Spreading rumors about coworkers can create a hostile environment that customers will pick up on. This is a good reason for avoiding gossip. Plus the fact that I've seen many deals go down due to gossip.

As advice columnist Dear Abby said, "It is almost impossible to throw dirt on someone without getting a little on yourself."

So clean up your act! The Triple Filter Test is simple to use. *Truth* alone is not enough reason to spread gossip. Who doesn't have an embarrassing truth that they want to remain private? And while *good news* may seem harmless enough, is it your news to share? But perhaps the most compelling reason to avoid gossip is the *usefulness* test. How will the information be used? I'm betting it won't be for positive reasons.

Maybe you've heard about the three ministers who went fishing. They were good friends, each of whom was a pastor at a different church in the same town. While they were fishing they began confessing their sins to each other.

The first pastor said, "Do you know what my big sin is? My big sin is drinking. I know it's wrong, but every Friday night I drive to a city where no one will recognize me, and I go to a saloon and get drunk. I know I shouldn't, but I can't help it. It's my big sin."

The second pastor said, "Well, to be honest with you, I've got a big sin, too. My big sin is gambling. As a matter of fact, you know all the money I raised for that mission trip to India? I took it to Las Vegas instead and lost it all. I'm so ashamed. My big sin is gambling."

Finally, it was the third pastor's turn. He said, "Guys, I probably should have gone first, because my big sin is gossiping."

MACKAY'S MORAL

A word can be more powerful than a sword.

27

FINAL THOUGHTS

THE OTHER SEVEN WONDERS OF THE WORLD

A group of students was asked to list what they thought were the present "Seven Wonders of the World." Though there were some disagreements, the following received the most votes:

1. Egypt's Great Pyramids
2. Taj Mahal
3. Grand Canyon
4. Panama Canal
5. Empire State Building
6. St. Peter's Basilica
7. China's Great Wall

While gathering the votes, the teacher noted that one student had not finished her assignment yet. So she asked the girl if she was having trouble with her list. The girl replied, "Yes, a little. I couldn't quite make up my mind because there are so many."

The teacher said, "Well, tell us what you have, and maybe we can help."

The girl hesitated, then read, "I think the 'Seven Wonders of the World' are:

1. To see
2. To hear
3. To touch
4. To taste
5. To feel
6. To laugh
7. And to love."

The room was so quiet you could have heard a pin drop. The things we overlook as simple and ordinary and that we take for granted are truly wondrous! A gentle reminder—that the most precious things in life cannot be built by hand or bought by man.

A reader sent me the above story. Wow! This is certainly something to think about.

We're so busy looking for the big picture that we sometimes miss the little pictures that make it up. It's true in all aspects of life, personal and professional. You can deal with the personal side; I'd like to explore the wonders of life at work.

If you look at what's important in your company, certainly a successful bottom line is right up there, but how do you get there? Can you be successful without a contented workforce? Products you believe in enough to use yourself? Sterling reputation? A real desire to be the best? These are the simple elements of any successful individual or company.

In other words, can you see your way to success? Can you feel it? Can you taste it? Can you smell it? Is it calling to you? Will you have some fun getting there, and will you love what you do?

In other words, can you see your way to success? Can you feel it? Can you taste it? Can you smell it? Is it calling to you? Will you have some fun getting there, and will you love what you do?

President Woodrow Wilson phrased it eloquently: "You are not here merely to make a living. You are here in order to enable the world to live more amply, with greater vision, with a finer spirit of hope and achievement. You are here to enrich the world, and you impoverish yourself if you forgot the errand."

Thomas Watson, Jr., former chairman of IBM, often told anecdotes about his father, Thomas Watson, Sr., founder of the company. One of them went like this: "Father was fond of saying that everybody, from time to time, should take a step back and watch himself go by."

I invite you to make a resolution to do just that. Then ask yourself some questions: Am I making things more complicated than they need to be? Am I getting a good look at everything that's going on around me? Am I using that information to improve my performance? Am I looking for big changes when little changes would make a bigger difference? Am I making more work for myself and others around me? Do I appreciate the simple gift that each day is?

The answers need not fly in the face of simplifying matters. Instead, they should help you see that, frequently, a simple solution will solve most problems. It's been said that making the simple complicated is commonplace, but to make the complicated simple requires creativity.

Like a great sculptor who chips away at a massive piece of marble to reveal its simple beauty, try to approach matters at work to get to the very core of the issue. It doesn't matter if you're talking about sales, manufacturing, marketing, management, or whatever. Keeping things simple will avoid a lot of complications down the road.

MACKAY'S MORAL

Simplicity is the eighth wonder of the world.

THE SECOND TEN COMMANDMENTS

We all know about the original Ten Commandments, but have you ever heard of "The Second Ten Commandments"? These pearls of wisdom, sent to me by a friend, have been often attributed to Elodie Armstrong. I have taken the liberty of putting my spin on them:

I. **Thou shall not worry, for worry is the most unproductive of all human activities.** You can't saw sawdust. A day of worry is more exhausting than a day of work. People get so busy worrying about yesterday or tomorrow, they forget about today. And today is what you have to work with.

II. **Thou shall not be fearful, for most of the things we fear never come to pass.** Every crisis we face is multiplied when we act out of fear. Fear is a self-fulfilling emotion. When we fear something, we empower it. If we refuse to concede to our fear, there is nothing to fear.

III. **Thou shall not cross bridges before you come to them, for no one yet has succeeded in accomplishing this.** Solve the issues before you right now. Tomorrow's problems may not even be problems when tomorrow comes!

IV. **Thou shall face each problem as it comes. You can only handle one at a time anyway.** In one of my favorite "Peanuts" comic strips, Linus says to Charlie Brown, "There's no problem too big we can't run away from it." I chuckle every time I think about it because it sounds like such a simple solution to a problem. Problem solving is not easy, so don't make it harder than it is.

V. **Thou shall not take problems to bed with you, for they make very poor bedfellows.** Just remember that all your problems seem much worse in the middle of the night. If I wake up thinking of a problem, I tell myself that it will seem lighter in the morning, and it always is.

VI. **Thou shall not borrow other people's problems. They can better care for them than you can.** I must confess that I have broken this commandment because I wanted to help someone out, without being asked, or I thought I was more equipped to handle a situation. But I wouldn't have to deal with the consequences, either.

VII. **Thou shall not try to relive yesterday. For good or ill, it is forever gone. Concentrate on what is happening in your life and be happy now!** We convince ourselves that life will be better after we get a better job, make more money, get married, have a baby, buy a bigger house, and so on. Yet the accomplishment of any of those events may not make any difference at all. The Declaration of Independence says we are endowed "with certain unalienable rights, which among these are life, liberty, and the pursuit of happiness." You are responsible for your own happiness.

VIII. **Thou shall be a good listener, for only when you listen do you hear ideas different from your own.** You can win more friends with your ears than with your mouth. Hearing is one of the body's five senses, but listening is an art. Your success could hinge on whether you have mastered the skill of listening. Most people won't listen to what you're saying unless they already feel that you have listened to them. When we feel we are being listened to, it makes us feel like we are being taken seriously and that what we say really matters.

IX. **Thou shall not become "bogged down" by frustration, for 90 percent of it is rooted in self-pity and will only interfere with positive action.** Seriously, has frustration ever improved a situation? Better to take a break, collect your thoughts, and redirect your attention to a positive first step. Then go on from there.

X. **Thou shall count thy blessings, never overlooking the small ones, for a lot of small blessings add up to a big one.** We all have something to be grateful for, even on the worst days. Hey, you're still on the green side of the grass, aren't you?

MACKAY'S MORAL

These may not be chiseled in stone, but try them—they'll make your life less rocky.

Things I've Learned in Life

There are three simple rules in life:

1. If you do not go after what you want, you'll never have it.
2. If you do not ask, the answer will always be no.
3. If you do not step forward, you'll always be in the same place.

I can't take credit for this; its source is anonymous. But it started me thinking about my own life and everything that I've learned over many decades in business.

The lessons I have learned could fill a set of encyclopedias. I would imagine anyone who has paid attention to the world around them could say the same. But there are several guiding principles that help me make decisions, plan strategy, and sleep at night.

For example, I know that you have to dig your well before you're thirsty. I believe it so completely that it became the title of my book on networking. This applies to both networking and planning. Here is the most important line in the book: "If I had to name the single characteristic shared by all the truly successful people I've met over a lifetime, I'd say it is the ability to create and nurture a network of contacts."

In the end, it's not the amount of money that you make or the buildings that you own that matter. It's the people on whom you can depend—and who can depend on you—that make your life better.

In the end, it's not the amount of money that you make or the buildings that you own that matter. It's the people on whom you can depend—and who can depend on you—that make your life better.

A close second for the top lesson of my life would be the following: "People don't care how much you know about them, once they realize how much you care about them." It's so important I made this the theme of my first book, *Swim with the Sharks Without Being Eaten Alive.* It's also central to my Mackay 66 Customer Profile, which is the cornerstone of all my speeches.

You have to learn as much about your customers and suppliers as you possibly can, because you can't talk about business all your life. You have to build those relationships and take it from a business level to a personal level. Knowing something about your customer is just as important as knowing everything about your product.

Many of my friends started out as customers. As our relationships grew, we discovered that we shared much in common. Our friendships are based on trust established in our business dealings. Trust is, after all, the most important word in business. And that extends to my personal life as well. You must be trustworthy to be a worthy friend.

Another key lesson: "Believe in yourself even when no one else does." I have never met a successful person that hasn't had to overcome either a little or a lot of adversity in his or her life. So who says that you can't accomplish your goals? Who says that you're not tougher and better and smarter and harder working and more able than your competition? It doesn't matter if they say you can't do it. The only thing that matters is if you say it.

Next, I've learned that we can't go it alone. The boat won't go if we all don't row. What is teamwork? It's a collection of diverse people who respect each other and are committed to each other's successes. The beautiful part of teamwork is that it offers us the opportunity to use our own special talents and abilities. We all have gifts to share.

The last thing I'll mention, and the way I finish all of my speeches, is to put some fun and creativity into your business and into your life. Don't be boring. Don't be predictable. You can take your work seriously, you can take your relationships seriously, but you should never take yourself too seriously.

The ability to laugh at yourself is one of the most endearing traits you can possess. Supremely confident people worry very little about being the coolest, smartest, most admired person in the room. They understand that by putting others first, they move to the front of the class. They have truly learned some of life's most important lessons.

In the end we only regret the chances we didn't take, the relationships we were afraid to have, and the decisions we waited too long to make. Learn from your mistakes. Be grateful for second chances and forgiving friends.

MACKAY'S MORAL

Make your life story a best-seller.

YOU GET WHAT YOU GIVE

Our country is seeing a volunteer need now the likes of which we have seen few times in our history. The response to the devastation after natural disasters is a testament to the desire we all possess to help out. We've seen this action before, but the need for help exists even when we are not in a time of crisis.

People who do volunteer work and help other people on a regular basis have a healthier outlook on life. They are more inclined to be go-getters and consistently report being happier. Young, old, professional, student, teacher—it doesn't matter. Volunteering is good for everyone.

I subscribe to the theory that 20 percent of your time should be devoted to volunteering. That sounds like a lot, until you find a cause that you can get passionate about. Then, there will never be enough time.

Think about what you can do besides donating cash. Don't get me wrong; I've never known an organization that didn't need money to keep the lights on. But there is a volunteer opportunity—and I use that phrase intentionally—to match the skills and commitment level of anyone who wants to give some time.

If you still think you are too busy to share some time, consider these points:

Volunteering is an opportunity to help. It's a chance to share your talents with people who need help. In my state, there is a need for people who can help immigrants learn to read. Can you imagine how hard it would be to navigate a new country without a working knowledge of the language—taking a driving test, filling out job applications, enrolling kids in school? In the bargain, you have the satisfaction of knowing that you contributed to their success, and you probably made a friend in the process. That's a win-win situation.

Volunteering is an opportunity to learn. Every organization has a job or two that no one really wants to do. Take on that chore! You will learn something new, to be sure. But even more important, you will discover that you can do all kinds of things you never thought you could. You'll begin to think bigger and see the possibilities in a whole new way. That will benefit both you and the organization.

Volunteering is an opportunity to crawl out of your shell. If you are afraid to join a club or are too timid to make a ripple at work, find a volunteer opportunity where you can contribute in a less threatening way. A gregarious personality is not a prerequisite, and can be detrimental in some situations. Organizations are begging for help; find out what you can do.

Volunteering is an opportunity to have some fun. Don't expect to be entertained, but at the same time, no one said volunteering had to be drudgery. After sitting in a windowless office all day, the prospect of helping weed the community garden can be mighty appealing. A change of pace is good; a change of pace that also does some good is a great combination.

Volunteering is an opportunity to sharpen your skills. One of my favorite examples here is accepting the fund-raising role. If you are selling the needs of a little-known non-profit to individuals and companies and organizations, you are honing sales skills that will be helpful, no matter what you do for a living.

Volunteering is an opportunity to clear your head. No matter where you decide to help out, you will find that there is a much larger world out there than your little corner. Volunteering provides a new perspective, and frequently takes you into a world you never really knew before. The change will do you good.

Volunteering is an opportunity to make a difference. I've hammered away at this theme forever: One person can make all the difference. Be that person.

Volunteering is a privilege. And you thought doing good deeds would make you look like a hero? Guess again. Non-profits don't need showboaters; they need worker bees. Approach volunteer work as a chance to be useful, and be grateful that someone thinks you are up to the task.

MACKAY'S MORAL

Life is like a game of tennis; the player who serves well seldom loses.

LIFELINES BEAT DEADLINES ANY DAY

When life feels a little off, it's a good thing to take time to re-evaluate our lives and the direction we're headed or have taken. Are you balancing out the different roles you have ... wage earner, spouse, parent, community member, and so on?

If you're like the average American, you devote 56 hours a week to work, including commuting; 70 hours to sleeping, eating, and other personal care; and 42 hours to leisure activities, of which 16 hours are spent socializing with friends and family.

WOW. That's not much personal time.

There are a lot of "supermoms" and "superdads" racing through the day. But balance isn't about speed. It's not a checklist. It's easy to leave kids or colleagues feeling slighted.

The good news is it's never too late to think about balance. And it's not always your choice. You and your family have to decide between unlimited personal success and a more evenly weighted life.

I choose balance, but it wasn't always that way. When I bought a distressed envelope company back in 1959, I blew a kiss to my wife, Carol Ann, and said, "I'll see you in five years." I figured it would take that amount of time to get the business where I wanted it. But I learned that the family moments are worth more than any time I lost at the office.

Here's a story that someone sent me that might help you think a little differently about balancing work and family:

A man came home from work late again, tired and irritated to find his five-year-old son waiting for him at the door. "Daddy, how much money do you make an hour?"

"That's none of your business. What makes you ask such a thing?" the man said angrily.

"I just want to know. Please tell me, how much do you make an hour?" pleaded the little boy.

"If you must know, I make $20 an hour."

"Daddy, may I borrow $10 please?"

The father was furious. "If the only reason you wanted to know how much money I make is just so you can borrow some to buy a silly toy or some other nonsense, then you march yourself straight to your room and go to bed. I work long, hard hours every day and don't have time for such childish games."

The little boy quietly went to his room and shut the door. The man sat down and started to get even madder about the little boy's questioning. After an hour or so, the man had calmed down, and started to think he may have been a little hard on his son. Maybe there was something he really needed to buy with that $10, and he really didn't ask for money very often. The man went to the little boy's room and opened the door.

"Are you asleep, son?" he asked.

"No, Daddy, I'm awake," replied the boy.

"I've been thinking, maybe I was too hard on you earlier," said the man. "Here's that $10 you asked for."

The little boy sat straight up, beaming. "Oh, thank you, Daddy," he yelled. Then, reaching under his pillow, he pulled out some more crumpled up bills. The man started to get angry again. The little boy slowly counted out his money, then looked up at his father.

"Why did you want more money if you already had some?" the father grumbled.

"Because I didn't have enough, but now I do," the little boy replied. "Daddy, I have $20 now. Can I buy an hour of your time?"

Share $20 worth of time with someone you love. Remember, the width of life is as important as the length. This is just a short reminder to all of us working so hard for our living. However, let us not let time slip through our fingers without having spent some quality time with those who really matter to us. Everyone is a house with four rooms—a physical, mental, emotional, and a spiritual room. Most of us tend to live in one room most of the time, but unless we go into every room every day, even if only to keep it aired, we are not complete persons.

MACKAY'S MORAL

Be sure not to let making a living interfere with having a life.

Happy people
make other people happy

There is a fable about a little girl who was feeling particularly lonely and blue when she happened across a gorgeous butterfly trapped in the thorns of a blackberry bush. Taking great care not to tear its fragile wings, the girl's nimble fingers finally worked the insect free, whereupon, instead of fluttering away, it turned into a golden fairy who offered to grant any wish.

"I want to be happy!" the little girl cried.

The fairy smiled, leaned forward, whispered something in her ear and vanished. And from that day forward there was no more happy spirit in the land than that child, who grew into a merry woman and a contented old lady. On her deathbed, her neighbors crowded around, desperate that the secret of happiness not die with her.

"Tell us, please tell us, what the fairy said to you," they pleaded.

The neighbor smiled benevolently, and whispered, "She told me that everyone—no matter how rich or secure or self-contained or successful they might appear—had need of me."

How true! Everyone needs to be needed. It brings tremendous satisfaction to know that you have such a vital purpose in life, one that surely contributes to your happiness and contentment.

Everyone needs to be needed. It brings tremendous satisfaction to know that you have such a vital purpose in life, one that surely contributes to your happiness and contentment.

I've learned over the years that happiness comes from making other people happy. Successful people, as well as successful businesses, take great joy in finding ways to spread happiness. Why is Disneyland the "happiest place on earth"? Is it any wonder that one of the biggest songs in recent years is Pharrell Williams' "Happy"? How many Happy Meals do you think McDonald's sells? Have you ever attended a happy hour at your favorite watering hole?

Businesses that are clued in to what customers want find ways to incorporate "happy" into the sale. A new car doesn't drive any better because the dealership was decked out in balloons and offered free hot dogs. But a happy experience beats an ordinary one most days.

Following that line of thought, it turns out that the conventional wisdom is wrong: It is possible to buy happiness—when you spend your money on others. Researchers at the University of British Columbia and Harvard University found that people who buy gifts for others and make charitable donations report being happier than people who spend their money primarily on themselves. The scientists studied 630 Americans and asked them to rate their general happiness, their annual income, and their monthly spending—including bills, gifts for themselves, gifts for others, and charitable contributions.

And again, it illustrates the point that knowing that others have need of you brightens your outlook.

Even our nation's Declaration of Independence places a premium on happiness, stating that we are "bestowed with certain unalienable rights, which among these are Life, Liberty, and the pursuit of Happiness." Thomas Jefferson and company left it up to us to figure out how to pursue happiness, but I have some thoughts for you. Here's my prescription for happiness. Use it regularly and you will see wonderful results:

- Don't let little things bother you. There is always something better to think about.

- Keep your perspective. Put first things first and stay the course.

- Only worry about what you can control. If you cannot do anything about a situation, worrying won't make it—or you—better.

- Do your best, but understand that you can't always be a perfectionist. Don't condemn yourself or others for not achieving perfection.

- When you are right, be gracious. When wrong, be even more gracious.

- Trust or believe people whenever you can, and when that isn't possible, accept them at their worst and weakest. You can keep your convictions without destroying others.

- Don't compare yourself to others, which is the guarantee of instant misery. People are different for many reasons.

- Brush away the chip on your shoulder so that when something happens to you that you don't like, you can take the high road.

- Give of yourself wholeheartedly or enthusiastically. When you have nothing left to give, someone will return the favor.

- Make happiness the aim of your life instead of bracing for life's barbs.

- Remember, you are responsible for your own happiness. Others can do kind things for you, but you must be open to being happy. But don't let that stop you from trying to make others happy!

MACKAY'S MORAL

You are only as happy as you decide to be.

Thoughts for a richer life

I've had this little gem tucked away for many years, and I refer to it from time to time to remind myself of what's really important. I've searched for the source, which I haven't been able to find, because I'd like to thank the author for these wonderful lessons.

Here are the original thoughts, followed by my impressions:

The most destructive habit: Worry.

The greatest joy: Giving.

The greatest loss: Loss of self-respect.

The most satisfying work: Helping others.

The ugliest personality trait: Selfishness.

The most endangered species: Dedicated leaders.

The greatest natural resource: Our youth.

The greatest "shot in the arm": Encouragement.

The greatest problem to overcome: Fear.

The most effective sleeping pill: Peace of mind.

The most crippling disease: Excuses.

The most powerful force in life: Love.

The most incredible computer: The brain.

The worst thing to be without: Hope.

The deadliest weapon: The tongue.

The two most power-filled words: I can.

The greatest asset: Faith.

The most worthless emotion: Self-pity.

The most beautiful attire: A smile.

The most prized possession: Integrity.

The most contagious spirit: Enthusiasm.

First, let's talk about worry. Did you know this word is derived from an Anglo-Saxon word that means to strangle or to choke? People do literally worry themselves to death ... or heart disease, high blood pressure, ulcers, nervous disorders, and all sorts of other nasty conditions. Worry can destroy your **peace of mind**. The best remedy? Remember that tomorrow is a new day, full of promise.

Giving/Helping others. These two go hand in hand. You are always in a position to give, just as you can always help someone. Never pass up an opportunity to share what you have. **Dedicated leaders** understand that they have tremendous power to help those they lead by setting a solid example and demonstrating the highest standards.

Selfishness. It is amazing what you can accomplish when you are willing to share the credit. An offshoot of selfishness is **self-pity,** which no one should waste time on anyway. Perhaps the worst effect is **loss of self-respect**. Self-respect is what motivates you to be the best you can be. And in turn, you can motivate others to be their best.

Encouragement is oxygen to the soul. People appreciate recognition, encouragement, and praise. Offering encouragement based on a person's character or actions inspires someone to perform in such a manner that invites additional praise. Be careful not to let **the tongue** undo the positive effects of encouragement. Use it for good.

Fear. Every crisis we face is multiplied when we act out of fear. When we fear something, we empower it. If we refuse to concede to our fear, there is nothing to fear.

Excuses. We all make excuses from time to time. However, the day you stop making them is the day you will move up in the world.

Hope is what gets many of us through our worst days. Hope is believing that every cloud has a silver lining, and when that cloud rains, it makes things grow. A perfect partner is **faith**, for without faith, hope is meaningless. **Love** completes this trio. Real power comes through when you love someone or something, whether it's a career or a cause.

A **smile** improves your looks. I learned years ago that one of the most powerful things you can do to have influence over others is to smile at them. It should be standard equipment for all people.

Integrity: either you have it or you don't. If you have integrity, nothing else matters. If you don't have integrity, nothing else matters. Doing the right thing is never the wrong thing to do.

Enthusiasm is the spark that ignites our lives. It's one of the most important attributes to success. It also leads to an attitude of **I can**, which provides the confidence required for achievement.

Pass as much **encouragement** as possible to **our youth**, the people who will inherit this world. I am constantly encouraged by the dreams and aspirations of the young people I mentor, and I want them to pass their experiences to future generations.

Finally, **the brain**. What a gift we have with our brains. Unlike your computer, it may not perform rapid-fire complex calculations. But attached to the heart, it can make better decisions and produce infinitely better results.

MACKAY'S MORAL

If you want life's best, see to it that life gets your best.

ABOUT THE AUTHOR

Harvey Mackay has written seven *New York Times* best-selling books, three reached #1, and two were named by the *New York Times* among the top 15 inspirational business books of all time—*Swim with the Sharks Without Being Eaten Alive* and *Beware the Naked Man Who Offers You His Shirt*. His books have sold 10 million copies in 80 countries and have been translated in more than 50 languages.

For the last 25 years, Harvey has been a nationally syndicated columnist. His weekly articles appear in 100 newspapers and magazines around the country.

He also is one of America's most popular and entertaining business speakers for Fortune 500–size companies and associations, plus he has spoken on six continents. Toastmasters International named him one of the top five speakers in the world. He is a member of the National Speakers Association Speakers Hall of Fame.

In addition, Harvey is chairman of MackayMitchell Envelope Company, a $100 million company he founded at age 26. MackayMitchell has 450 employees and manufactures 25 million envelopes a day.

The American Management Association listed Harvey among the top 30 leaders who influenced business in 2014. In July 2015, *Forbes* said, "Harvey Mackay is one of the world's top leadership experts who has accomplished more in business than most entrepreneurs could achieve in their lifetimes." In April 2004, Harvey received the prestigious Horatio Alger Award in the Supreme Court Chambers.

Harvey is a graduate of the University of Minnesota and the Stanford University Graduate School of Business Executive Program. He is an avid runner and marathoner, having run 10 marathons, and is a former #1 ranked senior tennis player in Minnesota.

Despite his busy work schedule, Harvey remains deeply committed to his wife of over 50 years, Carol Ann, their three children and their 11 grandchildren.

If you have thoughts, comments, or ideas about this book, I'd love to hear from you. (Please, no requests for personal advice.)

Write to me at the following address:
Harvey Mackay
MackayMitchell Envelope Company
2100 Elm St. SE
Minneapolis, MN 55414

I also can be reached electronically. My email address is
Harvey@Mackay.com.
My website address is www.harveymackay.com.

INDEX

A

Abdul-Jabbar, Kareem, 45
Accountability
  business basics and, 34
  for success, 245
Adversity, 1–9
  bouncing back from, 5–7
  importance of coping with, 3–4
  learning from failure, 8–9
Albert Einstein College of
    Medicine, 22
Alger, Horatio, 8
Ali, Muhammad, 168
Allen, Woody, 59
Alliance building,
    271–273
Amazon, 84
American Marketing Association,
    279
American Society for Quality
    Control, 222
American Sociological Review, 271
Andrews, Julie, 37
Apologizing to customers,
    85–86
Apple Computer, 5, 249
Aristotle, 168, 204
Armstrong, Elodie, 296
Arrogance, 18–20
Assessment, self-, 241–243
AT&T, 36

Attitude, 11–22

arrogance as detrimental to
    business, 18–20
happiness for success, 21–22
humor and laughter, 107–108
impact of language on,
    286–287
for improving job performance,
    101
for sales and marketing, 201
taking charge of, 13–15
teamwork and, 253–254
value of smiling, 16–17
Auerbach, Red, 39
Avis, 200
Awareness, 72

B

Backup plans, 189–190
Bailey, Greg, 25
Bannister, Roger, 25
Baum, Robert, 279
Becoming Real (Saltz), 191
Belief in yourself, 23–30
  for achievement, 25–26
  humility and, 27, 29–30
  improving job performance
    and, 102
  for self-confidence, 27,
    164–165, 238
Bell Atlantic, 36